A Landscape Photographer's Guide to
Zion National Park

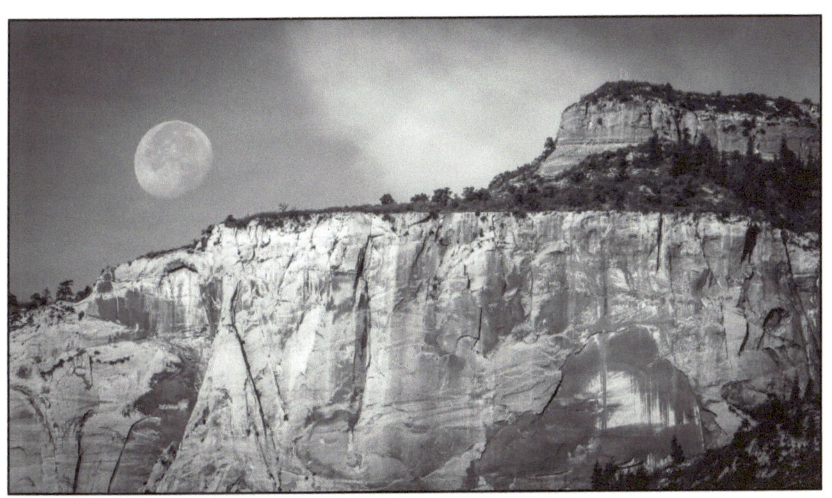

Anthony Jones

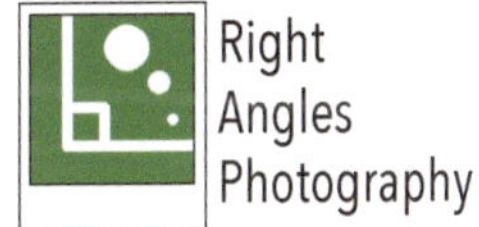

Contents

iv
To Cedar City, Cedar Breaks National Monument, and Salt Lake City
Gas station
Exit 42
15
Taylor Creek Trail
North Fork
Middle Fork
Taylor Creek
South Fork
PARIA POINT
Double Arch Alcove
Horse Ranch Mountain 8726ft 2659m
Exit 40
Kolob Canyons Road
Lee Pass Trailhead
Kolob Canyons Visitor Center
5074ft 1546m
Kolob Canyons Viewpoint
Timber Creek Overlook Trail
La Verkin Creek Trail
KOLOB CANYONS
Nagunt Mesa 7785ft 2372m
La Verkin Creek Trail
Willis Creek
Chasm Lake
BEAR TRAP CANYON
Kolob Reservoir 8118ft 2475m
OAK VAL
2455m
TIMBER TOP MOUNTAIN
Timber Creek
Gregory Butte 7705ft 2348m
Kolob Arch
Kolob Arch Trail
Beatty Spring
Langston Mountain 7408ft 2258m
Kolob Peak 8933ft 2739m
THE HARDSCRABBLE
KOLOB PLATEAU
La Verkin Creek
Hop Valley Trail
Burnt Mountain 7682ft 2341m
iii
Vehicles longer than 19 feet/5.8 meters are not allowed on Lava Point Road. Unpaved roads are impassable when wet.
UPPER
Blue Springs Reservoir 7921ft 2415m
Lava Point Rd
Lava Point
Lava Point Trailhead
Lava Point Overlook 7890ft 2405m
Spring
Sawmill Springs
HOP VALLEY
LOWER
Kolob Terrace Road
Beyond this point, road not plowed in winter.
Firepit Knoll 7265ft 2214m
Hop Valley Trailhead
Connector Trail
Wildcat Canyon Trailhead
Wildcat Canyon Trail
Northgate Peaks Trail
CAVE VALLEY
KOLOB PLATEAU
Spendlove Knoll 6895ft 2102m
LEE VALLEY
Viewpoint
North Guardian Angel 7395ft 2254m
Keyhole Falls
ZIO
SMITH MESA
Tabernacle Dome 6430ft 1960m
South Guardian Angel 7140ft 2176m
Double Falls
NATIO
To St George and Las Vegas, Nevada
Exit 27
Left Fork Trailhead
Unpaved roads are impassable when wet.
Left Fork
Right Fork
COUGAR MOUNTAIN
PAR
Toquerville
17
Grapevine Trailhead
Right Fork Trailhead
HURRICANE CLIFFS
HURRICANE MESA
Kolob Terrace Road
North Fork
Oilwell (ruins)
TOWERS OF THE
Altar of 7505ft 2288m
Zion Human His
The West Temple 7810ft 2380m
9
La Verkin
La Verkin Creek
Vehicles pulling trailers not recommended. Narrow winding road with steep grades. Upper section not plowed in winter.
Virgin 3550ft 1082m
Kolob Terrace Road
Crater Hill 5192ft 1582m
Spring
Mount Kinesava 7285ft 2220m
Sout
Zion Ca
Spr
To 15 exit 16, St George, and Las Vegas, Nevada
9
Springdale/Zion Canyon Shuttle and Zion-Mount Carmel Highway tunnel information
Virgin River
Chinle Trail
Hurricane
59
To Pipe Spring National Monument and Grand Canyon National Park
V
Coalpits Wash
Grafton (ghost town)
Rockville 3747ft 1142m
Bridge Road
Chinle Trailhead turn on A
Grafton Road
North
0 1 2 3 4 5 Kilometers
0 1 2 3 4 5 Miles
Unpaved roads are impassable when wet. Closed in winter.
Shuttle Information
Springdale shuttle route
Zion Canyon shuttle route and shuttle stop
Spring through fall, Zion Canyon Scenic Drive is open to shuttle buses only. Park your car and ride the shuttle.
Other Visitor Information
Paved road open to private vehicles
Unpaved road (impassable when wet)
Overlook/parking
Trail
Ranger station
Drinking water
Restrooms
Picnic area
Campground
Primitive campground
Smithsonian Butte Scenic Backway
To 59 Pipe Spring National Monument and Grand Canyon National Park

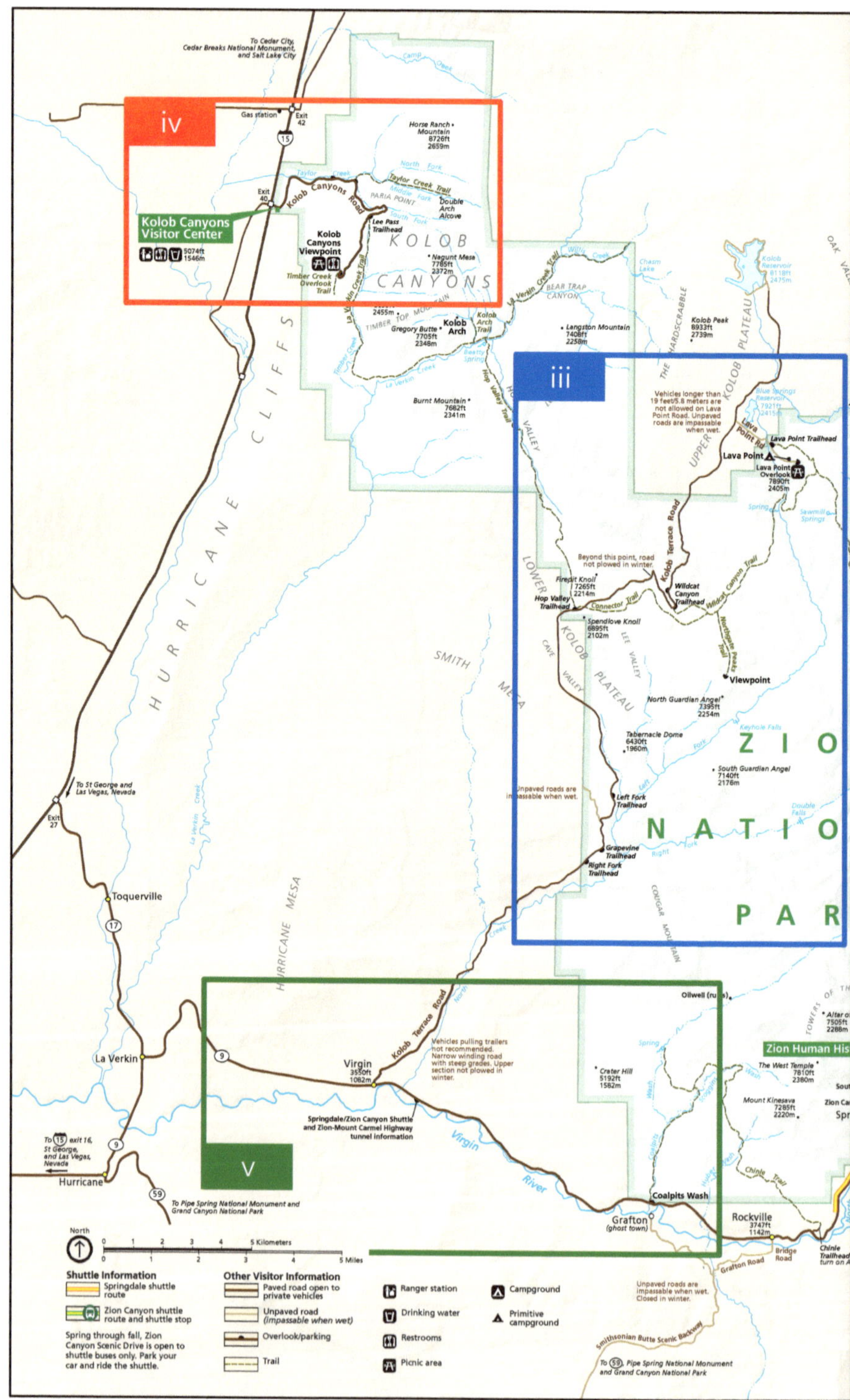

4

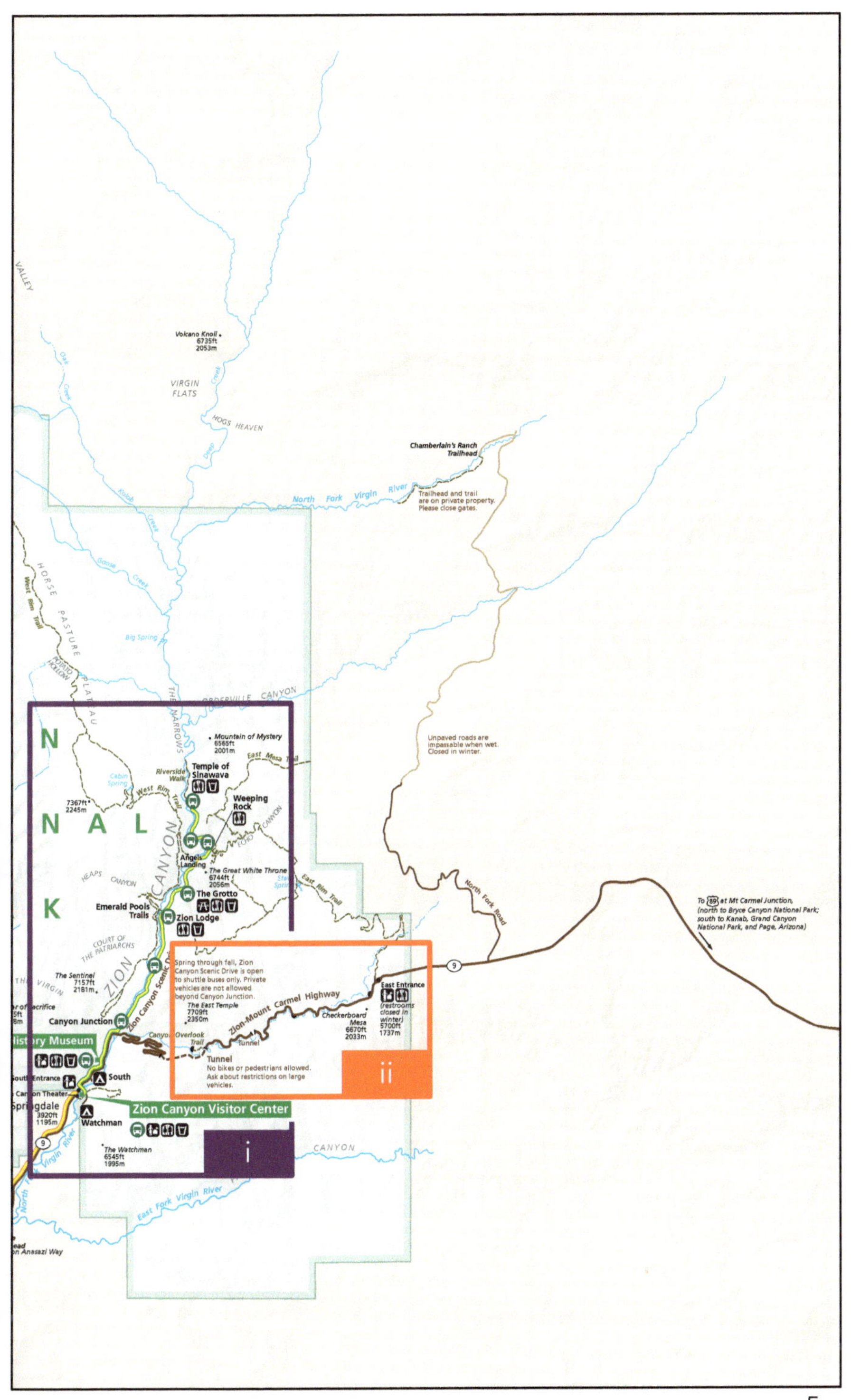

VALLEY
Volcano Knoll
6735ft
2053m
VIRGIN
FLATS
HOGS HEAVEN
Oak Creek
Deep Creek
Kolob Creek
Chamberlain's Ranch
Trailhead
North Fork Virgin River
Trailhead and trail
are on private property.
Please close gates.
Goose Creek
HORSE
PASTURE
PLATEAU
West Rim Trail
Big Spring
POND HOLLOW
THE NARROWS
GROSVILLE CANYON
Cabin Spring
7367ft
2245m
N
A
T
I
O
N
A
L
ORDERVILLE CANYON
Mountain of Mystery
6565ft
2001m
East Mesa Trail
Riverside Walk
Temple of Sinawava
Weeping Rock
West Rim Trail
ZION CANYON
Angels Landing
The Great White Throne
6744ft
2056m
Echo Canyon
HEAPS CANYON
K
The Grotto
Emerald Pools Trails
Zion Lodge
East Rim Trail
Stave Spring
COURT OF THE PATRIARCHS
ZION CANYON
Unpaved roads are
impassable when wet.
Closed in winter.
North Fork Road
To 89 at Mt Carmel Junction,
(north to Bryce Canyon National Park;
south to Kanab, Grand Canyon
National Park, and Page, Arizona)
The Sentinel
7157ft
2181m
THE VIRGIN
Spring through fall, Zion
Canyon Scenic Drive is open
to shuttle buses only. Private
vehicles are not allowed
beyond Canyon Junction.
9
East Entrance
(restrooms
closed in
winter)
5700ft
1737m
ar of Sacrifice
5ft
8m
The East Temple
7709ft
2350m
Zion-Mount Carmel Highway
Checkerboard Mesa
6670ft
2033m
Canyon Junction
Zion Canyon Scenic Drive
Canyon
History Museum
Overlook Trail
Tunnel
Tunnel
No bikes or pedestrians allowed.
Ask about restrictions on large
vehicles.
ii
South Entrance
South
Canyon Theater
Springdale
3920ft
1195m
Zion Canyon Visitor Center
Watchman
i
9
North Fork Virgin River
The Watchman
6545ft
1995m
CANYON
ead
on Anasazi Way
East Fork Virgin River

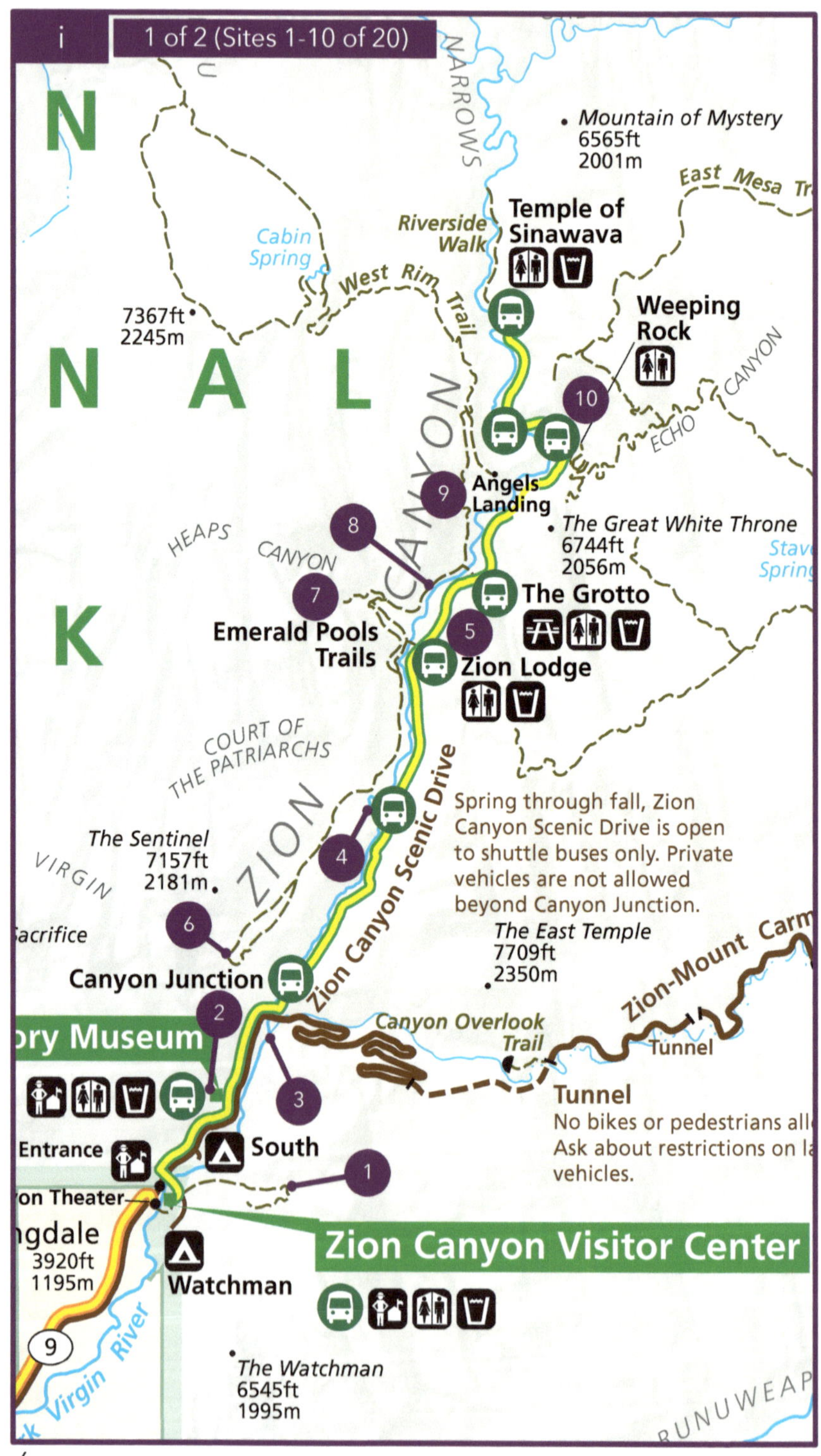

1 of 2 (Sites 1-10 of 20)
N
N A L
K
Cabin Spring
7367ft
2245m
West Rim Trail
NARROWS
Riverside Walk
Mountain of Mystery
6565ft
2001m
East Mesa Tr
Temple of Sinawava
Weeping Rock
10
ECHO CANYON
CANYON
9
Angels Landing
The Great White Throne
6744ft
2056m
Stave Spring
HEAPS
CANYON
8
7
Emerald Pools Trails
The Grotto
5
Zion Lodge
COURT OF THE PATRIARCHS
ZION
The Sentinel
7157ft
2181m
VIRGIN
Zion Canyon Scenic Drive
4
Spring through fall, Zion Canyon Scenic Drive is open to shuttle buses only. Private vehicles are not allowed beyond Canyon Junction.
The East Temple
7709ft
2350m
Zion-Mount Carm
Sacrifice
6
Canyon Junction
2
Canyon Overlook Trail
Tunnel
ory Museum
Tunnel
No bikes or pedestrians alle
Ask about restrictions on la
vehicles.
3
Entrance
South
1
gdale
3920ft
1195m
Watchman
Zion Canyon Visitor Center
on Theater
9
Virgin River
The Watchman
6545ft
1995m
RUNUWEAP

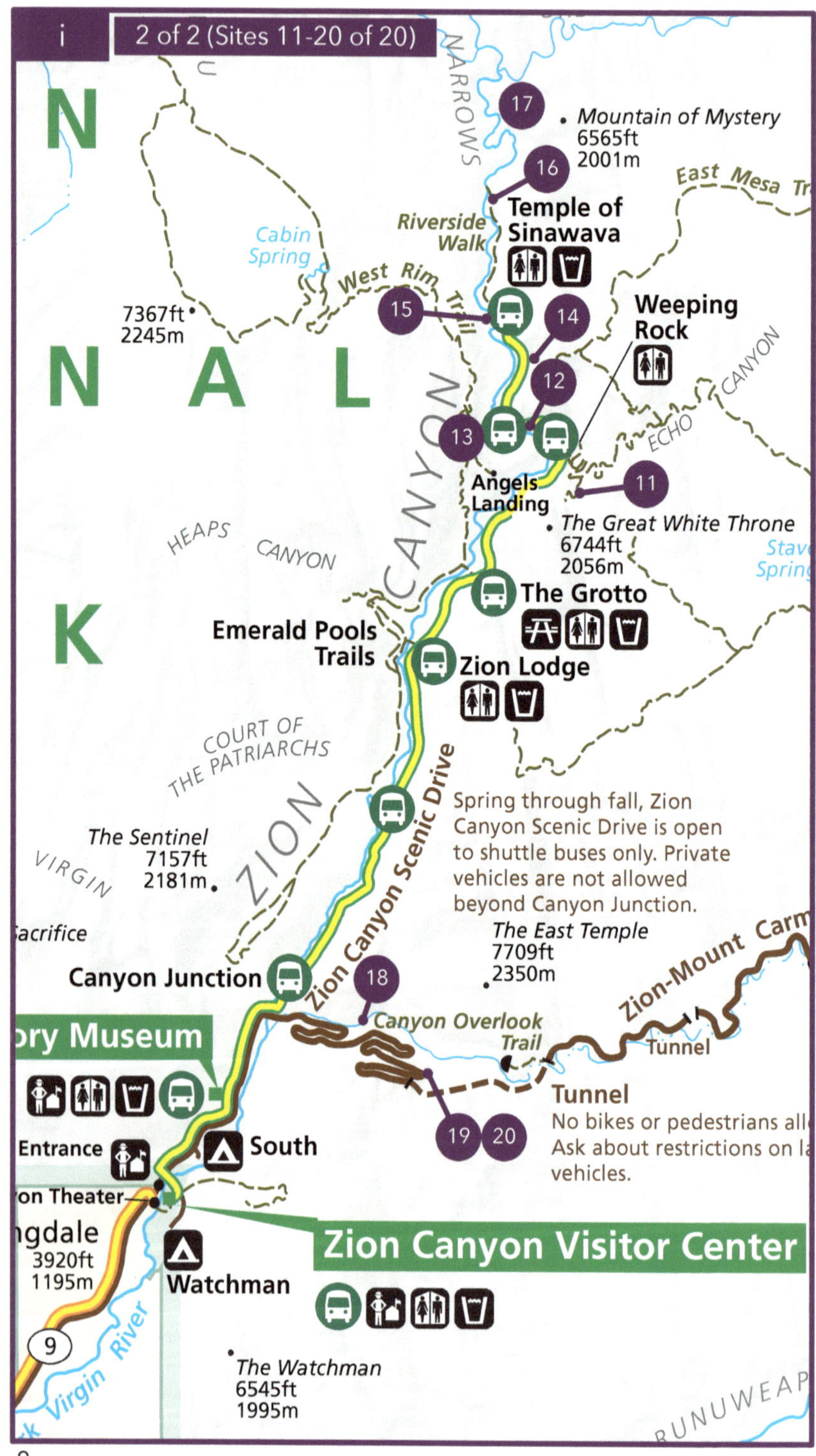
N
NAL
K
Mountain of Mystery
6565ft
2001m
East Mesa Tr
Cabin Spring
7367ft
2245m
Riverside Walk
17
16
Temple of Sinawava
Weeping Rock
West Rim Trail
15
14
12
ECHO CANYON
13
11
Angels Landing
The Great White Throne
6744ft
2056m
Stave Spring
HEAPS CANYON
CANYON
The Grotto
Emerald Pools Trails
Zion Lodge
COURT OF THE PATRIARCHS
ZION
The Sentinel
7157ft
2181m
VIRGIN
Zion Canyon Scenic Drive
Spring through fall, Zion Canyon Scenic Drive is open to shuttle buses only. Private vehicles are not allowed beyond Canyon Junction.
The East Temple
7709ft
2350m
Zion-Mount Carm
Sacrifice
Canyon Junction
18
Canyon Overlook Trail
Tunnel
ory Museum
Tunnel
No bikes or pedestrians all
Ask about restrictions on l
vehicles.
Entrance
South
19
20
on Theater
ngdale
3920ft
1195m
Zion Canyon Visitor Center
Watchman
9
Virgin River
The Watchman
6545ft
1995m
RUNUWEAP

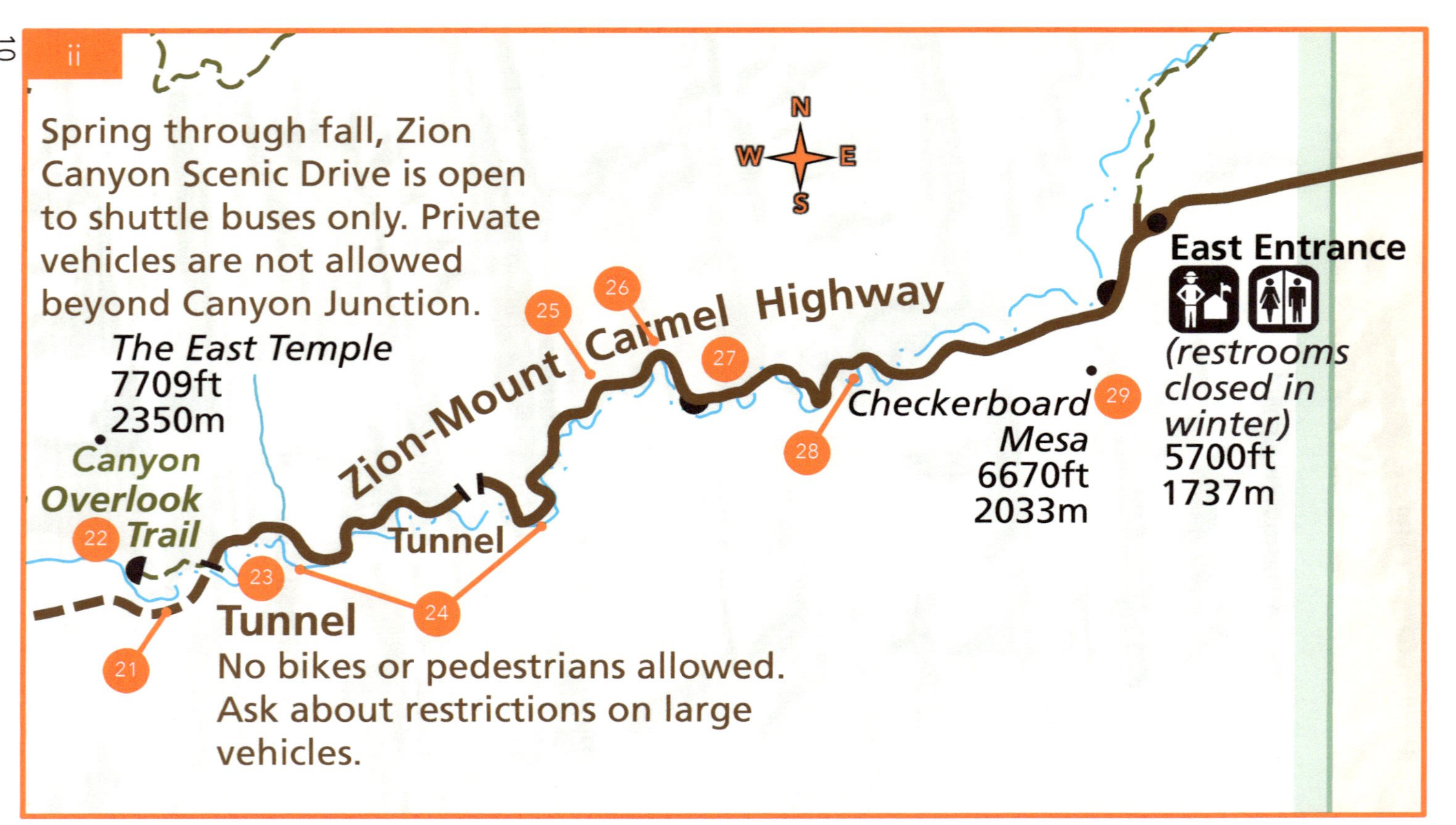
ii
Spring through fall, Zion Canyon Scenic Drive is open to shuttle buses only. Private vehicles are not allowed beyond Canyon Junction.
The East Temple
7709ft
2350m
Canyon Overlook Trail
Tunnel
Tunnel
No bikes or pedestrians allowed. Ask about restrictions on large vehicles.
Zion-Mount Carmel Highway
Checkerboard Mesa
6670ft
2033m
East Entrance
(restrooms closed in winter)
5700ft
1737m
N
W
E
S
22
21
23
24
25
26
27
28
29

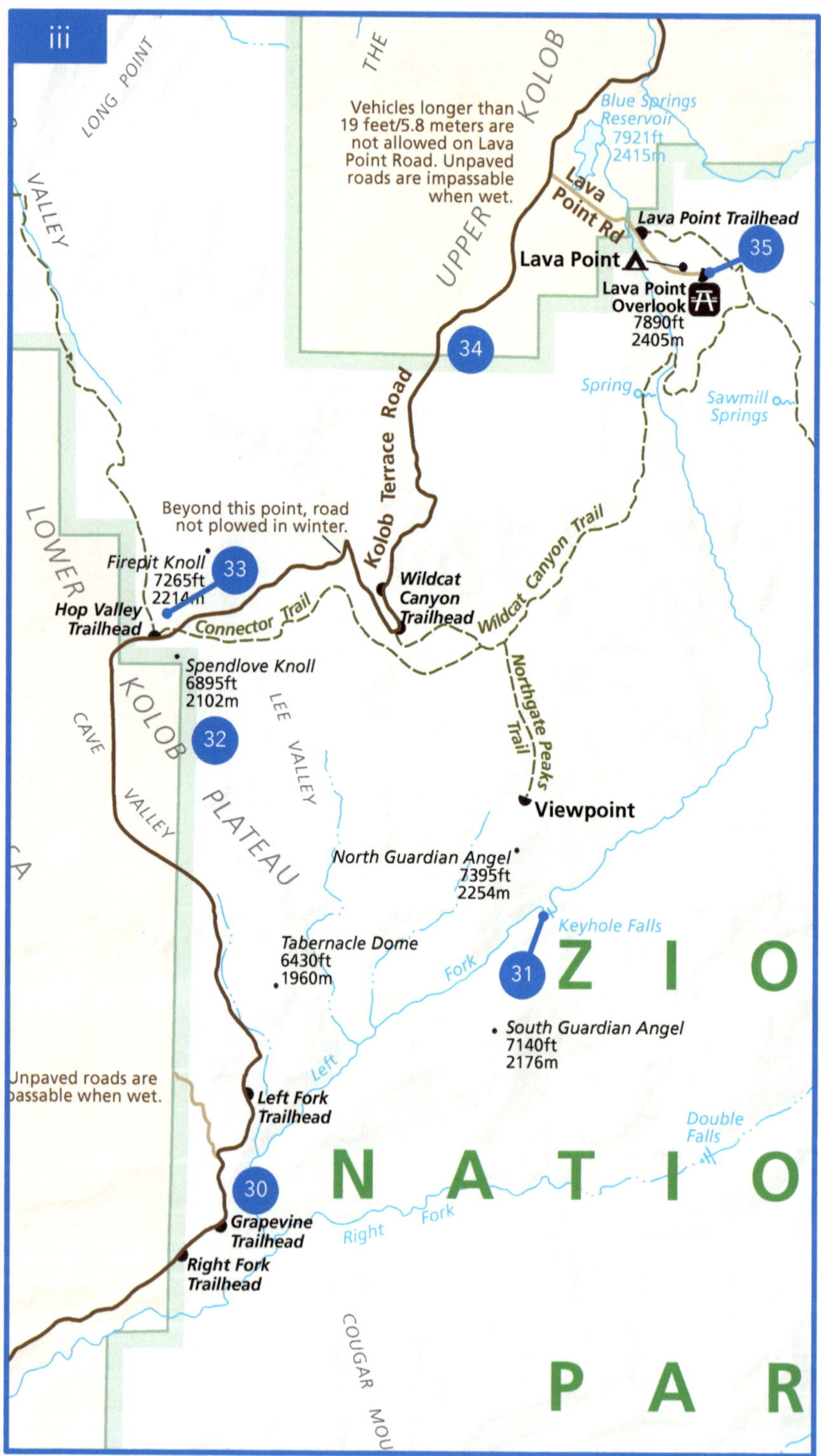
LONG POINT
VALLEY
THE
UPPER KOLOB
Blue Springs Reservoir
7921ft
2415m
Vehicles longer than 19 feet/5.8 meters are not allowed on Lava Point Road. Unpaved roads are impassable when wet.
Lava Point Rd
Lava Point Trailhead
Lava Point
35
34
Lava Point Overlook
7890ft
2405m
Spring
Sawmill Springs
Kolob Terrace Road
Wildcat Canyon Trail
Beyond this point, road not plowed in winter.
Firepit Knoll
7265ft
2214m
33
Wildcat Canyon Trailhead
Hop Valley Trailhead
Connector Trail
LOWER
Spendlove Knoll
6895ft
2102m
32
KOLOB
CAVE
LEE VALLEY
Northgate Peaks Trail
VALLEY
PLATEAU
Viewpoint
North Guardian Angel
7395ft
2254m
Tabernacle Dome
6430ft
1960m
Fork
Keyhole Falls
31
Z I O
South Guardian Angel
7140ft
2176m
Left
Unpaved roads are passable when wet.
Left Fork Trailhead
Double Falls
N A T I O
30
Right
Fork
Grapevine Trailhead
Right Fork Trailhead
COUGAR MOU
P A R

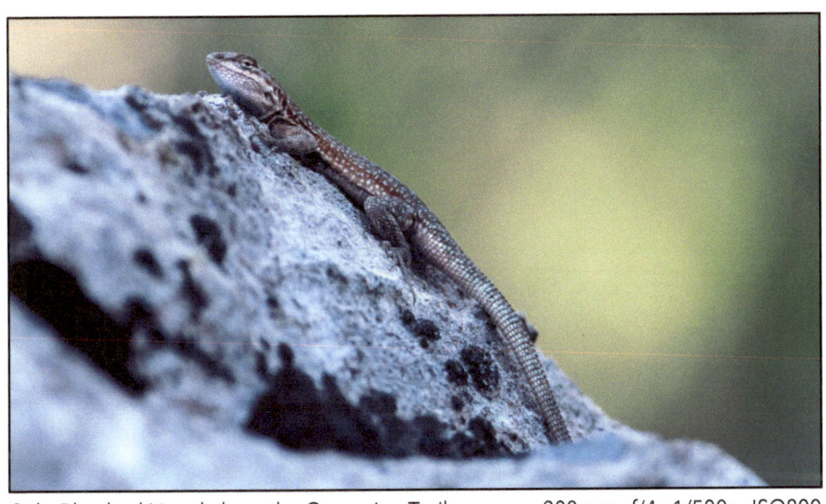

Side-Blotched Lizard along the Grapevine Trail   200mm f/4 1/500s ISO800

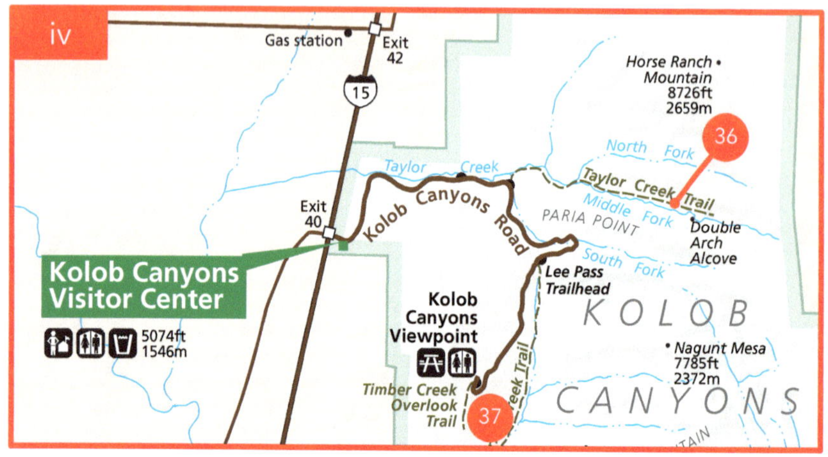

36. Taylor Creek Trail 128

Hike past two abandoned cabins to the gorgeous Double Arch Alcove.

37. Timber Creek Overlook 130

Experience a great perspective of the Kolob "Finger Canyons" formations.

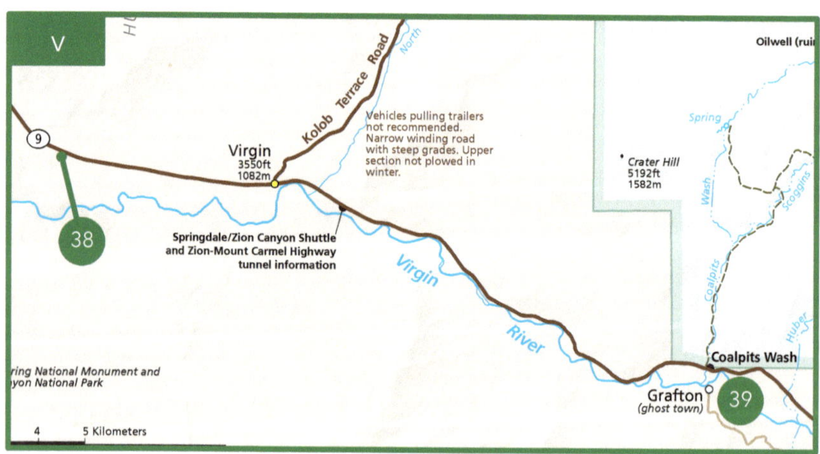

38. Park Approach from Virgin 132

A short section of Highway 9 that allows for an unobstructed, albeit distant, view of the West Temple and neighboring formations of Zion National Park.

39. Grafton 133

A ghost town on the south side of the Virgin River.

Introduction

Welcome to Zion National Park! Once at Number 5 on the most-visited list of America's national parks, as of 2021 it sits proudly at 3rd, having surpassed the Grand Canyon and Yosemite, only now behind Great Smokey Mountains and Yellowstone. What a jump!

Though if a list existed for most *widely* photogenic parks, I would expect to see it at Number 1. Magnificent red, orange & white slickrock textures, vegetation with greens in every shade imaginable, vibrant blue skies, and unique opportunities to hike *in* rivers all the way up to the canyons' edges above – this park offers a lot. For the landscape photographer, capturing its essence via camera is easily achievable. The variety of subjects and compositions is innumerable.

But I suspect that you already know a lot of this. And so, this guide isn't designed to persuade you to visit Zion National Park. Odds are that you have already made the decision to go. *Yes!*

Then what *is* this book's purpose?

Its core intent is to guide you **-the photographer-** throughout the park, to minimize "blind exploration" for sites, and to maximize the number of praiseworthy images you take home.

This book is especially catered towards those who I like to call "weekend photographers." Those who may visit the park only for 2-5 days – and for some people what may be their *only* visit to this national park. As such, the sites presented herein are more likely to be roadside or very short hikes, in order to maximize experiences, when time is limited. (There are some longer treks on the list, for those who do have the time.)

My style is also to provide honest information. Not every site is a "must see" / ★★★★. So sometimes the news is great; sometimes not so great. The idea is that you're armed with enough information to create a daily itinerary that meets or exceeds your goals as a landscape photographer on travel. My own philosophy as a traveling photographer, is that I seek destinations where the reward matches or exceeds the effort to get there. This is one of the governing philosophies of this book.

How to Use this Book

I have divided the park, for the photographer's needs, into 5 areas. For quick reference, please see that each area's color is consistent throughout the book. (This is for quickly finding maps, sections, etc.)

While a lot of literature you will come across may speak to the park's history, geology, flora, fauna, and so on, this book will focus mostly entirely on elements useful to the photographer. I'm no historian, geologist, or botanist, and it would be wasteful to reproduce a lot of that information in here, as it would only add to the volume's heft. I sincerely hope that you have room for this book in your camera bag, and that you take it along with you every step of the way.

I've also omitted the most basic "general" photography lessons in here as well. There are many excellent resources on that topic. I will, however, cover some intermediate-level topics that I think are relevant to making the most of your photography while at Zion National Park. The Tips & Techniques section is for exactly this.

So let's dissect the information presented for each of these hikes. The following is a sample, taken from The Three Patriarchs (4):

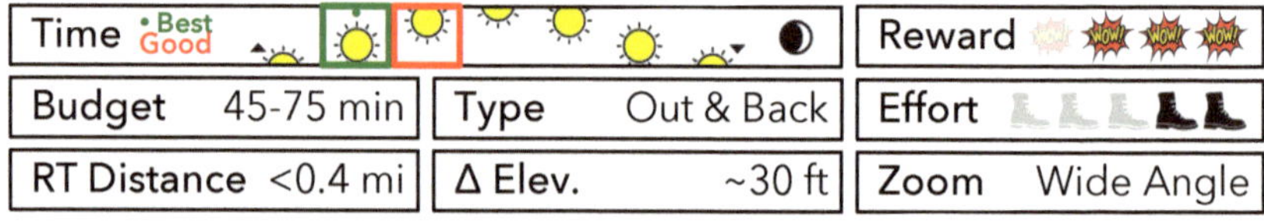

Time	Best Good							Reward	
Budget	45-75 min		Type		Out & Back		Effort		
RT Distance	<0.4 mi		Δ Elev.		~30 ft		Zoom		Wide Angle

Time: The icons represent sunrise, early AM, late AM, midday, early PM, late PM, sunset, and nighttime. The green box(es) represent the best time(s) of day to be there. The red box(es) represent good time(s). Ideally you are visiting during the "best" times, but itineraries do not always allow this, hence providing multiple options. The above site is best in early morning and also good in late morning. *One major caveat here: Clouds can change everything (and normally for the better!), offering softer, more accommodating light during other times of the day. Make impromptu adjustments, accordingly.*

Reward: One to 4 "Wow's." Now honestly, if it warrants printing in the book, then it's got merit, right? So a 1-Wow here isn't like a 1-star motel. It's just relative! The above site scores a 3.

Budget: Your time is valuable, and this is how much time you might expect to spend at this site (including getting there, if it is a hike). For the sample site, plan for between 45-75 minutes.

Type: This is the circuit that you will cover. "Roadside" involves some walking (but not hiking); you likely will work *near the side of the road.* "Meandering" means that there's not really a prescribed route, and so you should expect to explore the area via your own path. "Out & Back" is a route that you hike out one way, and then you turn around and hike back on the return. "Lollipop Loop" is an out & back with a loop at the far end. "Through" is a through-route, where the site is between the route's start and finish.

Effort: This is the physical effort required while on the hike. Here, we are using the "Boots" scale. Zero Boots highlighted is typical for everyday walks, then 1-5 Boots reflect the effort, similar to using the Easy-Moderate-Strenuous scale, but here with a 2-Boot representing Easy-Moderate, and a 4-Boot representing Moderate-Strenuous. For the sample site, as you will read about on page 45, some walking in shallow water is recommended, hence its rating of 2 Boots.

RT Distance: "RT" is Round Trip. This is the total hiking distance. (For "Through" hikes, since the trip does not begin and end at the same place, "RT" is removed.) Our sample site's round trip distance is less than ("<") 0.4 mile.

Δ Elev.: Change in Elevation. I need to be careful here. There are many ways to talk elevation and how it is recorded on a hike. For this book and this purpose, what is presented is simply the difference between your lowest elevation and your highest elevation. Some trails go up-and-down, and up-and-down, and so on. This value does not capture the summation of all those ascents and descents; it is merely the difference between the highest and your lowest points, while on the trail. For the sample site, the change in elevation is approximately ("~") 30 feet.

Zoom: I'm a firm believer in "less is more." Taking every lens on every hike can be backbreaking. And being weighed-down is no fun. So, in this box I'll suggest the key lens(es) you will want to take. Adding more is up to you. Using 35mm (full frame-equivalent) focal lengths, please consider "Wide" = Wide Angle (15-35mm), "Norm" = Normal (24-70mm), and "Tele" = Telephoto (70-200mm+).

Finally, each section will have photos of *hopefully* what you can expect to see and photograph – or do better than I could! Below these pictures are the camera settings that I used for the shot. Example:

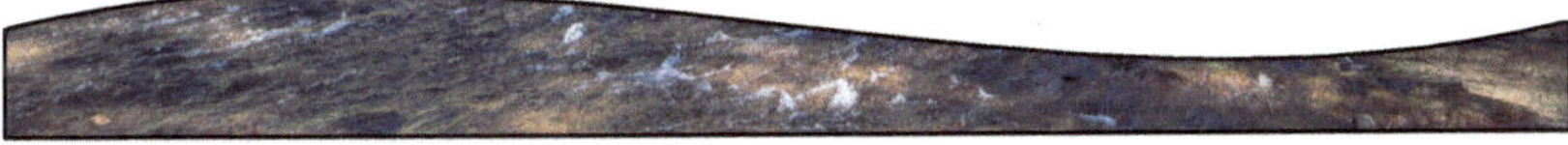

The Three Patriarchs   20mm f/11 1/80s ISO200

The Five Park Areas

The National Park Service divides Zion National Park into 3 ecological zones – rim, canyon, and river. These zones are found throughout most of the park. For your orientation, this book instead defines 5 geographic areas to work within – Zion Canyon, "East" (along the Zion-Mount Carmel Highway, between the Lower Pine Creek Canyon and the East Entrance), Kolob Terrace, Kolob Canyons, and finally "Outside Zion National Park."

Very many visitors to Zion National Park concentrate their time in Zion Canyon. This is where the crowds are during the peak months. Zion Canyon includes many "top" attractions, as far as park guides and other resources will suggest. I cannot disagree, but hopefully your time will permit exploring other areas as well – especially including Zion's east side.

If this is your first visit to Zion, then I recommend the following:

½ day	Stay longer!
1 day	Zion Canyon, and 1-2 hours devoted to the east side.
2 days	1½ days in Zion Canyon, and a ½ day on the east side.
3 days	Add a ½ day on the Kolob Terrace, and sprinkle left-over time elsewhere (Grafton a good option).
4 days	Add a trip to the Kolob Canyons or simply add more time in Zion Canyon and on the east side.

Let's take a look at each area...

Zion Canyon

Zion Canyon is the heartbeat of Zion National Park. Sites such as The Watchman, Temples of the Virgin, Emerald Pools, Angels Landing, and The Narrows provide remarkable opportunities for landscape photographers. Most of what you have seen in photography portfolios covering Zion National Park probably came from Zion Canyon.

While on this topic of suggested best-of-the-park, let's briefly cover The Subway and Archangel Falls. These two sites are breathtaking, and you have likely also seen photographs of them, but they are *not* found in Zion Canyon. Many first-time visitors confuse these two sites as being part of The Narrows. They are not. They are found on the Left Fork of North Creek, and are accessible from the Kolob Terrace. So more on The Subway and Archangel Falls in that section.

One last piece, before we dive into this subsection... During peak months, Zion Canyon, from Canyon Junction north, is only served by the Zion Canyon Shuttle System. You cannot drive this stretch. See the Tips & Techniques section for detailed information on shuttles.

The South Entrance to Zion National Park is adjacent to the town of Springdale. About 200 feet before the two entrance booths is an awesome stone-and-timber park entrance sign. I enjoy having one of these signs in the beginning of my photo album – it makes for a nice "introduction" to your portfolio of park photos. There is a parking lot just in front of this sign for your use.

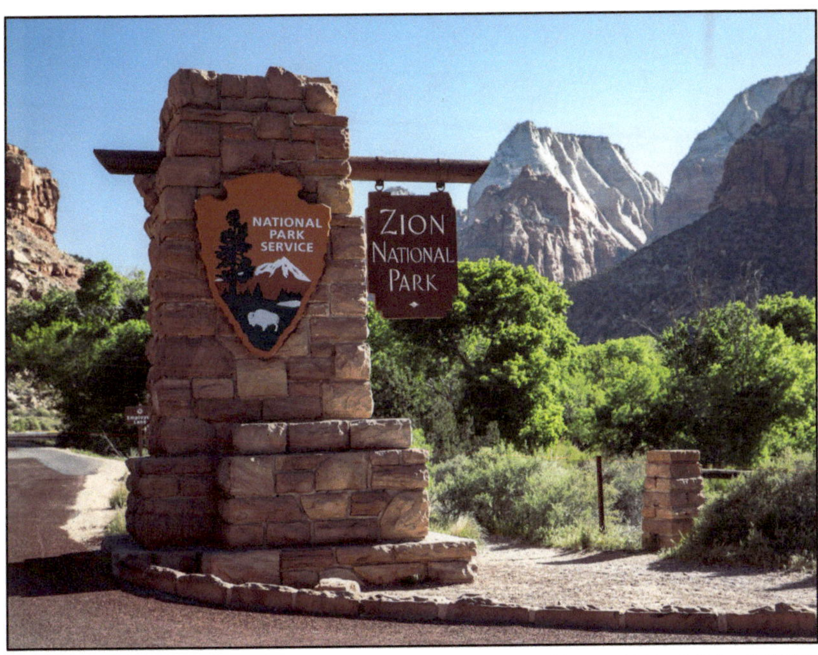

Zion National Park – South Entrance Sign   50mm f/5.6 1/80s ISO100

Once through the entrance, the Zion Canyon Visitor Center is the hub for park information, hiking permits, and the southern-most stop of the Zion Canyon Shuttle System. Also in this area are two campgrounds – the Watchman Campground and the South Campground. (Never mind that the South Campground is the north one of the two. I have yet to figure this out.) I have camped in the Watchman Campground and really enjoyed it.

How deep is this canyon? The elevation at the Temple of Sinawava is about 4,500 feet (above sea level). As we follow the Virgin River as it continues south to the Zion Canyon Visitor Center, the elevation drops to about 4,000 feet. Many of the surrounding peaks up-and-down along the Virgin River in the Canyon are between 6,500-7,000 feet. Though the West and East Temples are at a whopping 7,800 and 7,700 feet (respectively). So, generally speaking, the canyon is on average 2,500 feet deep. That's half a mile!

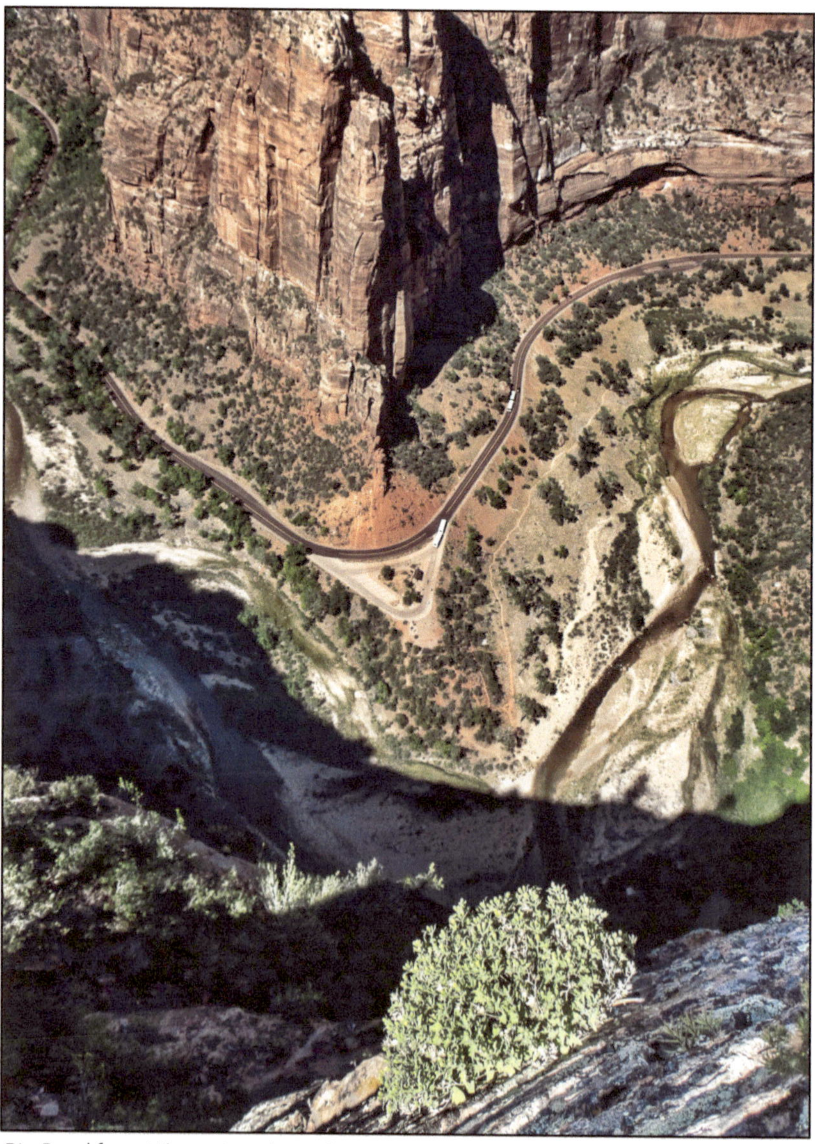

Big Bend from Hike to Angels Landing   28mm f/5.6 1/1200s ISO100

With this depth brings a few lighting limitations. First, don't expect to be on the canyon floor and see a conventional sunrise or sunset! At the time the sun traverses the canyon's edge, it is still so high in the sky that the most fantastic colors are either long gone (if morning) or some time away (if afternoon). Now this isn't to say that you can't benefit from first- and last-light colors... But you will not be able to capture a prairie-style sunrise or sunset from down inside the canyon. Second, there is a simple rule of thumb to consider for adequate lighting along the canyon walls and on its adjacent peaks – photograph the west-side features in the morning, and the east side features in the afternoon. (To say it another way, do not shoot into the direction of the sun.) There are always exceptions, depending on what you may be trying to achieve – but this rule generally holds true. Shoot westerly in the morning; easterly in the afternoon.

The two most common, interesting wildlife you will see in Zion Canyon are wild turkey and deer. Both prefer early morning and evening to midday hours for their daily adventures out-and-about. Do keep an eye out. Also keep your camera ready while in the car, and have your telephoto lens mounted and other camera settings ready, so that if the opportunity presents itself, you're not wasting time getting your camera ready for a shot.

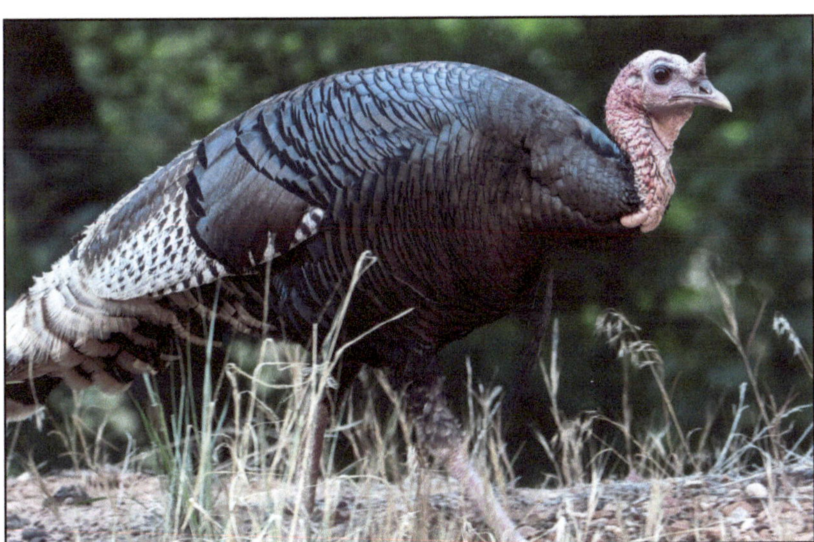

Wild Turkey near Court of the Patriarchs Shuttle Stop 300mm f/5.6 1/100s ISO1600

Zion Canyon is magnificent, and the good news here is that despite its many hikes with a lot of elevation change, there are just as many sites that are very easy to reach with fantastic photographic potential.

East

I love this area.

Surprisingly, along the 5½ miles between the East Entrance and the Zion-Mount Carmel Tunnel there is only one formal hike and one formal "vista" – Canyon Overlook Trail and Checkerboard Mesa, respectively. And these two happen to be at each end!

This area has all the makings for great hiking and great photography. So why aren't there any more formal sites? My suspicion – because of the topography and existing infrastructure, it is not really feasible to expand parking options, and that which is there is already quite limited. But shhhhh... The **good news** is that because this area lacks formal stops, most people are pacified with simply driving through it and gawking at the radical topography on the move. So you now know better... Parking is usually not even a problem!

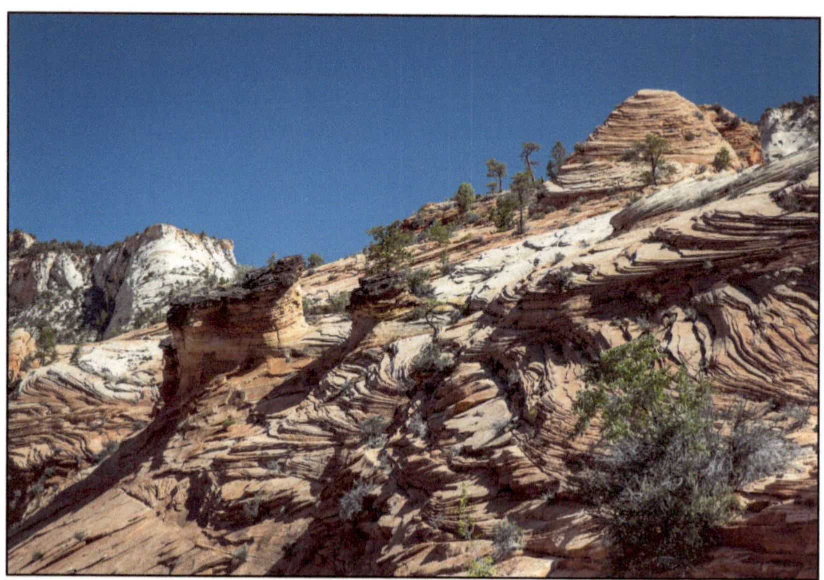

Fantastic East Side Slickrock   70mm f/8 1/160s ISO200

The slickrock (sandstone) in this area is really weirdly-shaped but quite wonderful. It's hard to describe, so I'll allow the photographs to do the talking for me! If you are coming into this area by way of the Zion-Mount Carmel Tunnel, when you exit that tunnel you will swear that you've been transported to another world! It is that different. I get a kick out of it every time.

One of the more prized finds along here is Desert Bighorn Sheep. Morning and evening, they seem to typically move in a herd, eating vegetation along this wild terrain. Midday, they'll often roam singularly to find a warm spot to soak in the sun's rays. So as you make your way through this area, do be on the lookout. Same rule applies as mentioned in the Zion Canyon section – have your camera ready before you spot one!

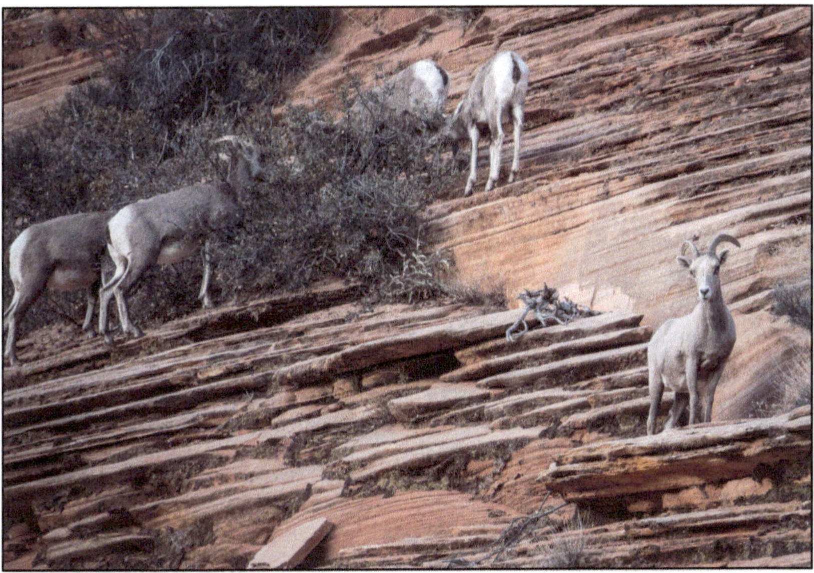

Big Horn Sheep

400mm f/5.6 1/100s ISO800

The good news is that there's really not a bad time of day to visit this area. I have had success during all daylight hours – and even some at night! (See page 88.) So where Zion Canyon may not be as forgiving with limited "right" times of day to visit, as you build your itinerary the east side can be more flexible to your schedule's needs.

Kolob Terrace

Access to the Kolob Terrace is along the Kolob Terrace Road, which tees into Highway 9 at Virgin. (There is good signage on Highway 9 alerting motorists of the turnoff.)

This is a windy road with a substantial amount of elevation gain. Be sure to have enough fuel, and monitor your gauge regularly. I was caught off-guard on a trip all the way to the Kolob Reservoir one time, and with ¼ tank at the turnoff in Virgin I found myself rolling all the way back down and into La Verkin with the needle pointed to empty. That was not fun.

Now, since I have mentioned the Kolob Reservoir, I want to save you time and recommend against going that far up the road. There is zero photographic potential there, unless your thing is shooting people fishing or on jet skis.

The road does enter and exit the national park multiple times, so be cognizant of where you are – what is public / national park land, and what is private land – especially if you are exploring Aspens (34) and while out of your car at Cave Knoll (32).

For a casual, few hours afternoon visit, head all the way up to the Lava Point Overlook (35) first, making note of interesting sites along the way to stop at on the way back.   Expect a 10-20 degree drop in temperature when you arrive – always a refreshing sensation! Head back down, stopping at Hoodoo Hill (33) and spending time on foot exploring there. Finally, drive a little further and enjoy the prairie and rock formations at Cave Knoll. If you have time for a sunset, double-back to Hoodoo Hill after Cave Knoll and hang there for the show.

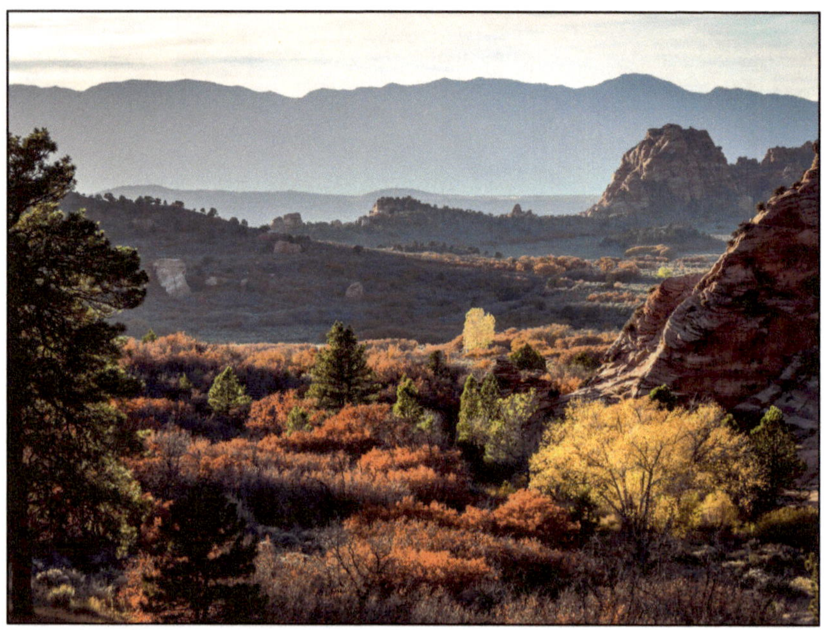

Soft Light and Fall Color near Hoodoo Hill   135mm f/5.6 1/400s ISO200

In the Zion Canyon subsection, I mentioned The Subway and Archangel Falls... These sensational places are accessed on the Left Fork of North Creek, and while there are multiple routes to take, I have included the most straightforward one, known as the "Bottom-Up" route to The Subway (31), beginning and ending at the Left Fork Trailhead. This is a permit-only trip, so do be sure to study these details closely on that site's narrative. Hiking this route isn't quintessential "Kolob Terrace," even though that is how you access it.

24

So, if your itinerary includes a day on the Left Fork of North Creek, and you do have time elsewhere, see about coming back and exploring the upper elevations of Kolob Terrace some more.

Kolob Canyons

If Zion Canyon, the east side, and the Kolob Terrace combine to make Zion's "big picture," then Kolob Canyons is the national park's featurette. It even feels this way – a park within a park, so to speak.

The Kolob "Finger Canyons" area serves 3 primary sites – the Taylor Creek Trail (and its picturesque Double Arch Alcove), the Kolob Canyons Viewpoint (and its adjacent Timber Creek Overlook Trail), and finally the La Verkin Creek Trail (serving the Kolob Arch Trail and its namesake arch). The first two are covered in this book; the last one is not. (Visiting the Kolob Arch requires about 13 miles of hiking with some substantial gains and losses in elevation.)

I had visited Zion National Park multiple times before finally visiting the Kolob Canyons area. Its relative remoteness had been my deterrent. I was thrilled when I finally did make it there... Its quaintness and its sites are enjoyable, just like other areas of the park. And like other areas of the park, it's slightly "different" as well. So if you're looking to add still some more variety to your Zion National Park portfolio, make time for both the Taylor Creek and Timber Creek Overlook Trails.

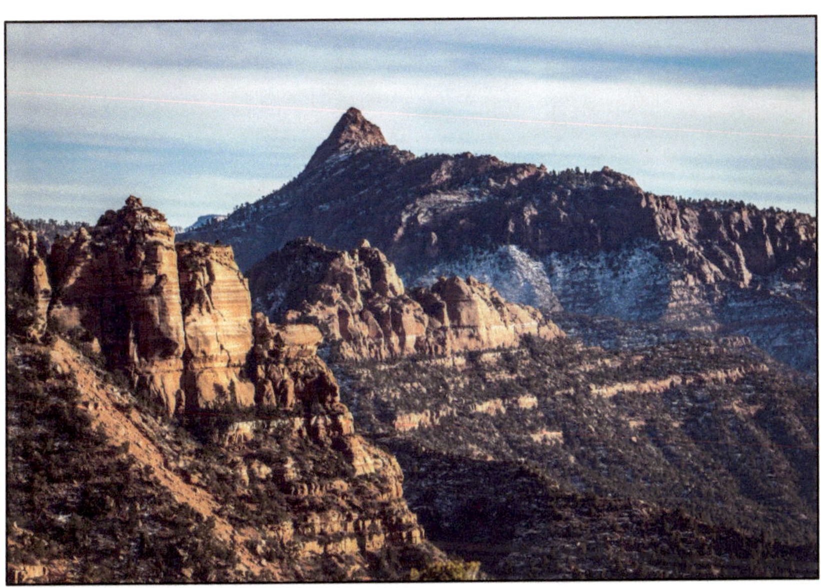

Kolob Canyons Viewpoint   200mm f/8 1/320s ISO100

Outside Zion National Park

I have stayed inside the park, in Springdale, in La Verkin, and also in Hurricane. Lodging prices and trip logistics play a role in the decisions that I made. I suspect the same will be true for many of you as well.

The good news is, for those of you staying in La Verkin or Hurricane (or perhaps even St. George), on a pre-sunrise drive into the park, you're often treated to some gorgeous colors in the east, with a silhouette of the West Temple and other adjacent peaks. This happened so regularly, I started paying closer attention to the best places to see this along the highway and decided to share records of these details in this book – even though you're still quite a way outside the park. See page 132.

Sunrise Silhouette   200mm f/5.6 1/125s ISO100

The other "outside the park" site is more obvious – Grafton Ghost Town. This place is just plain neat! While a bumpy and not exactly a short drive there, I do believe it's worth it, and warrants placement on any 3+ day trip itinerary.

Tips & Techniques

As briefly mentioned in the "How to Use this Book" section, I want to share with you what I think are some of the more unique pieces of advice for your trip to Zion National Park. Some of this information is park-specific (logistics and planning, mostly), while other information is photography-related (i.e. techno-talk).

Let's get straight to it...

Additional Resources
Please do not skip this!

My goal, in writing this book, is to minimize the resources that you must seek-out, purchase or print, and ultimately rely on in order to enjoy *photography* at Zion National Park. So, along with the purchase of this book I recommend three additional resources:

1. The Zion National Park Website (www.nps.gov/zion/index.htm),

2. A printed copy of the National Park Service map of Zion National Park, and

3. A purchased copy of National Geographic's "Trails Illustrated" Topographical Map of Zion National Park (map #214).

The Website...

I'm not going to guide you through the whole website – that would be silly. Though, it is in your best interest to make some time and explore it completely, or very close to. Also, a disclaimer – some of these subcategories listed here may change names over time, as the website evolves, so if you cannot find what you're looking for based on my guidance here, try finding it outside the website with your favorite search engine. Just be sure that when you follow the results, you're staying within the www.nps.gov domain. It is the most reliable.

Alerts

On the top banner there is a link to park alerts. This could be abnormal weather or road conditions, or any upcoming or emergency activities that visitors need to be aware of. Check this ahead of your trip, and as connectivity allows, check it regularly during your trip.

Weather

A direct link is available on the homepage. Weather conditions can change very rapidly in this region. Again, as connectivity allows, check this regularly during your trip.

Maps

Again on the top banner, follow the maps link for an abundance of great information. Your first mission is to find and download the PDF of the park map that you will be provided once you arrive at a park entrance pay station. I advise to print in color your downloaded copy on the largest paper possible. The copy you will receive at the park, unfolded, is approximately 24 x 16 inches. This is the same map used on pages 4-14 of this book, and the same map that I listed as Item 2 above for you to carry during your visit.

Unfortunately, the aforementioned map lacks adequate detail in some places, especially for use while driving (and seeking topographic waypoints). Its scale is approximately 1 inch = 2.1 miles. Though not a "must," I strongly encourage purchase of the National Geographic map listed on the prior page. It provides 3.5 times more resolution. This is a lot! (Its scale is 1 inch = 0.6 mile.) It is easy to find online and in many national stores.

The maps that I provide later in this book, for select sites, are mostly for planning purposes, and while on foot are for orientation only. These maps should not be used for navigation. (Orientation at sites without a provided map is either described in the site's text, adequately depicted on the free park map, or in the case of the Sand Bench Loop – provided by your tour guide.)

Driving Information

Some typical distances and driving times for your reference:

Town of Springdale to East Entrance	12 mi	30 min
Town of Springdale to Temple of Sinawava (Restrictions Apply*)	9 mi	25 min
Town of Springdale to Town of Virgin	13 mi	20 min
Town of Virgin to Lava Point Road	21 mi	40 min
Town of Virgin to Kolob Canyons Road	26 mi	30 min

* See next section on Zion Canyon Shuttle System

The Zion National Park website provides information on driving (and parking) do's and don'ts. Since this topic isn't really an opinion piece and you probably won't need to understand it more than once, I'll leave it to you to consult the website for this information.

There is, however, one thing to share... This fits squarely in the "hint" category. If you will be visiting during peak months, where crowds can be very challenging, consider staying at the Zion Lodge. Guests of the Zion Lodge are allowed personal vehicle access to and from their accommodations, which also includes *parking in the Zion Lodge area*.

Zion Canyon Shuttle System

Zion National Park employs a no-fare shuttle system from the Zion Canyon Visitor Center to the Temple of Sinawava during the spring, summer, and fall seasons. (There are some transition periods between fall and winter, and winter and spring, where the shuttle only operates on the weekends. Be sure to check the Zion National Park website if your itinerary includes travel in November, December, February, or March.)

Nine stops are present – **(1) Visitor Center, (2) Museum, (3) Canyon Junction, (4) Court of the Patriarchs, (5) Zion Lodge, (6) The Grotto, (7) Weeping Rock, (8) Big Bend**, and **(9) Temple of Sinawava**. Each stop allows loading and offloading.

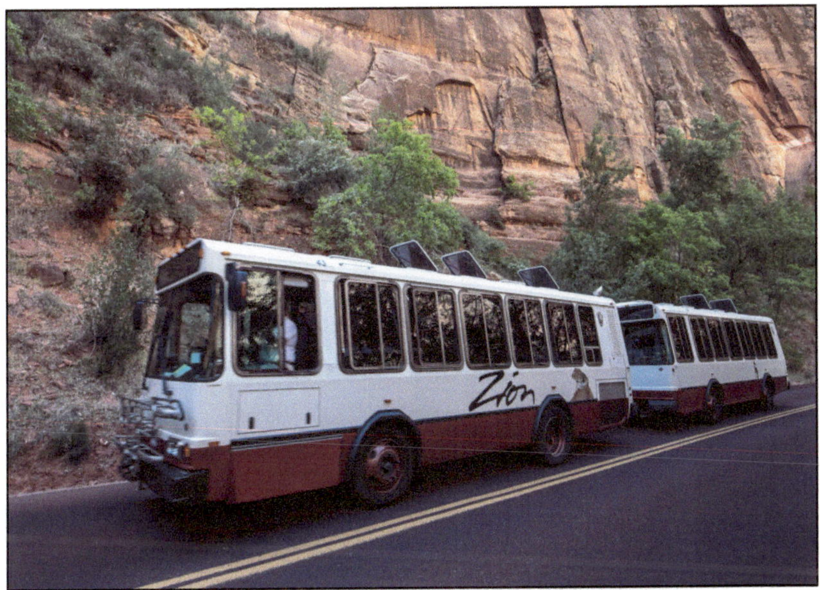

The Zion Canyon Shuttle   16mm f/5.6 1/200s ISO800

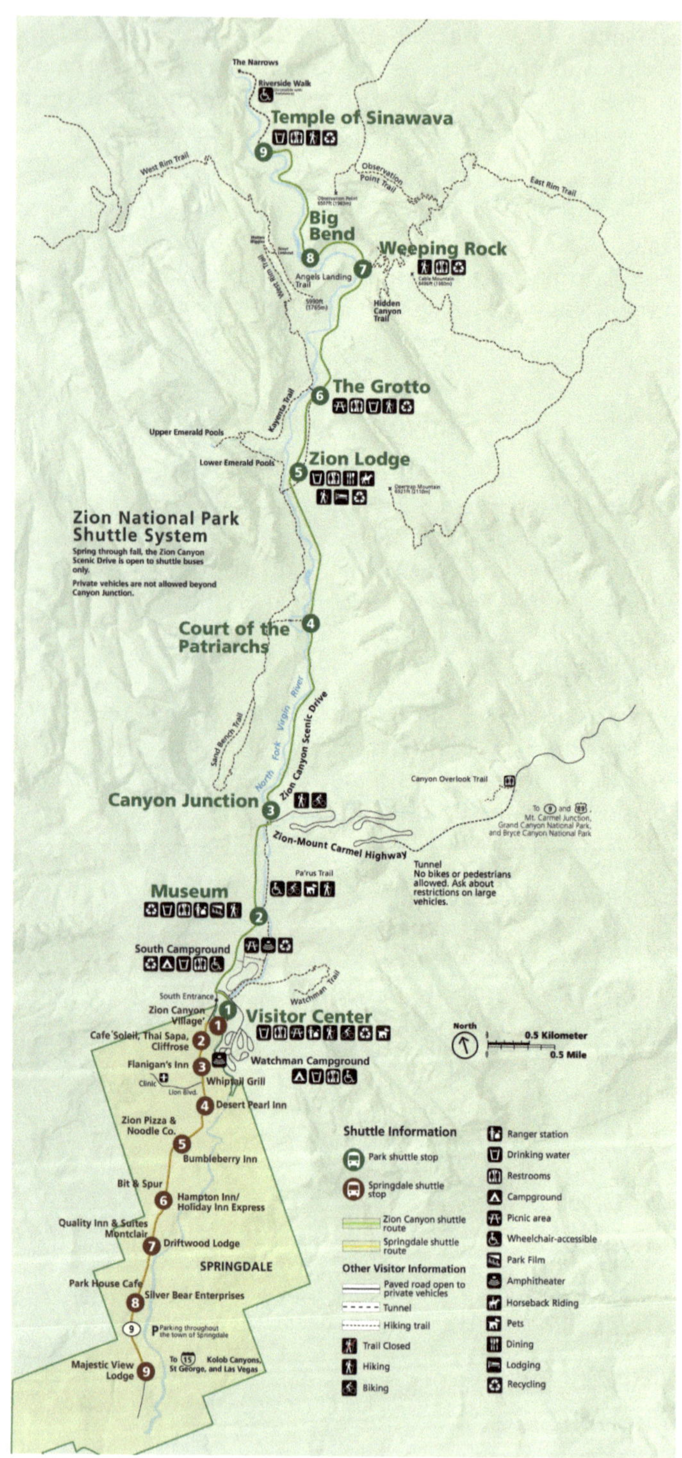

The Narrows
Riverside Walk
Temple of Sinawava
9
West Rim Trail
East Rim Trail
Observation Point Trail
Observation Point 6521ft (1983m)
Big Bend
8
Weeping Rock
7
Cable Mountain 6496ft (1980m)
Angels Landing Trail
5990ft (1765m)
Hidden Canyon Trail
The Grotto
6
Kayenta Trail
Upper Emerald Pools
Zion Lodge
5
Lower Emerald Pools
Deertrap Mountain 6921ft (2118m)
Zion National Park Shuttle System
Spring through fall, the Zion Canyon Scenic Drive is open to shuttle buses only.
Private vehicles are not allowed beyond Canyon Junction.
Court of the Patriarchs
4
Sand Bench Trail
North Fork Virgin River
Zion Canyon Scenic Drive
Canyon Overlook Trail
Canyon Junction
3
To 9 and ,
Mt. Carmel Junction,
Grand Canyon National Park,
and Bryce Canyon National Park
Zion-Mount Carmel Highway
Tunnel
No bikes or pedestrians allowed. Ask about restrictions on large vehicles.
Pa'rus Trail
Museum
2
South Campground
Watchman Trail
South Entrance
Zion Canyon Village
1
Visitor Center
2
Cafe Soleil, Thai Sapa, Cliffrose
North
0.5 Kilometer
0.5 Mile
Flanigan's Inn
3
Clinic
Lion Blvd.
Whiptail Grill
Watchman Campground
4
Desert Pearl Inn
Zion Pizza & Noodle Co.
5
Bumbleberry Inn
Bit & Spur
6
Hampton Inn/ Holiday Inn Express
Quality Inn & Suites Montclair
7
Driftwood Lodge
SPRINGDALE
Park House Cafe
8
Silver Bear Enterprises
9
P Parking throughout the town of Springdale
Majestic View Lodge
9
To 15 Kolob Canyons, St George, and Las Vegas

Shuttle Information
Park shuttle stop
Springdale shuttle stop
Zion Canyon shuttle route
Springdale shuttle route
Other Visitor Information
Paved road open to private vehicles
Tunnel
Hiking trail
Trail Closed
Hiking
Biking

Ranger station
Drinking water
Restrooms
Campground
Picnic area
Wheelchair-accessible
Park Film
Amphitheater
Horseback Riding
Pets
Dining
Lodging
Recycling

Bus arrival varies, but usually is not ever more than a 15 minute wait. Check latest published information for times on first and last buses in the canyon.

"Up Canyon" represents buses traveling northbound; "Down Canyon" represents southbound travel.

Buses can become crowded at times and lines to board them at certain stops (especially Visitor Center, Zion Lodge, and Temple of Sinawava) can become long. Do your best to exercise patience. The good news is that when visitation is high, the park deploys additional buses in the circuit to help move things along more efficiently.

Some visitors to Zion Canyon may also utilize the companion (and also free) Springdale Shuttle System. Entering the park, you will offload at **(1) Zion Canyon Village** stop (on the Springdale system) and walk along a wide, paved path to a footbridge crossing the Virgin River. Just on the other side of the river is the pedestrian entrance to Zion National Park – there is an entrance station here for your use. If boarding the Zion Canyon shuttle is your goal, walk north through the Visitor Center grounds to shuttle stop **(1) Visitor Center.**

Seasons

Zion National Park is a true 4-season destination. The only exception is the upper elevations along the Kolob Terrace road – not far beyond Hoodoo Hill (33) the road is not plowed, once snow arrives. It typically re-opens in March, though this may vary.

Spring

Temperatures are on a warming trend (coming out of winter), but still moderate. Greens are vibrant, as grasses and leaves return. Water flow in the Virgin River can be high, as snow melts from higher elevations. The best months are April and early May, as crowds still will not be as high.

Summer

Temperatures become hot, and unbearable at times in midday and afternoon direct sunlight. Wildflowers bloom in many places within the park – be on the lookout. Summer is usually dry, though like any season in Zion National Park, swift-moving thunderstorms can appear. So while water flow in the Virgin River is at its lowest during this season, pay close attention to park and weather alerts for forecasted rain or river events. Crowds can be stifling, but mostly only in Zion Canyon.

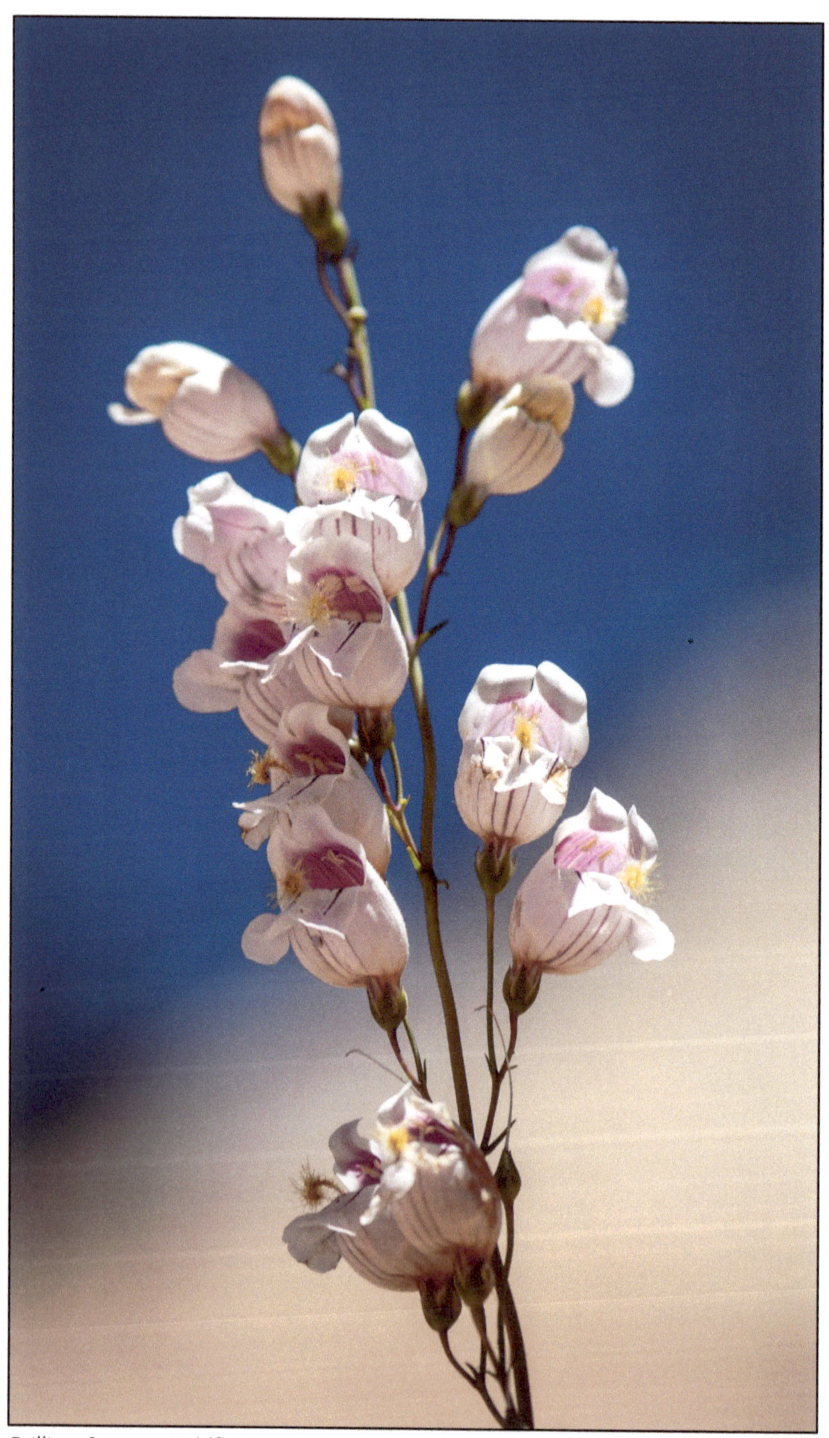

Brilliant Summer Wildflowers

Fall

Temperatures return to comfortable. Splashes of trees' leaves in fall color are everywhere in park. Color comes first at the highest elevations, and last in the canyons below. The Virgin River depth again is on the rise. Visitation numbers to Zion National Park in the fall (especially September and October) do remain high.

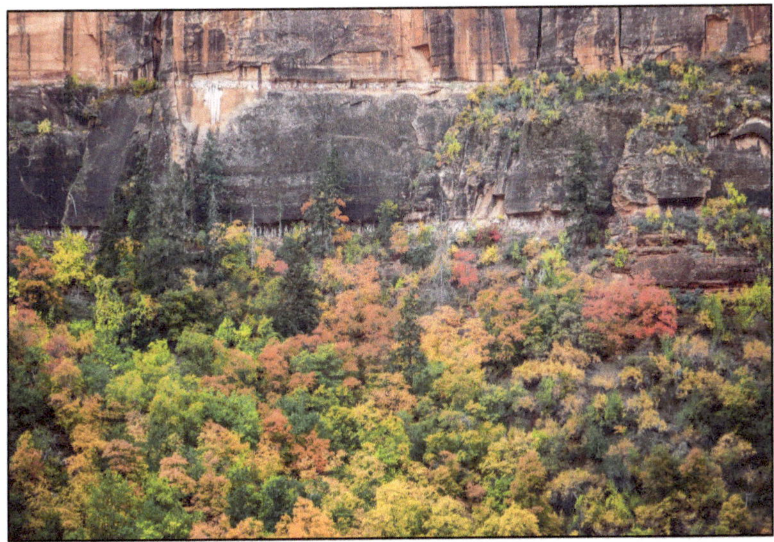

Fall Color above Clear Creek   135mm f/4 1/500s ISO400

Winter

Temperatures drop, and while many nights are near or below freezing, daytime temperatures can still be pleasant. Snow events occasionally occur, but any accumulation in Zion Canyon usually melts quickly. Longer nights allow the photographer more sleep... Or some downtime before nighttime photography activities ensue! Winter is the most tranquil season at Zion National Park, especially January and February, where visitation is at its lowest. The Zion Canyon Shuttle System is idle, and thus visitors are allowed to drive and park in the canyon.

My advice is this: If hiking The Narrows (17) is a must during your visit, schedule a summer visit. Brave the crowds. They are workable, with some extra effort on timing (particularly earlier starts to your day). If you are willing to forego The Narrows (or at least be at the mercy of more unpredictable conditions), April is my favorite month for knock-your-socks-off, truly vibrant greens. October is a close second, for its fall color potential. Though January is oh so quiet... And the freedom to drive into the Zion Canyon is divine.

Filters

Polarizing Filter

Do not leave home without your polarizing filter. There are lengthy articles on linear polarizing filters vs. circular polarizing filters – the topic is in my opinion too scientific for this book... If in doubt, use a circular polarizing filter. Most modern cameras will not meter correctly with a linear polarizer. (If you are still curious on this topic, seek further wisdom online.)

Aside from a functioning camera, a polarizing filter is the most important tool in your camera bag. Most are round and are threaded to screw onto your camera lens. Though, not all cameras and camera lenses have threads to accept accessory filters. Adapters are available for nearly every configuration. Once again, check online for availability for such adapters, if necessary.

A circular polarizer has a rotating front element, that when turned (and while you're looking through it – either by itself or through the camera) reduces glare and reflection of light. It also tends to enrich colors. And while colors' "pop" may be simulated using saturation and hue adjustments during post-processing, there does not exist a computer program to date that can effectively simulate a polarizer's effect on water. This is where it really shines. On a water scene, look to the polarizing filter to reduce glare, to see "into" the water, and sometimes enhance the reflections on the water's surface that you do want.

Two caveats to polarizing filters...

First, they really only work when the light source (the sun) is at a substantial angle, relative to the lens. At sunrise and sunset, you will not experience its effects. During very early morning and late afternoon, its effect will be minimal. Mid-morning through mid-afternoon, they work best.

Second, and perhaps the more important one of the two, is to **be careful of its effect on a blue sky at higher elevations.** Too much polarization can result in a very dark sky. Admittedly, I learned this the hard way on Zion's east side. On my first visit to the park, I was in the habit of simply leaving a polarizing filter on my lenses nearly all the time. In looking at my captured images, I realized that something was wrong. The sky was a strange, dark blue. I learned, on the more precious compositions, to shoot both with the filter and without. Then I could select which one I preferred later.

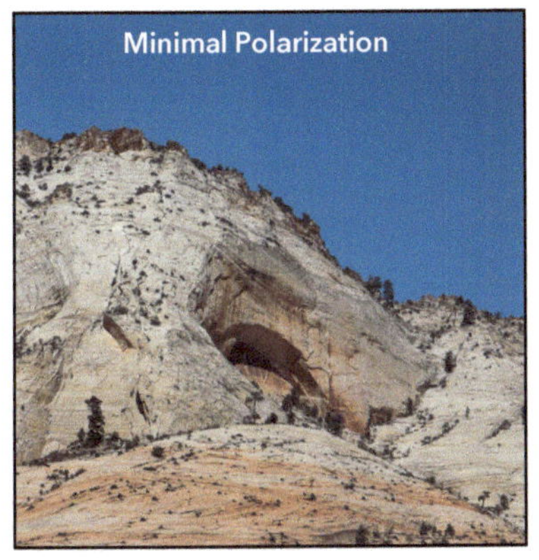

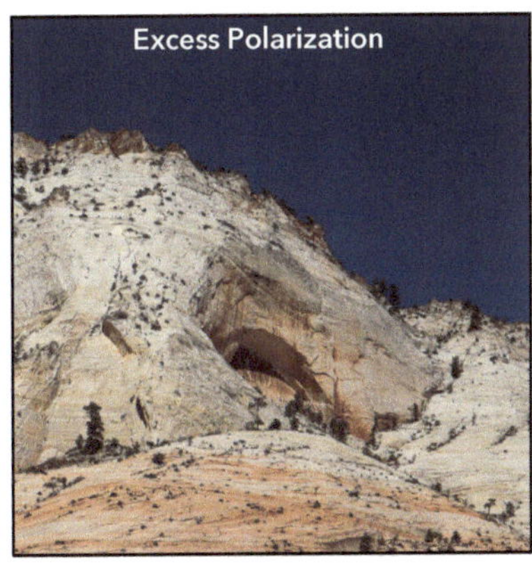

Neutral Density Filter

A neutral density (ND) filter is like a pair of sunglasses for your lens. Its purpose is to filter light, so that you can apply longer shutter speeds. This is the "density" part of its name. The "neutral" piece implies that its use won't impact the color tone of your photograph, but in reality they all do somewhat. And typically, the darker they are, the more un-neutral they become.

Why use a ND filter? When lowering your ISO and setting or stopping-down your aperture for your desired depth of field cannot get you to the shutter speed you desire. For the landscape photographer the most common application is for use with flowing water. If your desire is to create that silky-looking flow, you need to really slow your shutter speed down. My rule of thumb is 0.5 to 2 seconds. Any more isn't doing as much for the look of the water, but perhaps the rest of your scene benefits otherwise. Conversely, if your goal is to capture the more natural "tumble" of water, try between 1/60-1/100 second.

Like circular polarizers, the most typical format are those that screw onto the front of the lens. They come in an abundance of varieties, but if you are just starting out, my recommendation is to select a 4-stop (1.2) neutral density filter.

Capture vs. Final

When capturing an image, I pay close attention to its histogram, and I encourage you to as well. (Go research this topic if necessary.) None of the photographs in this book are "straight from the camera." But then again, none have what some might call "voodoo" applied either. Just basic adjustments to shadows, highlights, saturation, contrast, etc. – to mimic, as best I can, what I remember seeing.

Wait, what's this? This wasn't in the Table of Contents!

I have a few of these throughout the book... Offbeat topics, usually that can apply anywhere – maybe even beyond Zion National Park. They're "just for fun."

This one provides an alternative to your traditional self-portrait. (I'm not wild about self-portraits, but I recognize that occasionally it's fitting to reflect that you were actually there!)

The concept is simple. With lighting behind you, and in front of an interesting vista or subject, capture your shadow or silhouette against the adjacent surface.

Here, I was mesmerized by the apparent, inverted silhouette of a person, cast on the canyon wall to my right. So I joined the party!

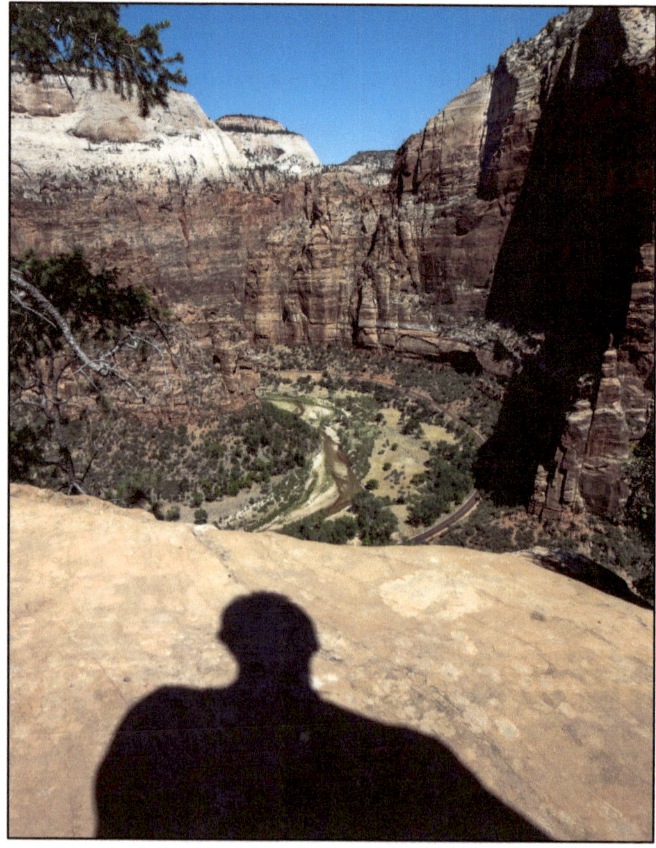

En Route to Hidden Canyon   16mm f/22 1/160s ISO200

Zion Canyon

South Entrance to Temple of Sinawava and ZMC Tunnel

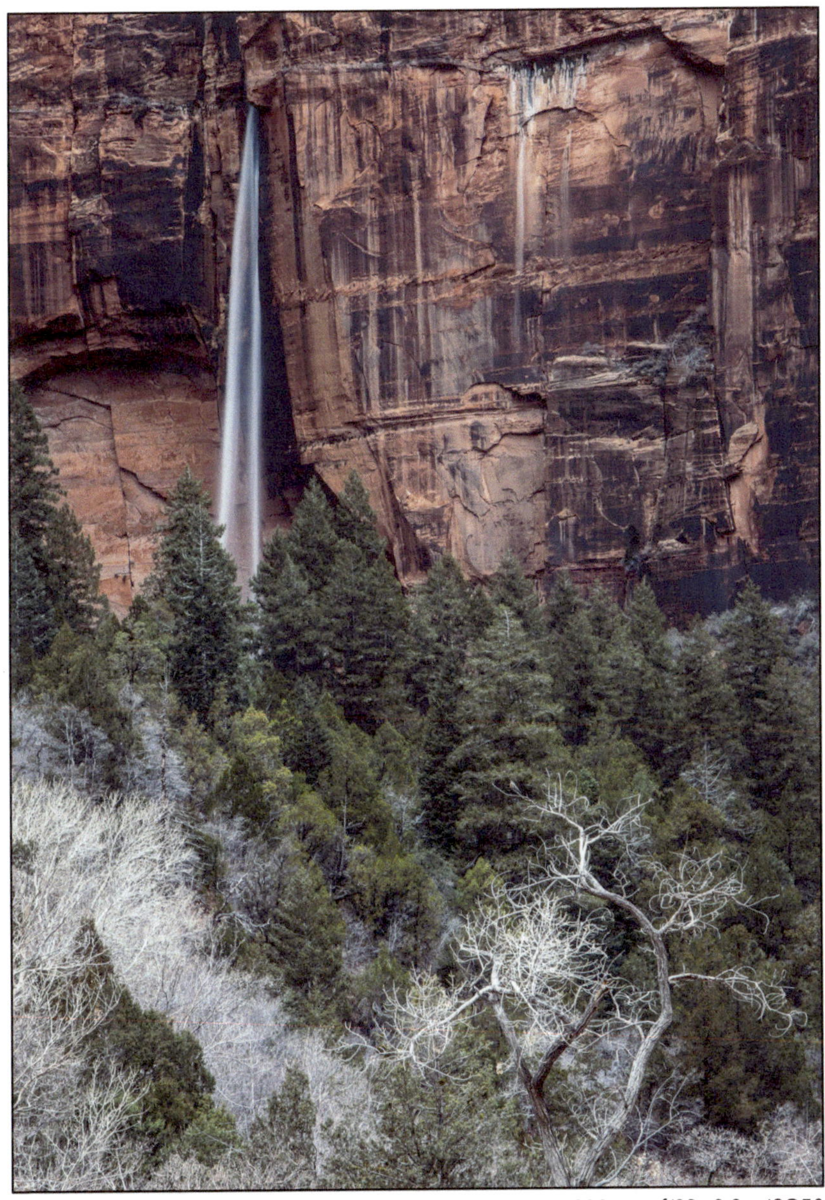

Upper Emerald Pool Waterfall   200mm f/22 0.8s ISO50

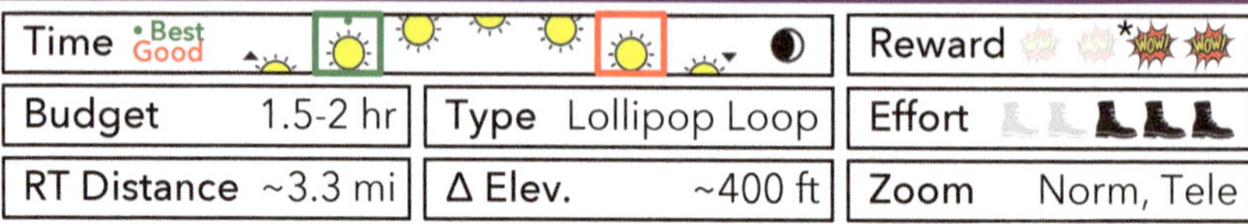

Time	•Best Good	☀ ☀ ☀ ☀ ☀ ☀ ●	Reward	*WOW WOW WOW WOW
Budget	1.5-2 hr	**Type** Lollipop Loop	**Effort**	👢 👢 👢
RT Distance ~3.3 mi		**Δ Elev.** ~400 ft	**Zoom**	Norm, Tele

Zion offers several opportunities to capture The Watchman – this one gets you the closest to it. (I should help clarify, since it confuses some visitors... This trail does **not** take you up The Watchman, but rather alongside it.) And you can see in the photo at the right, it also offers an interesting foreground.

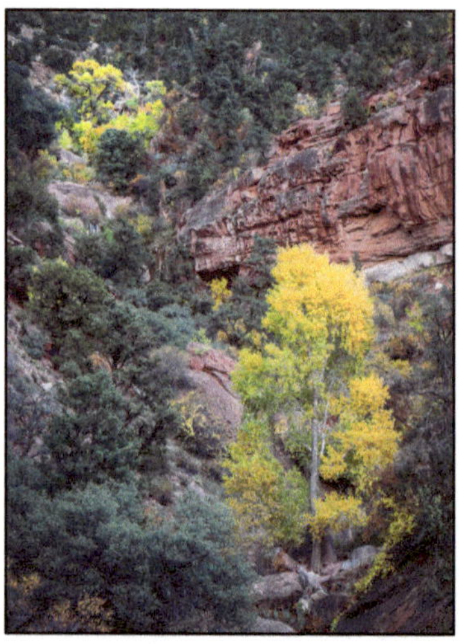

For the first site description in the book, I'm already breaking stride with an asterisk (*) next to the "Wow" factor. For spring, summer, and winter visitors it's a solid "2," but for fall it would earn a "3." On the hike up along the adjacent creek are some beautiful trees that turn brilliant shades of yellow, normally in mid-October.

70mm f/8 1/60s ISO800

The map below helps to outline the trail route. First, it is not instinctive to start in the direction that you will (northeast, alongside the Virgin River). Also, there is a park-maintained loop at the end, which I have never seen on any of the National Park Services' maps.

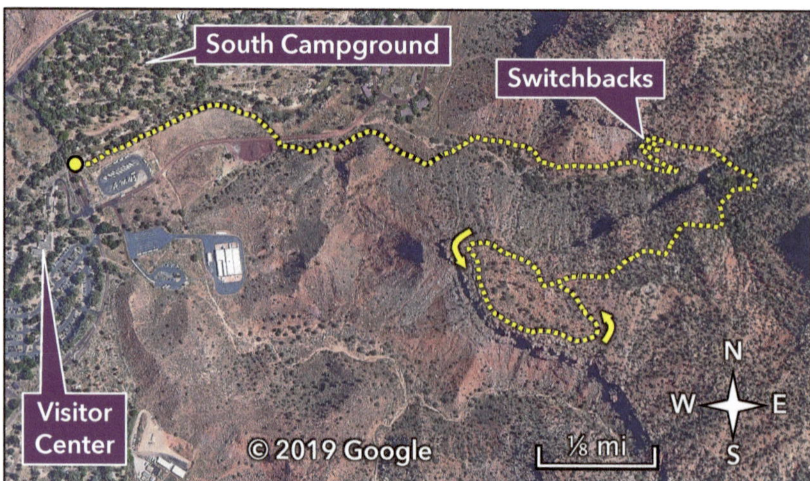

Your timing is important for this hike. If you elect to go in the morning, the goal is to reach the loop at the end before the sun crests the east terrain. Once it does, not only does it heat up very quickly, but the lighting will be too bright for your Watchman composition. (If you find yourself descending under direct sunlight, this isn't as bad, and likely your photography work is already complete.) If conversely, you go in the late afternoon, as the sun is making its way over the west horizon, the lighting can be good here as well, just be sure to take a light for possible use on the return trip down. (And likely also an extra layer of clothes to stay warm!)

Once atop this mesa, enjoy the panoramic views. A small sign will inform you of the loop... I recommend going in a counter-clockwise direction. Since your primary subject is The Watchman, this direction will allow you to curve around and approach various compositions head-on. (Walking clockwise, and you will be more often looking over your shoulder to study your scene.)

Now, we all see things differently – that's the beauty of photography and all forms of art. Personally, I prefer color photography most of the time, but when a dead or decaying tree is my subject matter I tend to switch to my camera's black and white filter. The monotone translation reflects the tree's finality.

Record your work, take a nice break up top, and head back down.

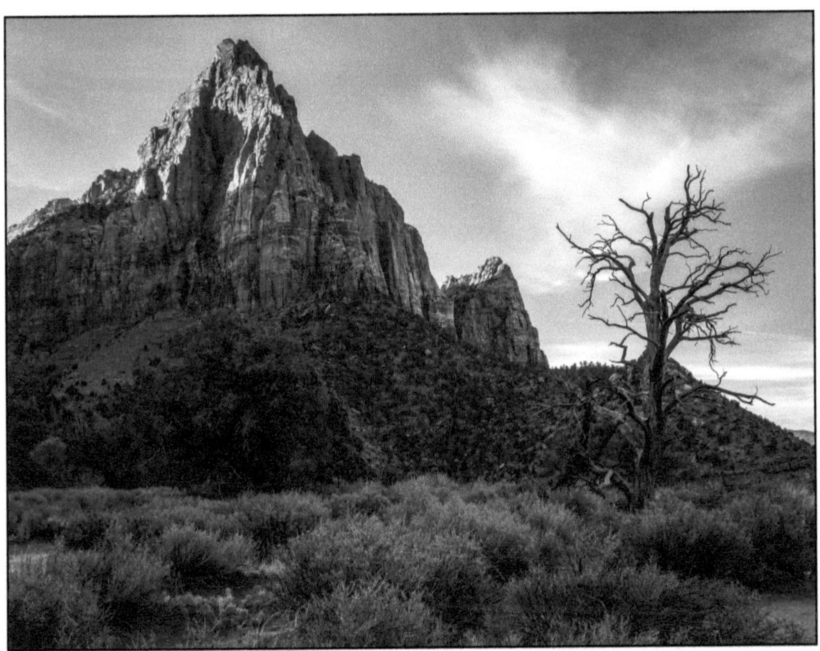

The Watchman   50mm f/11 1/125s ISO800

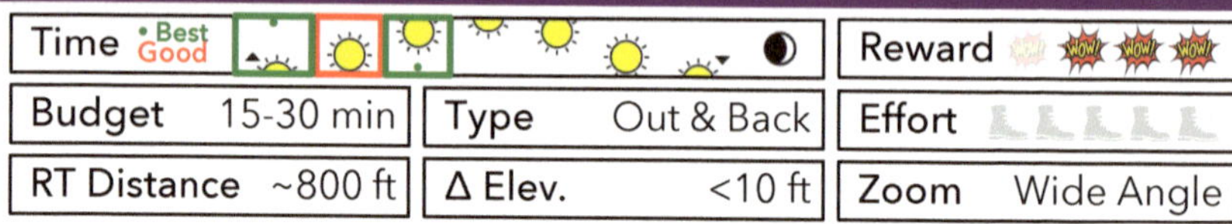

Time	Best / Good		Reward	
Budget	15-30 min	Type	Out & Back	Effort
RT Distance	~800 ft	Δ Elev.	<10 ft	Zoom	Wide Angle

The common advice for this photo is to capture first light (from the rising sun behind you) on the Towers of the Virgin for sensational color. One problem... the magic is heavily dependent on the presence of clouds in the east to filter the incoming, bright light. I have found most mornings to be uncooperative. However!.. I have had repeatable success mid- to late morning at this vista. So, consider either or both for your own itinerary. Below is the late morning variety... See page 95 (from Canyon Overlook Trail [22]) for the seemingly-rare, more colorful showing of light.

The vista is accessed from the backside of the Zion Human History Museum. This museum is on the west side of Highway 9 between the Zion Canyon Visitor Center and Canyon Junction. Parking here is normally not an issue, however if none is available then a shuttle bus ride may be required. (The bus stops at the museum.) When you reach the museum, walk to its right side around to the back for the view.

The best place to position yourself is at the far left end of the short stone wall (near the corner).

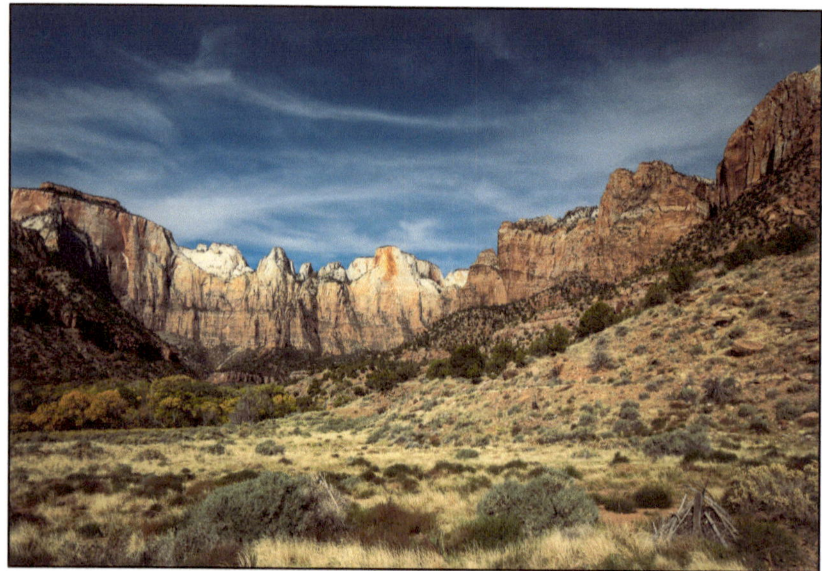

Towers of the Virgin   24mm f/11 1/125s ISO100

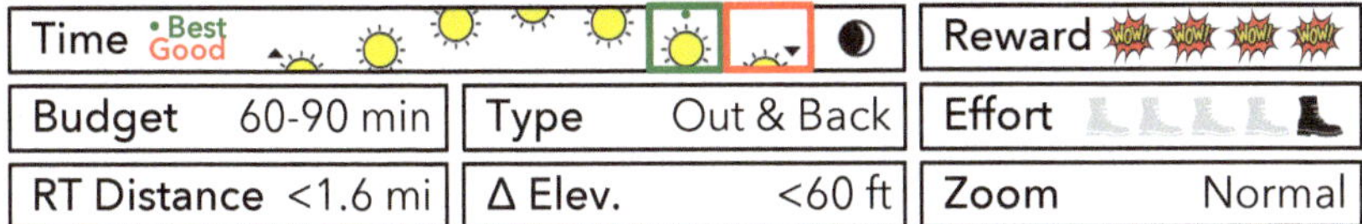

Time	•Best Good							Reward
Budget	60-90 min		**Type**		Out & Back		**Effort**	
RT Distance	<1.6 mi		**Δ Elev.**		<60 ft		**Zoom**	Normal

The Watchman and the Virgin River... The composition below is one of the hallmark images of Zion National Park. It *was* on the cover of the first edition of this book, and I sure was proud of it. Clearly though, as you hold this later edition in your hand, you recognize a different image on the cover – now that of the Virgin River and The Three Patriarchs (4), covered next.

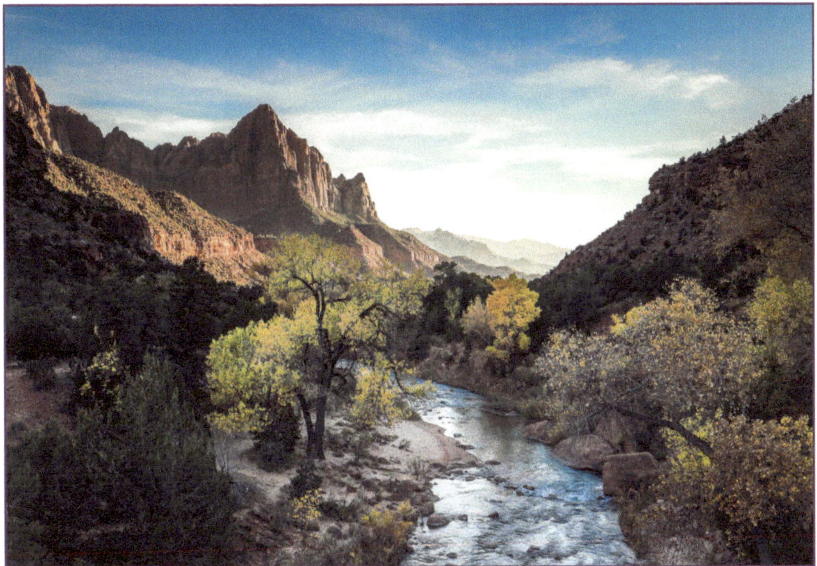

The Watchman - From Vehicle Bridge in October   35mm f/8 1/80s ISO200

This iconic composition of The Watchman and the Virgin River is taken from the vehicle bridge at Canyon Junction. In 2020 the National Park Service posted new signage at this location... **Stopping, standing, or walking on the vehicle bridge is no longer permitted.**

I have updated this site's narrative to adhere to this new, posted restriction. The good news is that the combination of elements within this popular composition is still possible along the very nice **Pa'rus Trail**.

The Pa'rus Trail is a gentle, mostly-paved path alongside the Virgin River between the Zion Canyon Visitor Center and Canyon Junction. There are a few interesting sites along the route, and I considered even renaming this site to "Pa'rus Trail," but still I want the focus to be the pursuit of a similar composition to the above, so I left it as-is.

The north end of the Pa'rus Trail begins at the Canyon Junction Shuttle Stop (along a sidewalk on the west side of the road). The mileages listed on these pages begin at 0.00 from this shuttle stop. ...Of course, you can walk from the visitor center or elsewhere, but if time is critical then beginning at the shuttle stop is the most efficient place to start.

The southbound path veers away from the road's edge and down to continue underneath the vehicle bridge at ~0.08 mile (400 ft). It is worth noting that a shot from the west bank (opposite side) of the Virgin River captures the same elements of the picture on the prior page, but when at the water's edge the perspective of the trees from below dwarf The Watchman. Also, since walking across this bridge is prohibited and the next closest shuttle stop is at the museum this riverside option leaves a bit to be desired.

Bridge 1: Reach this northernmost bridge at ~0.14 mile. This bridge crosses over Lower Pine Creek, just before it merges with the Virgin River. This viewpoint is different than the rest, as the Virgin River is mostly out of sight. However, if you like instead a bridge in the composition and typically lighter crowds, this one has merit.

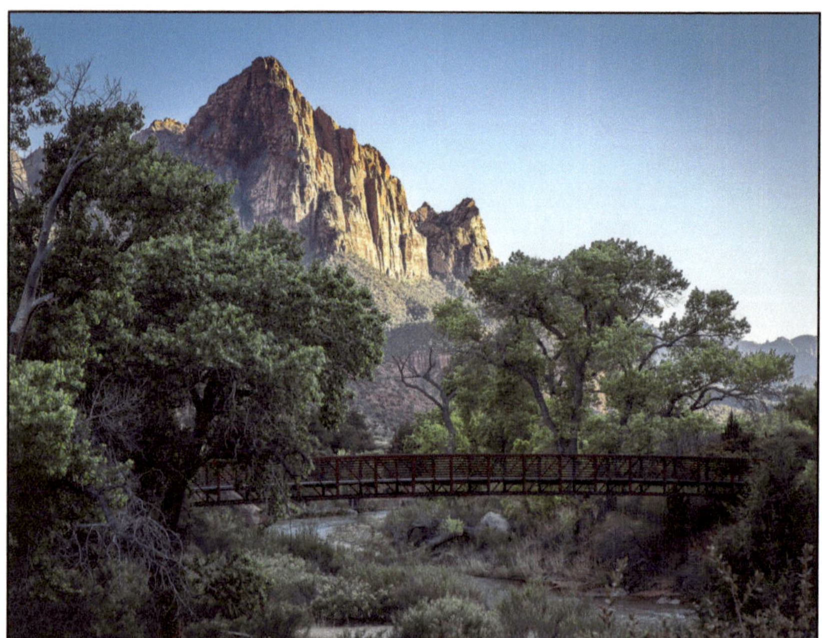

The Watchman - From Bridge 1 in April   70mm f/8 1/160s ISO200

★ **Bridge 2:** Reach this bridge at ~0.22 mile. I would award this vantage second place among the four. It is a bit lacking on the left side of the frame but has the most unobstructed view of The Watchman. Downriver you can see the diversion dam, in place for

42

Springdale's water supply. (Locate an information board regarding this dam at ~0.34 mile.) An upriver composition is very nice from Bridge 2, capturing Lower Pine Creek flowing into the Virgin River.

★ **Bridge 3:** Reach this bridge at ~0.38 mile. This bridge takes first place on my list with The Watchman, trees on both sides of the water, and the Pa'rus Trail (parallel to and complimentary of the Virgin River). This view, more than any other, is sensitive to exactly where you position yourself on the bridge. Sample accordingly.

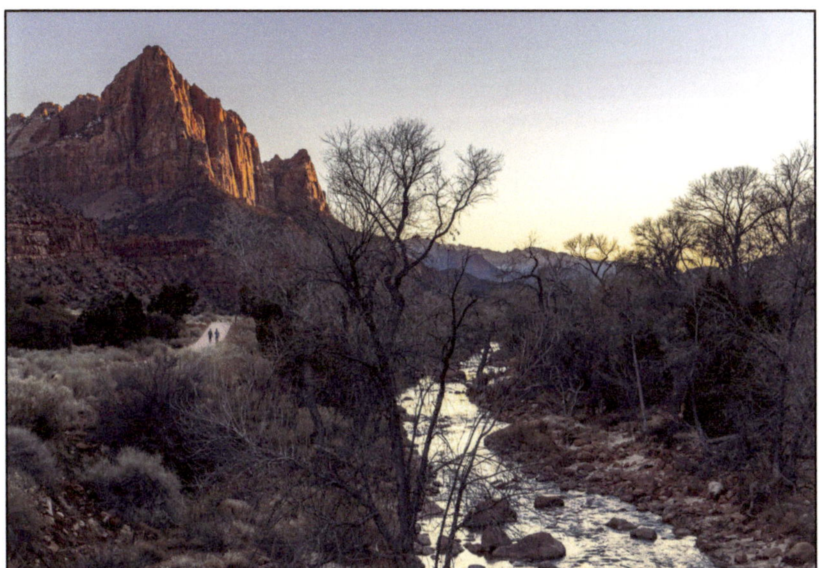

The Watchman - From Bridge 3 in January　　　　　50mm f/11 1/20s ISO100

Once having crossed Bridge 3, en route to Bridge 4, enjoy a broad meadow at your left. Wildlife frequents this area during sunrise and sunset. If looking for an alternative view of The Watchman, perhaps more entirely filling your frame, this stretch is a nice option.

Bridge 4: Reach this bridge at ~0.79 mile. This is my least favorite of the four because the trees along the river have thick trunks and really dominate the "weight" of the scene. If this though is of interest to you, then check it out! Like Bridge 2, the view upriver is interesting, so don't forget to look in that direction if at this location.

In a nutshell, I recommend heading out from the shuttle stop and at minimum checking out Bridges 1, 2, and 3. Study Bridge 2 closely before continuing to Bridge 3. Once at Bridge 3, decide to stay or double-back. (Or continue to Bridge 4 if you're still not sure!)

The Cottonwoods' leaves (color, or lack thereof) impact the scene greatly, as you can see across these images taken over three seasons.

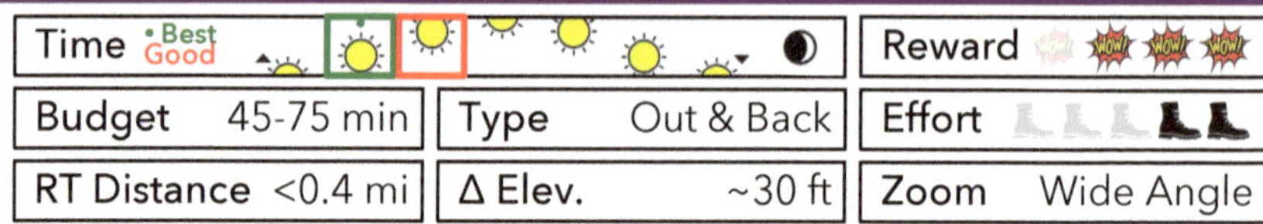

Time	Best Good										Reward	WOW WOW WOW
Budget	45-75 min			**Type**	Out & Back		**Effort**					
RT Distance	<0.4 mi			**Δ Elev.**	~30 ft		**Zoom**	Wide Angle				

Zion's "Three Patriarchs" peaks are named, from left to right, after the biblical figures Abraham, Isaac, and Jacob.

The phrase "Court of the Patriarchs" is used in 3 places, and so I want to provide some clarity here...

The actual Court of the Patriarchs is an open space near the bottom of these peaks, on the west side of the Virgin River, about 0.2 mile from the Zion Canyon Scenic Drive. That's not where we're going. However, if you take the Sand Bench Loop on Horse (6), you will stop here.

Court of the Patriarchs is also used to define one of the shuttle stops. This is the stop that serves our particular destination, so do take it!

On the east side of this same shuttle stop is the much-trafficked short, paved climb to the Court of the Patriarchs Viewpoint. While popular, it provides no interesting foreground. Use your time elsewhere.

So where are we going? Not to any "court," but simply a superb perspective of the Three Patriarchs, from the Virgin River!

At the south end of the west (down canyon) side of the shuttle stop find a set of stone steps leading down to a trail towards the Virgin River. Pick up the main, wide path heading westerly. Horse stables are to your left as you walk. Once closer to the water tower the trail will narrow but does remain obvious. At the pedestrian bridge, carefully follow the path down to the east bank of the river.

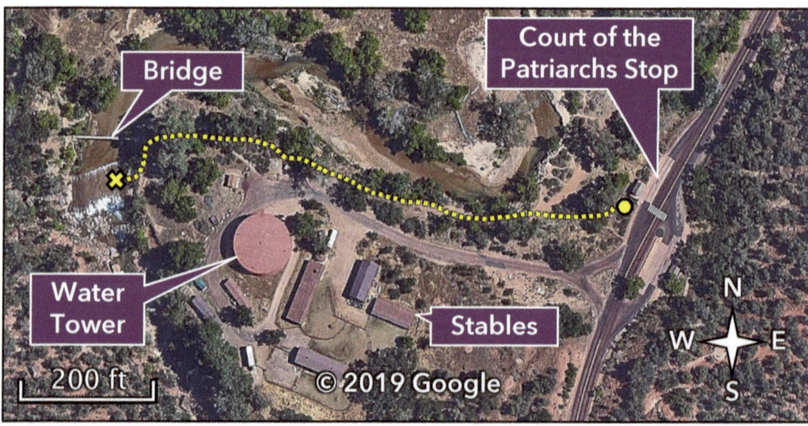

Now you have some options. The first one is binary – to either walk into the river or not. The best compositions are from within the river. If you elect this route, be equipped with shoes or rugged sandals that may be submerged, and of course be careful where you step – the features beneath the water can be slippery.

Next is which route to take and where to position yourself. There are two options here – after that first gentle cascade on top of the more course river bottom, or in the more smoothly-flowing section of water under the bridge. (Any further downstream, and the vista is crowded by adjacent trees.)

The first option, further back, allows for the cascade to be a part of the composition.   Here it is easy to compose with all three peaks, though a wide angle lens is a must.

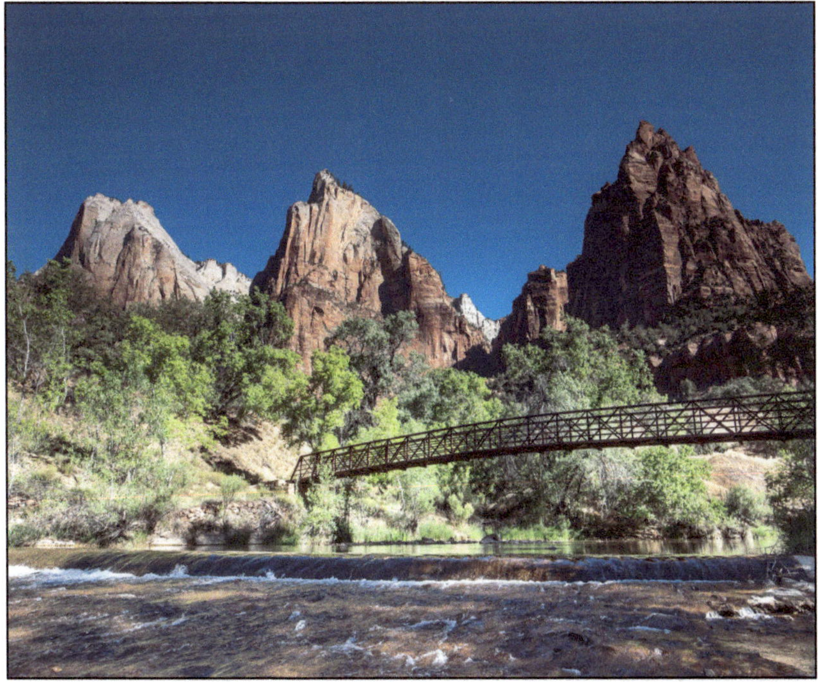

The Three Patriarchs   20mm f/11 1/80s ISO200

The second option, closer to the bridge, allows for a reflection of the peaks and bridge to be captured in the water, though it may be hard to capture all three peaks at once. If this is the case, you can concentrate on Isaac with your composition. See page 90 for this result.

Try them both!

Time	Best Good		Reward
Budget	15-30 min	Type	Meandering	Effort
RT Distance	<0.2 mi	Δ Elev.	<10 ft	Zoom	Normal

Zion National Park, like many national parks, is home to early 20th century rustic-themed architecture – buildings designed both for function and to celebrate the natural surroundings in which they reside. The most-easily accessible and the arguably the best at Zion are at The Grotto and around the Zion Lodge areas.

My favorite is the Artist-in-Residence cabin at The Grotto. It's a humble structure, completed in 1924. It has been used for a variety of purposes in the last century, at times a welcome center and a museum. Today it is a residence for visiting artists in its program.

South of The Grotto area is the Zion Lodge, including its hotel and rustic cabins. While the two hotel buildings aren't really all that fantastic, the lodge itself and the quaint little cabins are. Coupled with lodge's gigantic courtyard Cottonwood plus deer and wild turkeys that frequent the area, and you have the possibility of a sensational photograph. Crowds of people may make this challenging, but here the lighting and potential for wildlife are at their best early in the morning and late in the afternoon, normally when most of the visitors have departed.

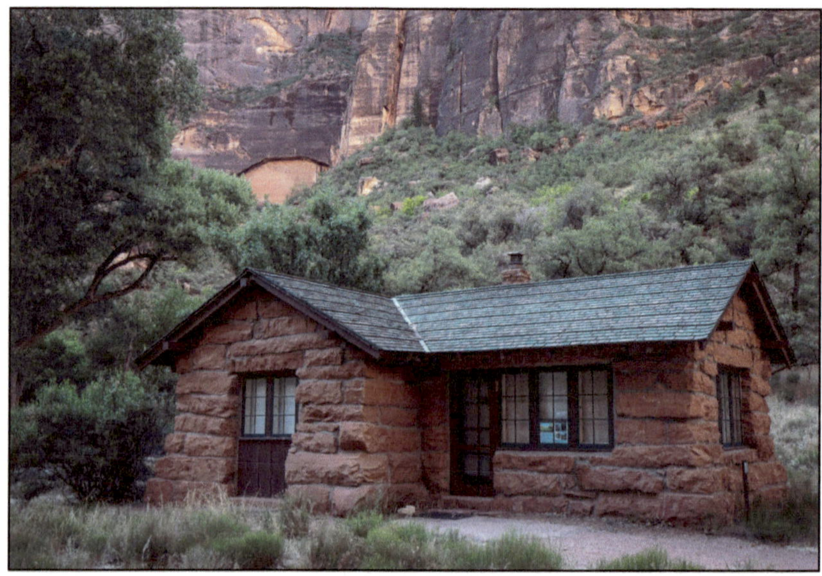

Artist-in-Residence Cabin at The Grotto   35mm f/11 1/50s ISO800

Time	Best Good			Reward	WOW! WOW! WOW!
Budget	3-3.5 hr	Type	Lollipop Loop	Effort	Yeehaw!
RT Distance	~7.6 mi	Δ Elev.	~500 ft	Zoom	See Text

I am very excited to share this horseback and photography experience with you. I wholeheartedly recommend it if you're looking to add some variety to your Zion visit.

Canyon Trail Rides is the outfitter and guide. They offer this experience at multiple national parks, so perhaps the fastest way to find them on the Internet is to simply search for "Zion Horseback Riding."

Their service is to provide guides, orientation to horseback riding (beginners welcome!), a saddled-up horse (or mule), the ride, and a water break about halfway through. Their trail rides are not crafted to cater to photographers. This is important to recognize and respect. Their responsibility is your safety and enjoyment, and to keep the pace of the riding party on schedule.

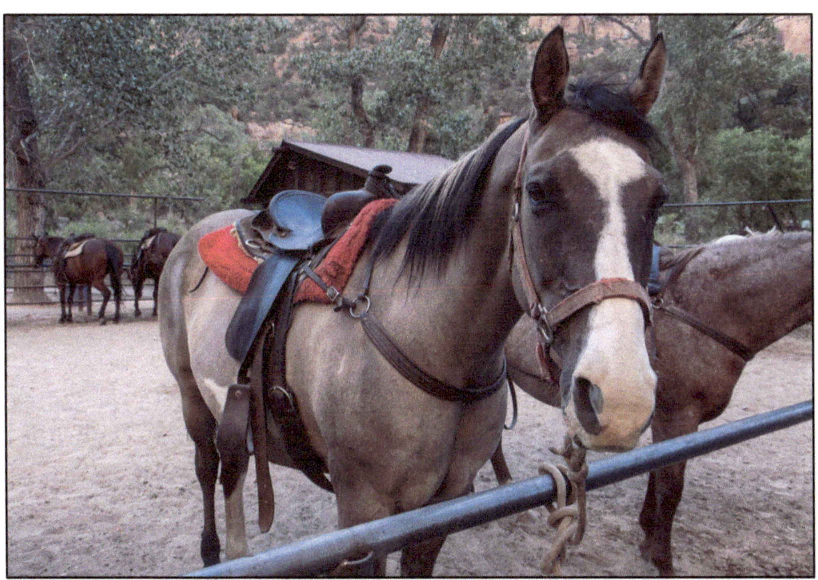

Saddled-Up and Ready to Ride   28mm f/4 1/60s ISO100

This section covers the 3 hour ride. You depart from and return to the corral across the road from the Zion Lodge area. You'll immediately cross the Virgin River and meander up to the Court of the Patriarchs and onto the Sand Bench Loop.

Their website has many details, including rider age and weight limitations, as well as departure times. I strongly recommend a morning ride, due to canyon temperatures and lighting.

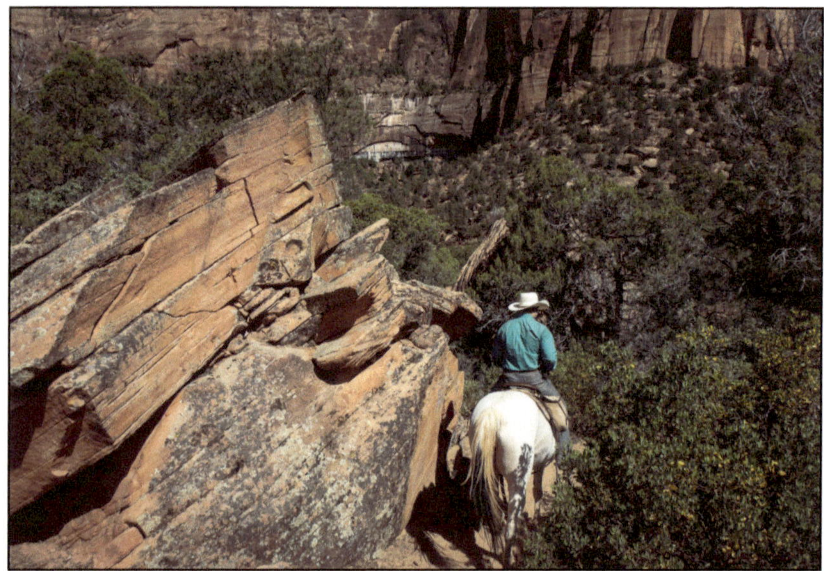

Along the Ride   28mm f/5.6 1/1250s ISO100

Please note – bags and backpacks are not allowed! My advice is to leave your big camera behind. Instead, take along either a point-and-shoot or simply use your phone's camera. Either must be tethered to your body. My setup was a point-and-shoot coupled to a shoulder strap, but hung over my head and one shoulder for a secure fit. First, you will be using your arms while riding. Dropping a camera (or anything for that matter) is inexcusable. Second, the ride can be very dusty, so a camera without external moving parts will far less likely be damaged from this environment.

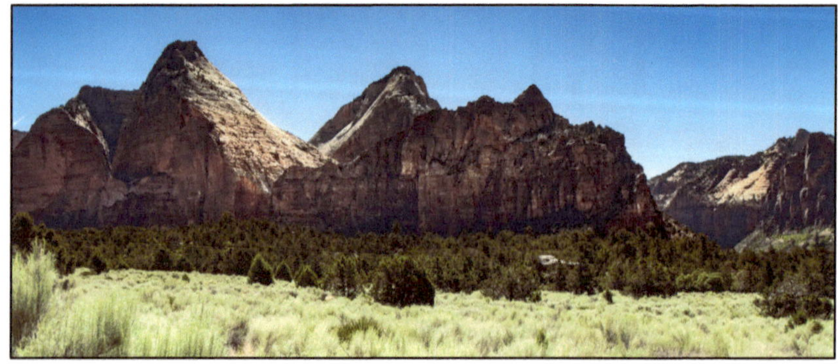

The Sand Bench   28mm f/4 1/600s ISO100

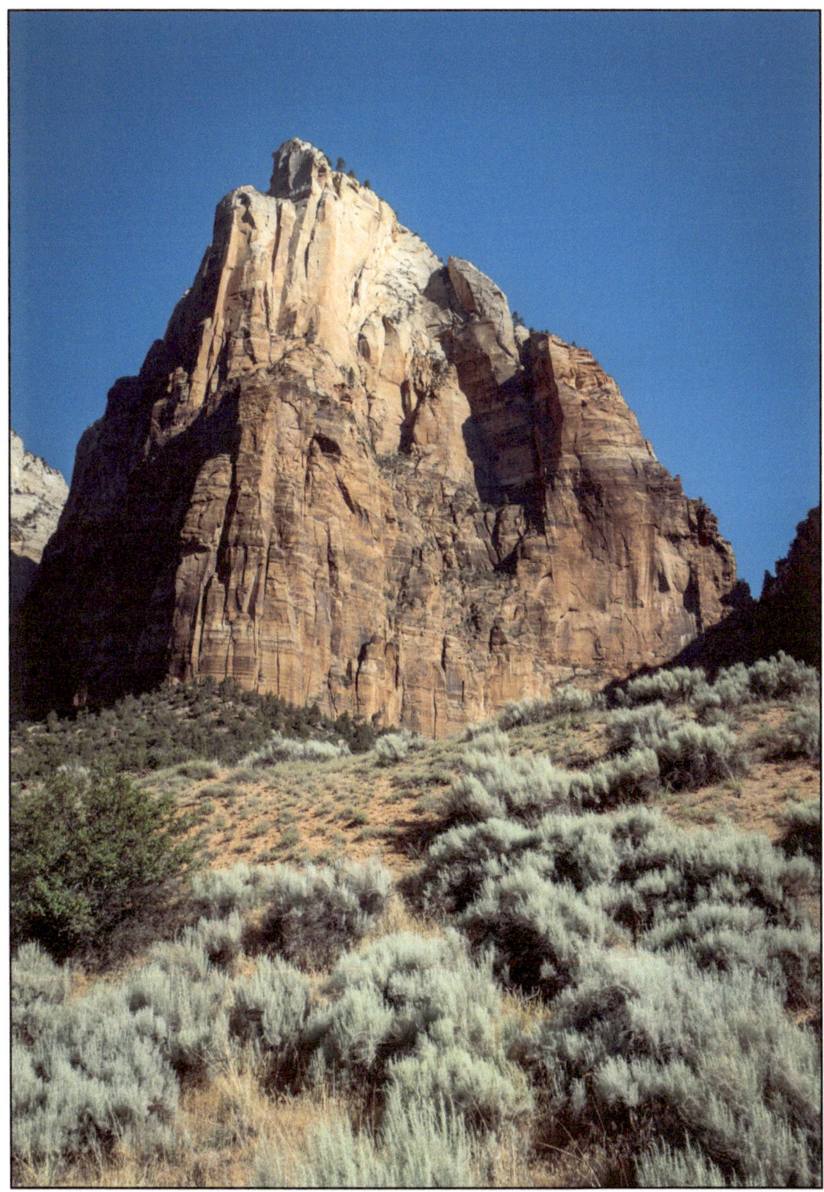

Sagebrush on Court of the Patriarchs   35mm f/5.6 1/1250s ISO100

Really, as stated before, your tour guides' priorities are safety, your enjoyment riding and sightseeing, and timeliness. If fumbling with your camera interrupts any of these elements, they probably will ask that you stow it for the duration of the ride. Be competent and efficient in your handling of your camera. Practice with one hand how you will use your camera before you arrive at the corral.

The photography along the way is straightforward. Listen to your guides for interesting features and information. Look for compositions that are unique to your riding experience.

After the conclusion of your ride, consider tipping your guide or guides. An amount of $10 or $20 (or more or less) is greatly appreciated, and it may help encourage the continued ability for future visitors to use their cameras too!

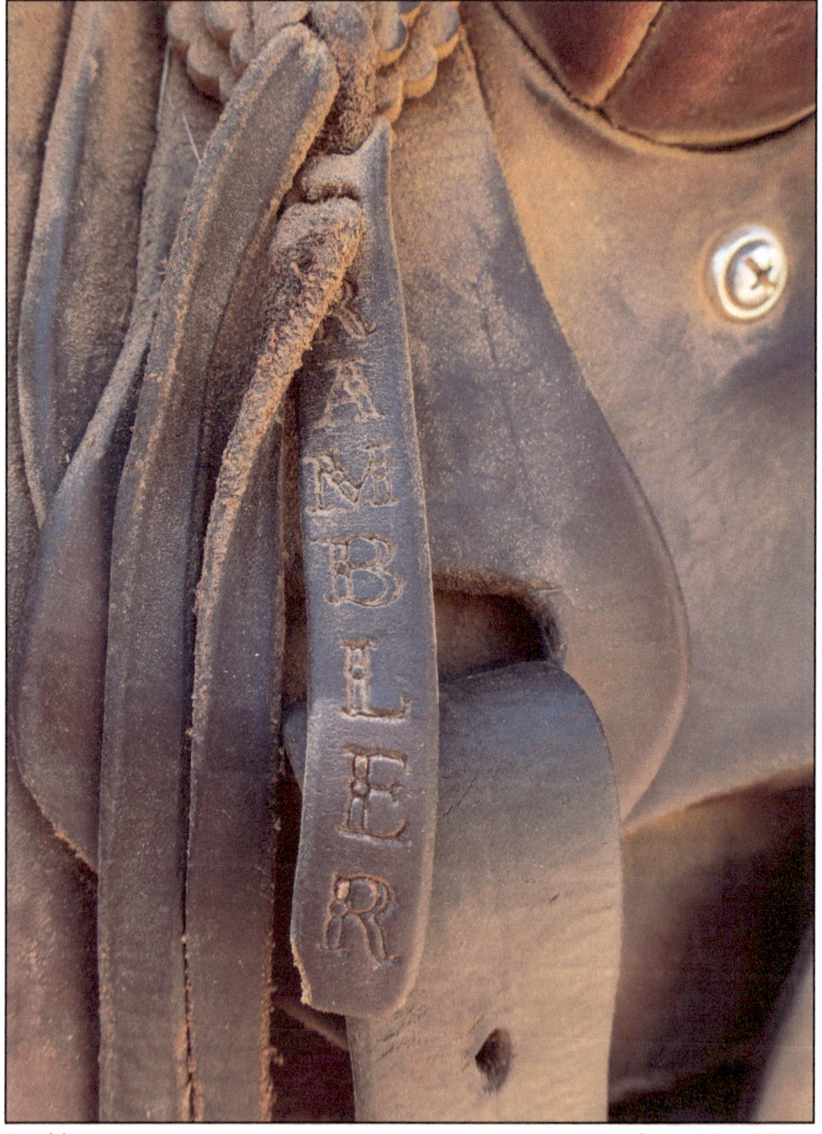

Rambler   28mm f/4 1/80s ISO100

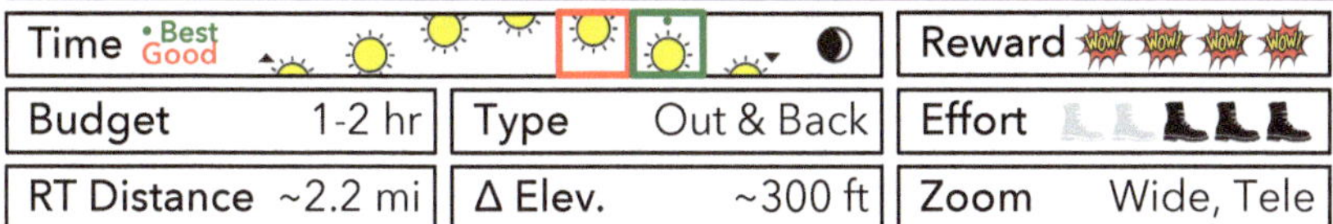

On my first trip to Zion National Park, my stepfather and I rolled into the park mid-afternoon, checked into our cabin at the Zion Lodge, readied our photo bags, and crossed the street to check out the Emerald Pools Trail. Wow! Superb choice.

I was immediately hooked on Zion.

If you're like us and arrive in the afternoon, this is a great place to start. Perhaps the best. Couple it with a subsequent hike back down via the Kayenta Trail (8) even closer to sunset, and you have an extraordinary introduction to Zion National Park.

The hike begins across the footbridge over the Virgin River, adjacent to the parking lot that serves the horse corral.

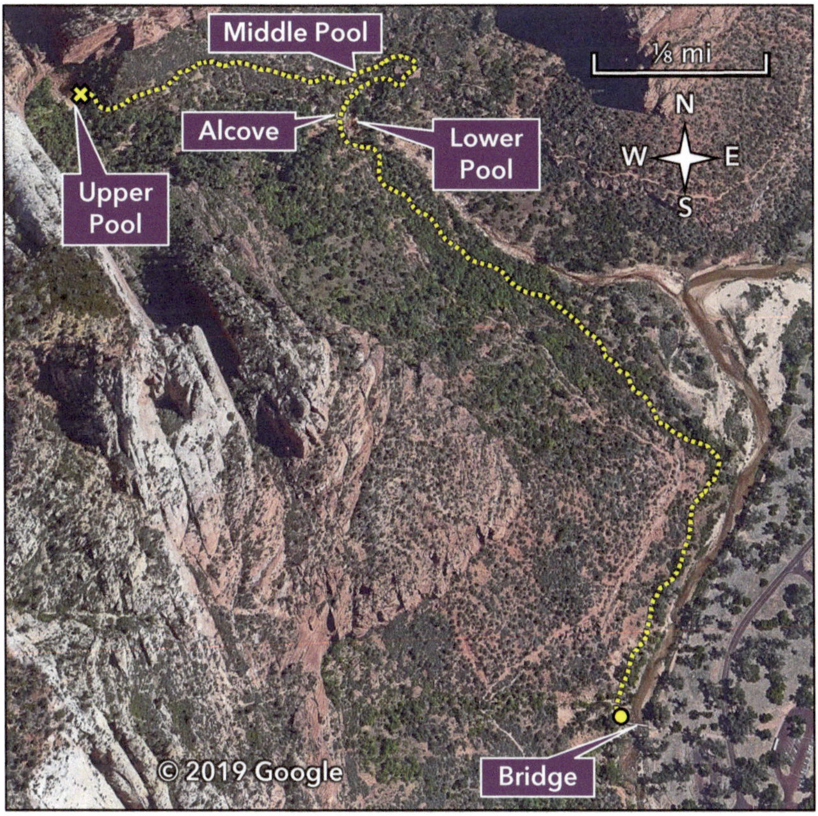

The walk to the alcove doesn't really have much photographic potential, but that's OK, because once you arrive at the alcove things get interesting quickly.

The Lower Emerald Pool becomes visible, down below the path. Try photographing it, from alongside the handrail, with a telephoto lens.

Continuing forward, a very light waterfall is normally raining water right around and onto the path. This can be a fun subject to photograph – just be mindful of the water spray and your camera kit.

Back on the move, walk under the large alcove. You will be able now to see the rest of the Lower Emerald Pool. (I have yet to find a good composition to capture it from here, but perhaps your creativity will provide otherwise.)

The trail bends to the right. Now you're on the beginning of an ascent to the Middle Emerald Pool... This section is where it gets good. And I mean really good. You will spot multiple larger places alongside the trail to take some shots of the sweeping and colorful alcove. While still well "below" the Middle Emerald Pool (the source of the nearest waterfall), either shoot ultrawide (12-16mm) or create a panorama. This sweeping view is so awesome.

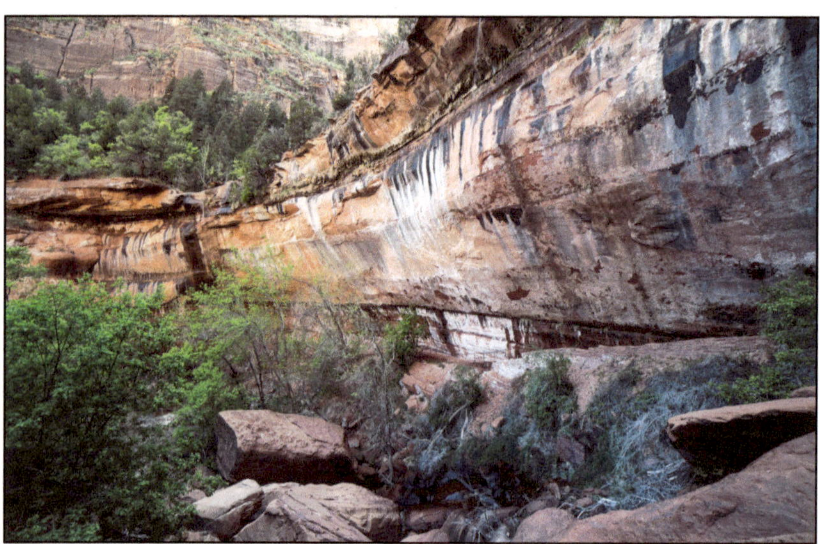

Alcove at Emerald Pools - From Below   14mm f/8 1/30s ISO200

Time for a little stair-climbing. Up a ways, and you'll now find yourself at about the level of the top of this waterfall. There is another space for your work, and here you can capture a similar scene, but with a different perspective. Amazing how a slight shift in elevation has so much impact – another absolutely marvelous view!

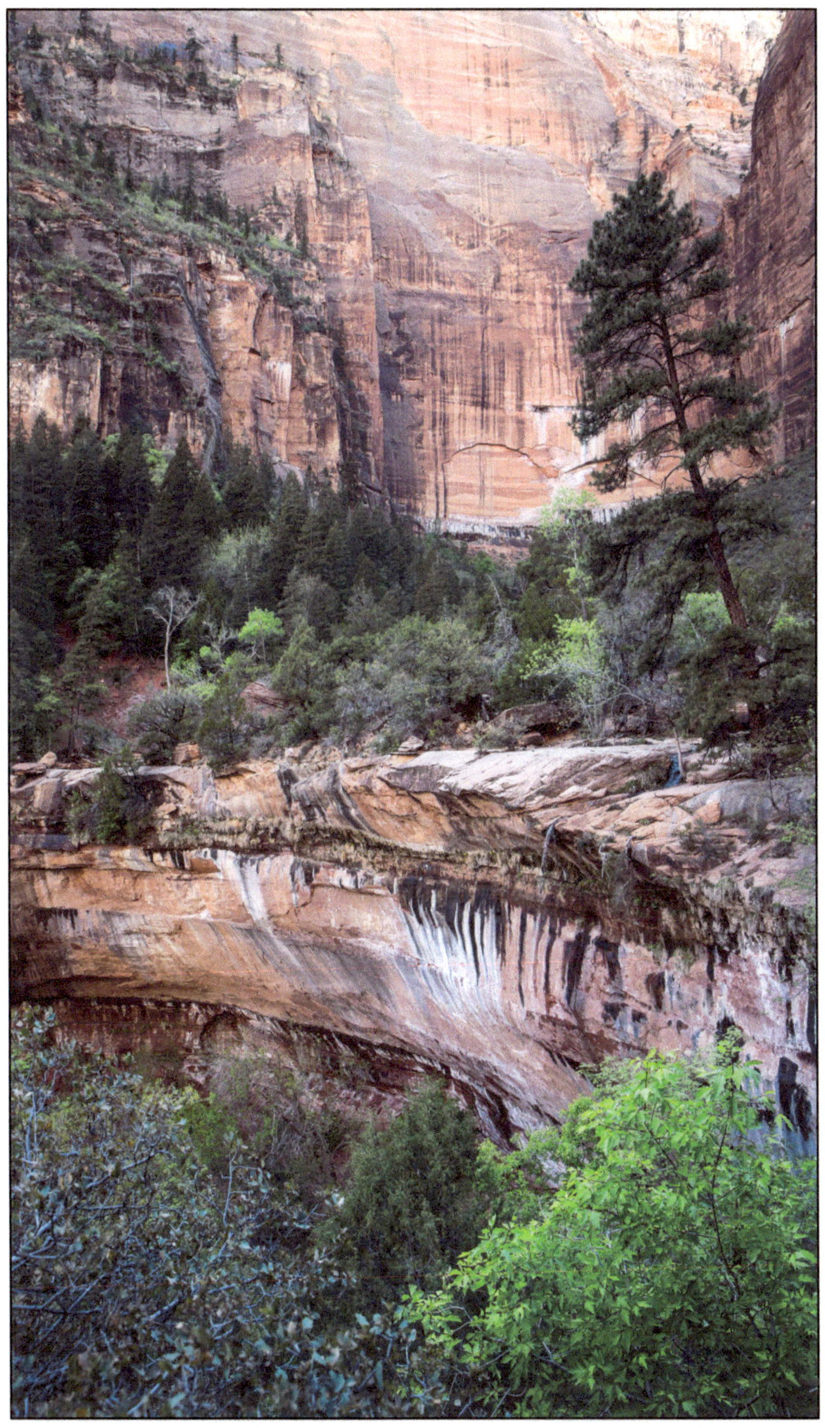

Alcove at Emerald Pools - From Above 24mm f/5.6 1/125s ISO400

Back on the trail, the next destination is the Middle Emerald Pool. On the way you will walk up some more stone steps and through two large boulders with a confident, slender tree growing in this narrow space. Both the steps and the gap between the boulders make for interesting subjects as well. Good places for more composition experimentation.

You will reach the Middle Emerald Pool. Truth is, there are actually two Middle Emerald Pools, but the one near the edge is the only one that warrants attention. Be careful here – the wet ground can be slippery. Adhere to the sign's warnings of the dangers in the water and on this high-up edge.

A reflection of Deertrap Mountain can be captured in this pool's water, but the lighting contrast can be challenging, to say the least.

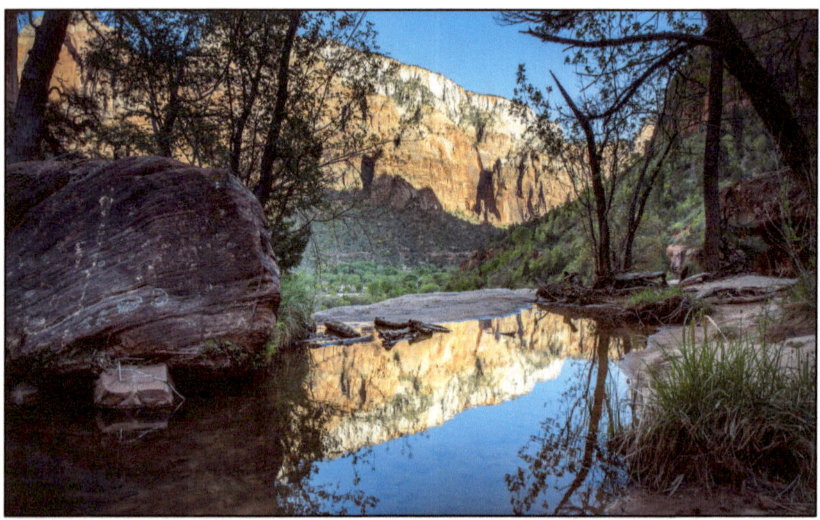

Middle Emerald Pool   24mm f/11 1/30s ISO100

Time again to stow your gear, because now the hike gets a bit more technical to the Upper Emerald Pool, and there's really nothing to shoot along the way.

When you arrive, take a break, and enjoy this hike's final destination. Crowds can form here, so a bit of patience may be required – especially for still water within the pool, as many people like to cool their feet and stir it up a bit. Once calm, and likely with a tripod, use a slower shutter speed to help smooth it and capture this tall alcove.

That's basically it! Either retrace your steps completely, or after the two boulders and tree where the signs point to The Grotto, take it if you wish to explore the Kayenta Trail (8) instead on the way down.

54

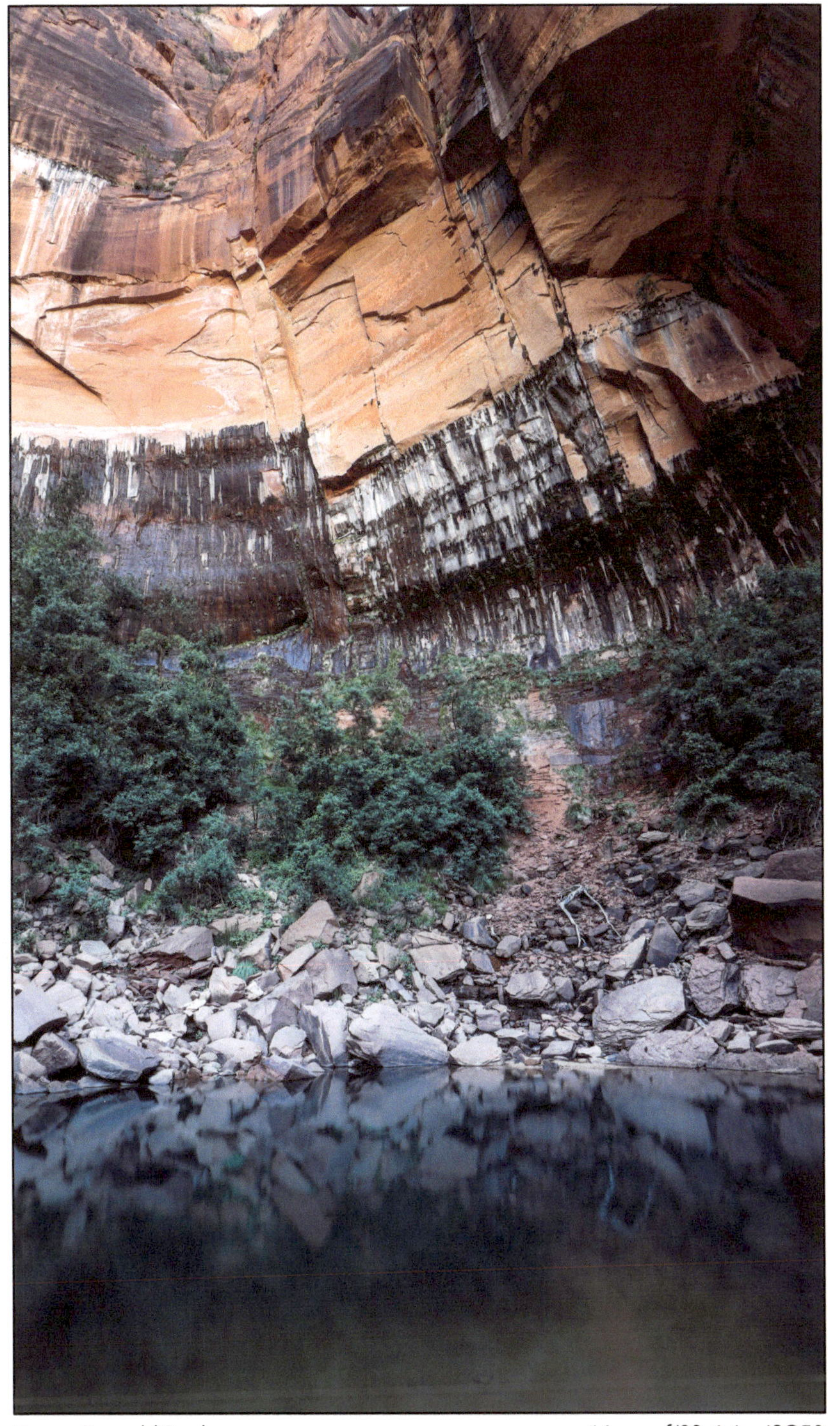

Upper Emerald Pool

16mm f/22 1.6s ISO50

Time	• Best Good			Reward
Budget	1-1.5 hr	Type	Out & Back	Effort
RT Distance	~2.0 mi	Δ Elev.	~150 ft	Zoom	Norm, Tele

If we were to consider the Kayenta Trail as a "standalone" hike, its beginning is directly across the pedestrian bridge from The Grotto, and its end is near the Middle Emerald Pool. This one-way distance is approximately 1 mile. So for consistency's sake, in our legend above, the round trip distance is double this, approximately 2 miles.

That said, I recommend that you enjoy the Kayenta Trail after visiting the Emerald Pools. (However many Emerald Pools you desire!) Begin with the Emerald Pools Trail, visit the lower pools, the alcove area, then either also include the middle and upper pools or do not – but then descend via the Kayenta Trail to The Grotto.

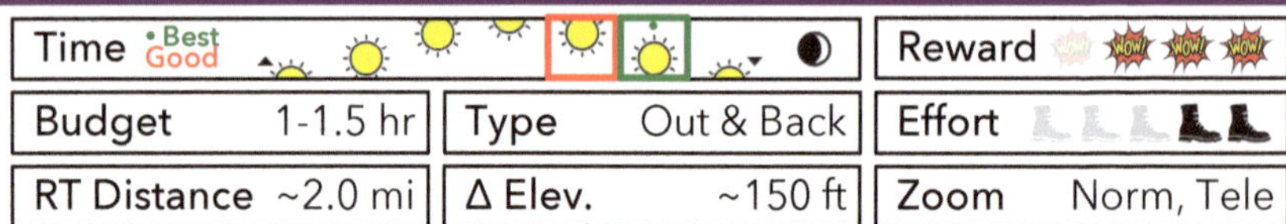

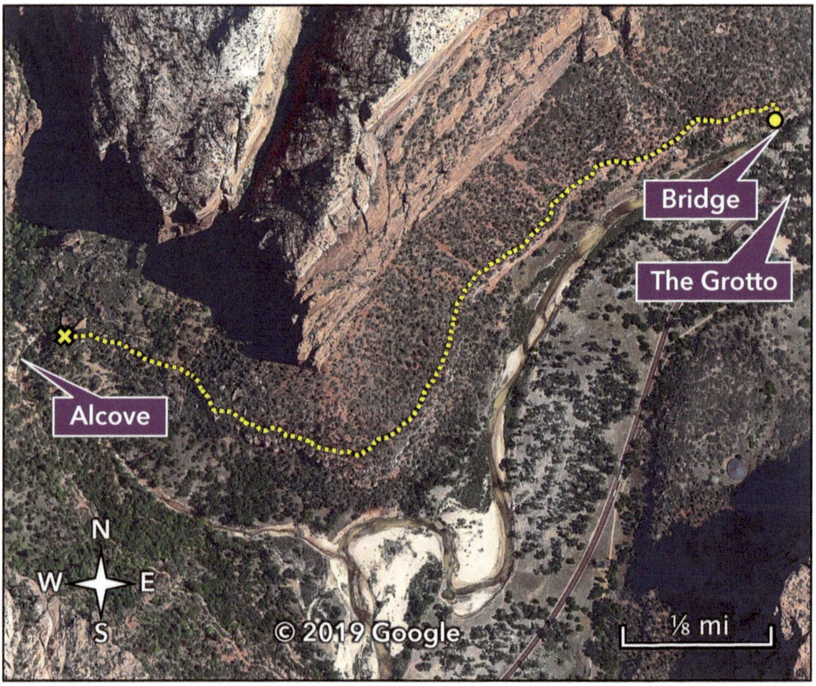

The Kayenta Trail skirts the Virgin River, but at a higher elevation than the water, with many steep drop-offs and as many dynamic views of the canyon.

The lighting on the adjacent page is worth waiting a little bit for, if you find yourself somewhat early.

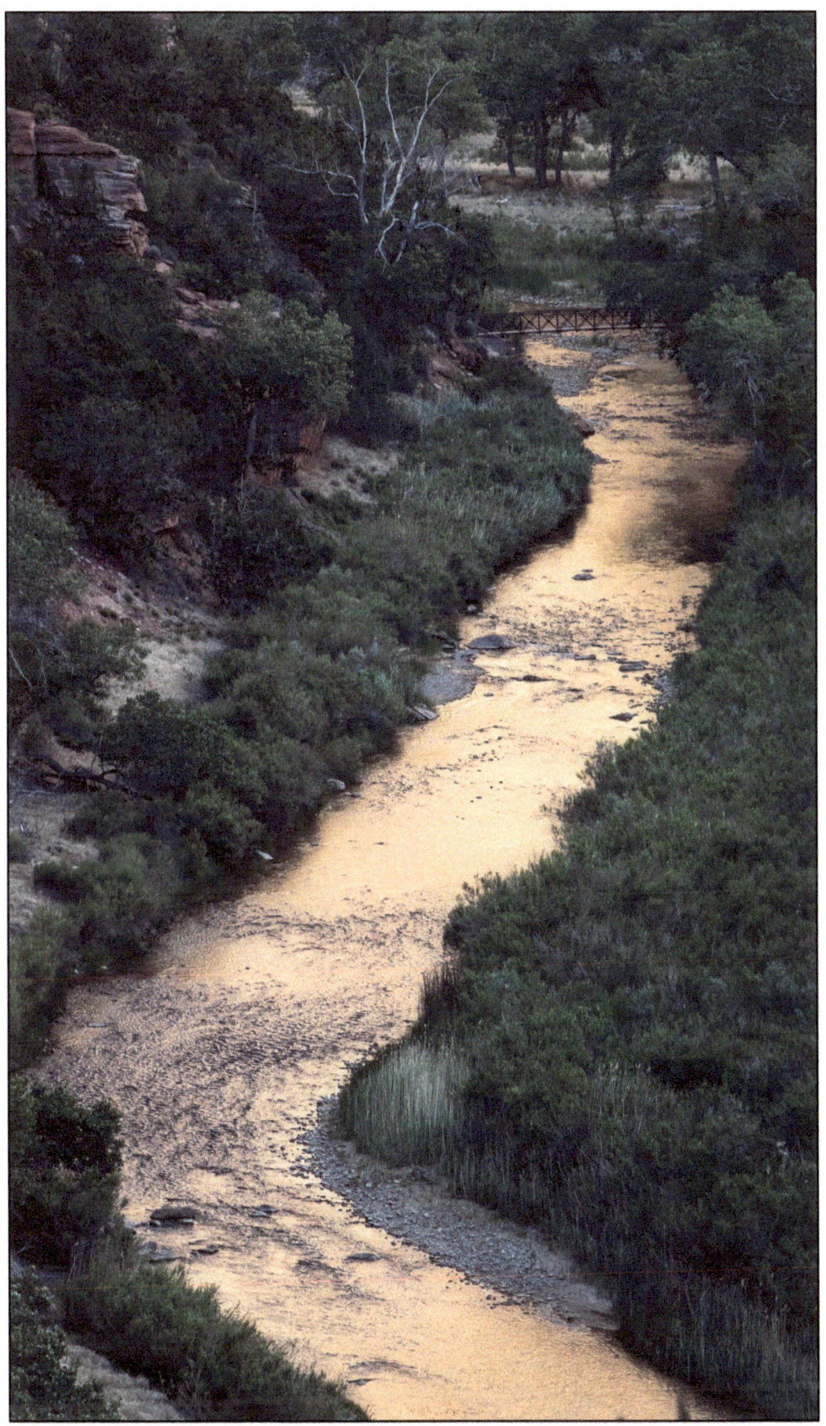

Reflected Golden Light on the Virgin River   200mm   f/5.6   1/320s   ISO800

The Kayenta Trail offers photographers two unique opportunities...
1) Lines of sight with sensational lighting on the Virgin River and
adjacent trees during the very late afternoon, and 2) Additional,
fantastic views of the alcove at Emerald Pools. All of it gorgeous!

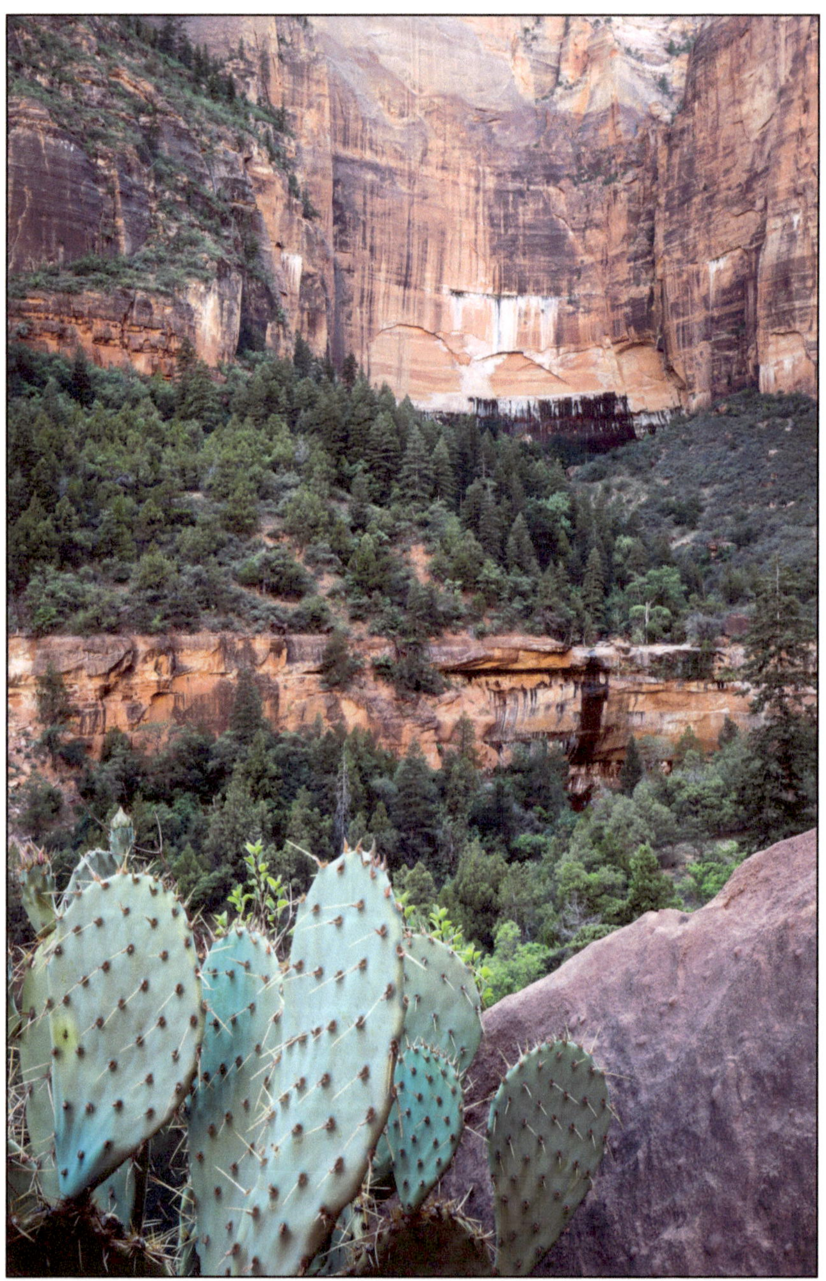

Emerald Pools Alcove from the Kayenta Trail   35mm f/22 0.5s ISO100

Time	**Best Good** ☀	Reward 💥 💥 💥 💥
Budget	3-5 hr	Type	Out & Back	Effort 👢👢👢👢👢
RT Distance ~5.4 mi	Δ Elev. ~1,500 ft	Zoom	Normal

Angels Landing is quintessential Zion, and I highly recommend it, as long as you're up for it physically and mentally. *We'll explore this last component in a moment...*

Some good news here – if after reading the below you feel like hiking Angels Landing in its entirety is too much, Scout Lookout offers some fantastic views as well. I would still fit it in the "strenuous" category getting there, but hiking to it is not technical. So, if you have some people in your group who would like to go to the top, and others don't, part of your party can hang loose at Scout Lookout while others summit Angels Landing.

Alright, let's explore my physical and mental readiness statement above. From The Grotto to Scout Lookout, you will have gained about 1,000 feet in elevation over 1.7 miles (over a mostly-paved path). Consider this your legs' and lungs' warm-up. Continuing upward, past Scout Lookout, is a section of the hike known as Hogsback, or The Spine. The path is narrow, and very uneven. Chains are used in many places on one side of the route to hold on to and steady your step. You'll find yourself holding on tightly, because many places a fall would likely be fatal. Occasionally, you

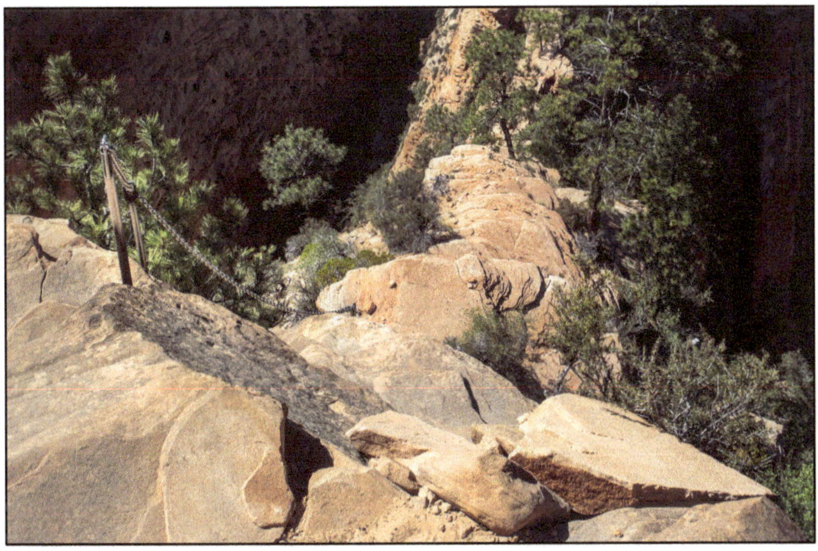

Steep Route & Precipitous Drops   28mm f/5.6 1/1250s ISO100

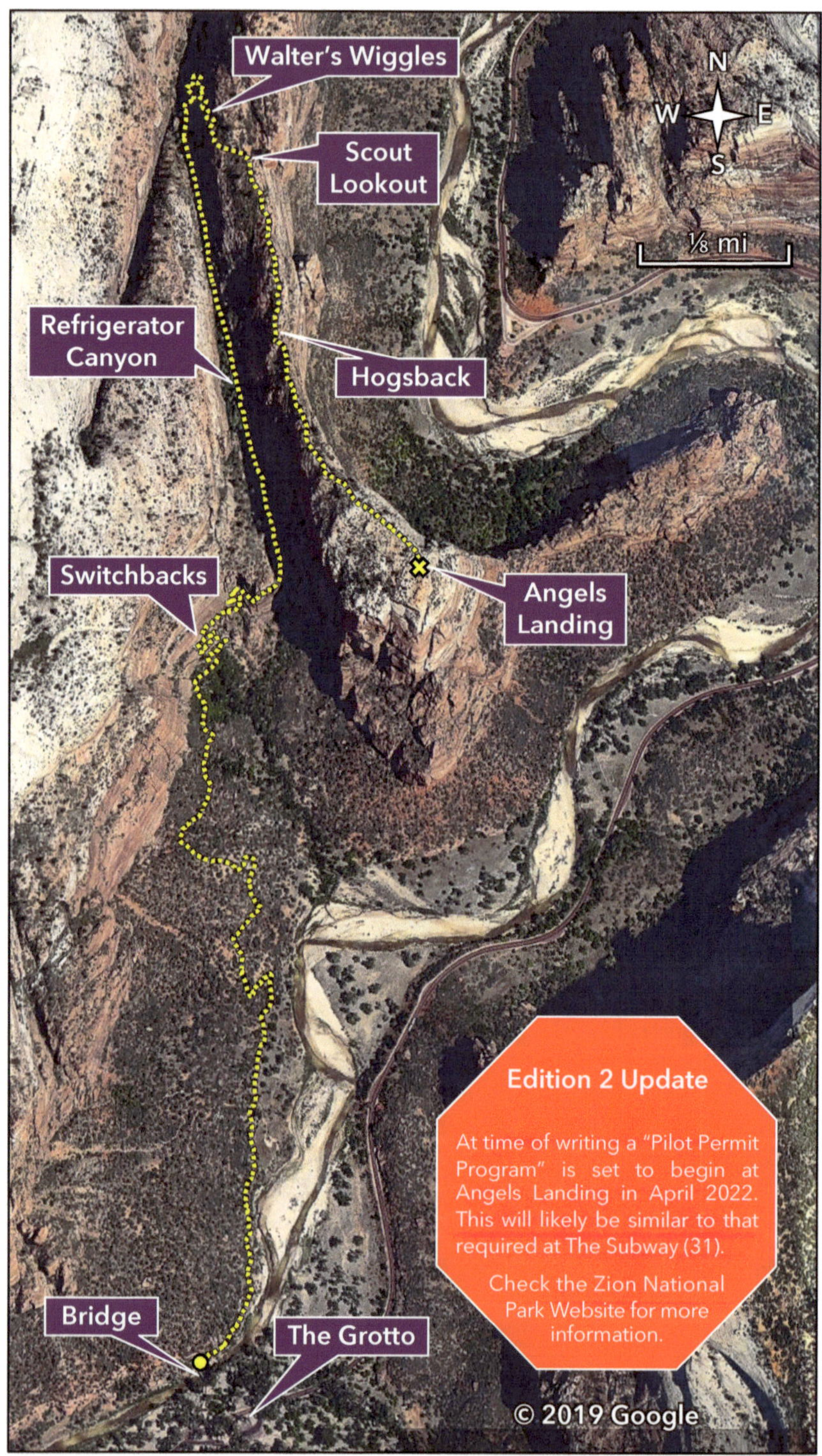

Walter's Wiggles
Scout Lookout
Refrigerator Canyon
Hogsback
Switchbacks
Angels Landing
Bridge
The Grotto
N
W
E
S
⅛ mi
Edition 2 Update
At time of writing a "Pilot Permit Program" is set to begin at Angels Landing in April 2022. This will likely be similar to that required at The Subway (31).
Check the Zion National Park Website for more information.
© 2019 Google

will be using the chains to help hoist your body up and over large rocks. You'll be timing short sections of ascent (and later descent) with passing hikers. It can feel like rush hour in a busy city at times. Once past Hogsback, you near the summit. Angels Landing has better space to move about, but you must still be careful of your footing, as the drop-offs now everywhere around you are seemingly straight down and 1,500 feet to the canyon floor below.

Check with a Park Ranger for more information or status on current conditions.

The hike begins across the Virgin River bridge at The Grotto. The first section will warm your legs and lungs up quickly, as you zig-zag and ascend towards Refrigerator Canyon. I find this section a bit taxing, because you don't have adrenaline at your side, as you will later in the hike. Also, there are not any noteworthy photographic subjects, so set your pace, rest as often as required, and walk, walk, walk.

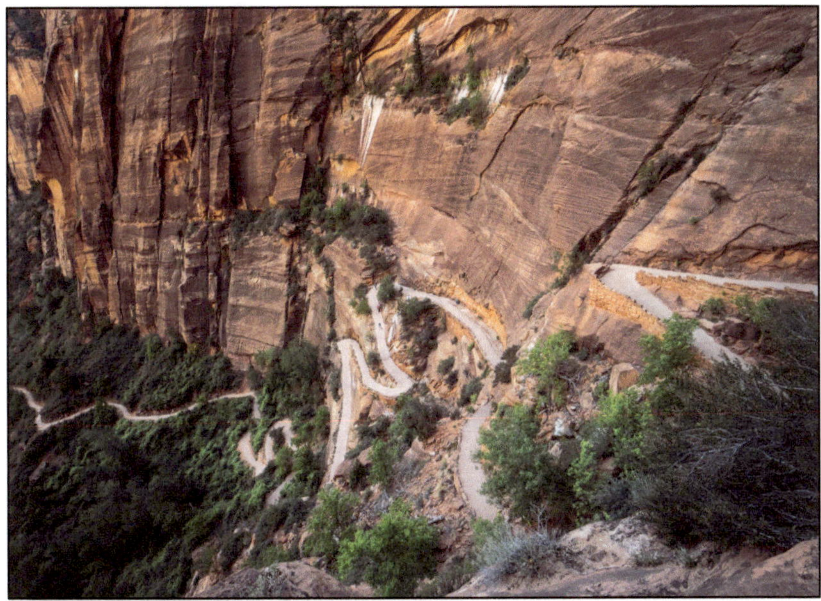

Switchbacks to Refrigerator Canyon   16mm f/22 1/20s ISO1600

Refrigerator Canyon is the next section, and a wonderful reprieve from the heat and relentless climbing. Here, there are some interesting eroded features along the canyon wall at your right, as well as some pleasant views into the canyon below at your left. There may be some compositions to be made here with your camera, but generally on strenuous hikes such as this one, I recommend taking all or most of it in with your eyes alone on the way up, and save any photographs for your descent.

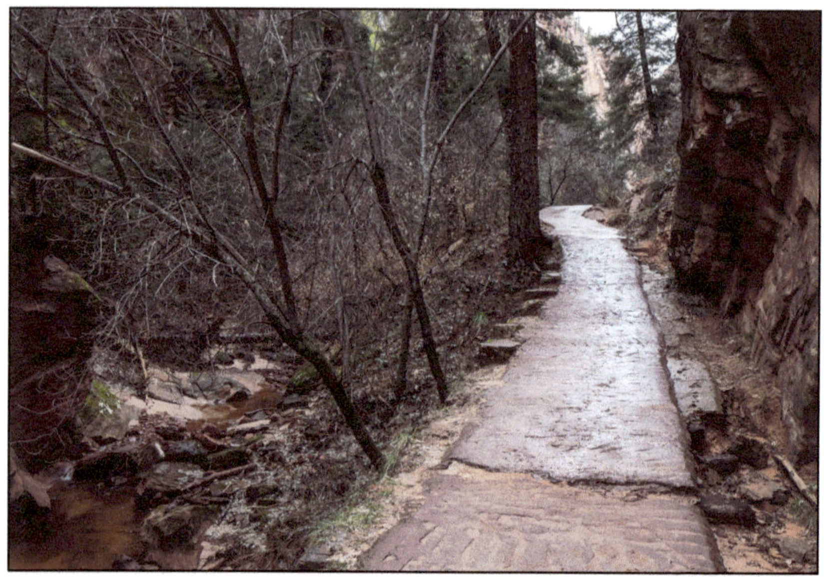

Cooling Down in Refrigerator Canyon   35mm f/11 1/30s ISO1600

At the end of Refrigerator Canyon is the well-renowned "Walter's Wiggles," a series of 21 switchbacks that will quickly get your legs and lungs re-engaged on your effort upward. Sad to say, the popular photograph seen here is not possible to take while on this hike. In order to capture that photo of Walter's Wiggles, it is necessary to hike quite a bit north on the West Rim Trail. The best composition of Walter's Wiggles that you can achieve while on this hike is from the top (or near the top), looking down. Remember to try this alternative shot on your descent later.

Atop Walter's Wiggles, welcome to Scout Lookout! This is a great place to take a break and photos. Along the east edge are nice views below... Use close-by plants and stones for a foreground.

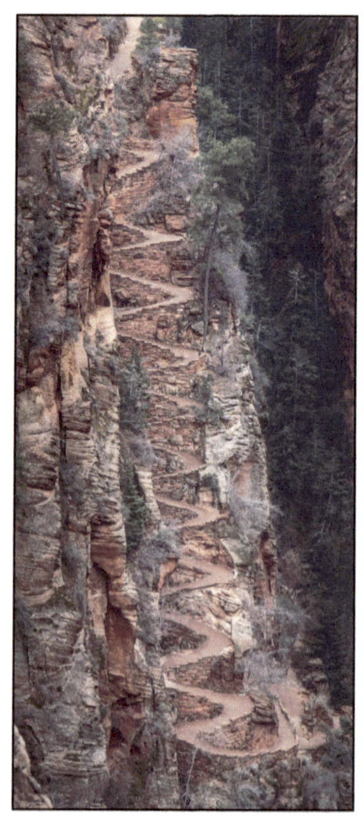

Walter's Wiggles as seen from the West Rim Trail
(3/4 mile north of Scout Lookout)
300mm f/5.6 1/200s ISO400

Back to the ascent, it's time for Hogsback. My photographic advice here is straightforward – stop and do so only if safe, and simply be on the lookout for interesting (including harrowing!) compositions of the route.

Finally, atop Angels Landing. As noted earlier, here at least there is some room to move around a bit. The classic shot is taken near the end, facing south (down canyon). However, there are many vistas. Make your way around, and enjoy exploring different compositions.

Once finished with your work and hopefully a large snack (a well-deserved one!), your route back down is the same one you came up. The return journey will continue to tax your legs, though your lungs can breathe a sigh of relief. Their hardest work is behind them.

"What time of day do I go?" Good question. Assuming your visit is during hot weather, there is a tradeoff to be made... Either depart in the morning for cooler temperatures on your ascent, or depart in the early afternoon for *slightly* better lighting once you reach the top. Or perhaps forecasted weather and/or clouds will aid your decision. (Consider these variables as well.)

I'll elaborate on my lighting comment... Morning and afternoon light ultimately produce very similar results at the summit – a canyon with shade either on the west or east side. From my experience and research, the afternoon light is a little better than that of the morning, all else being equal. Midday, the least shade is present, but the result is not as great as the light is quite harsh.

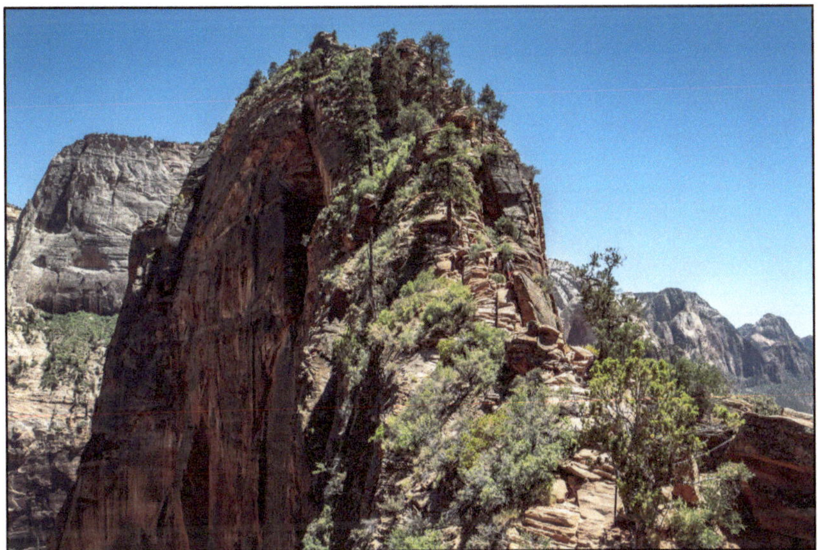

Hogsback   28mm f/5.6 1/800s ISO100

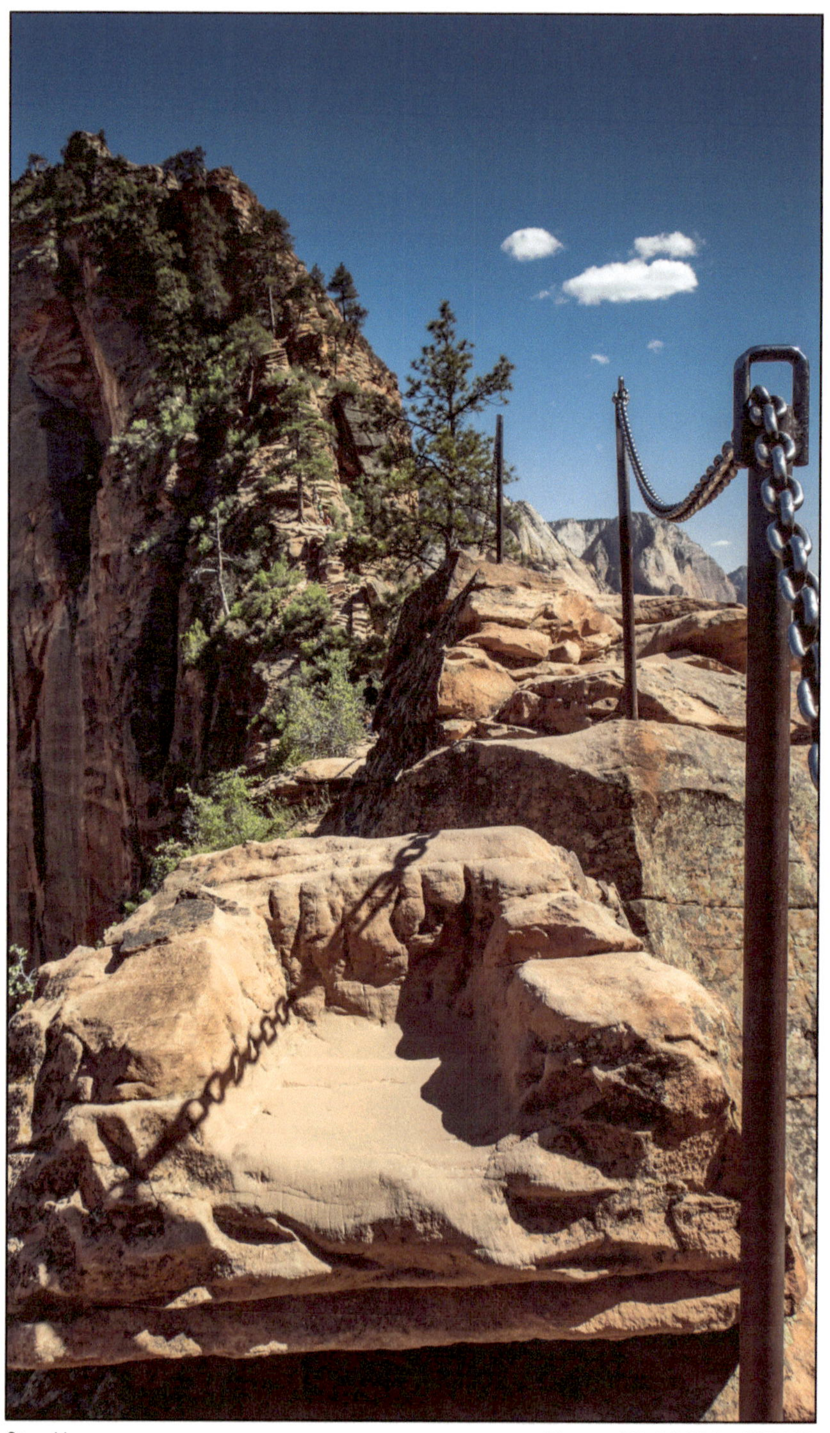

Step Here

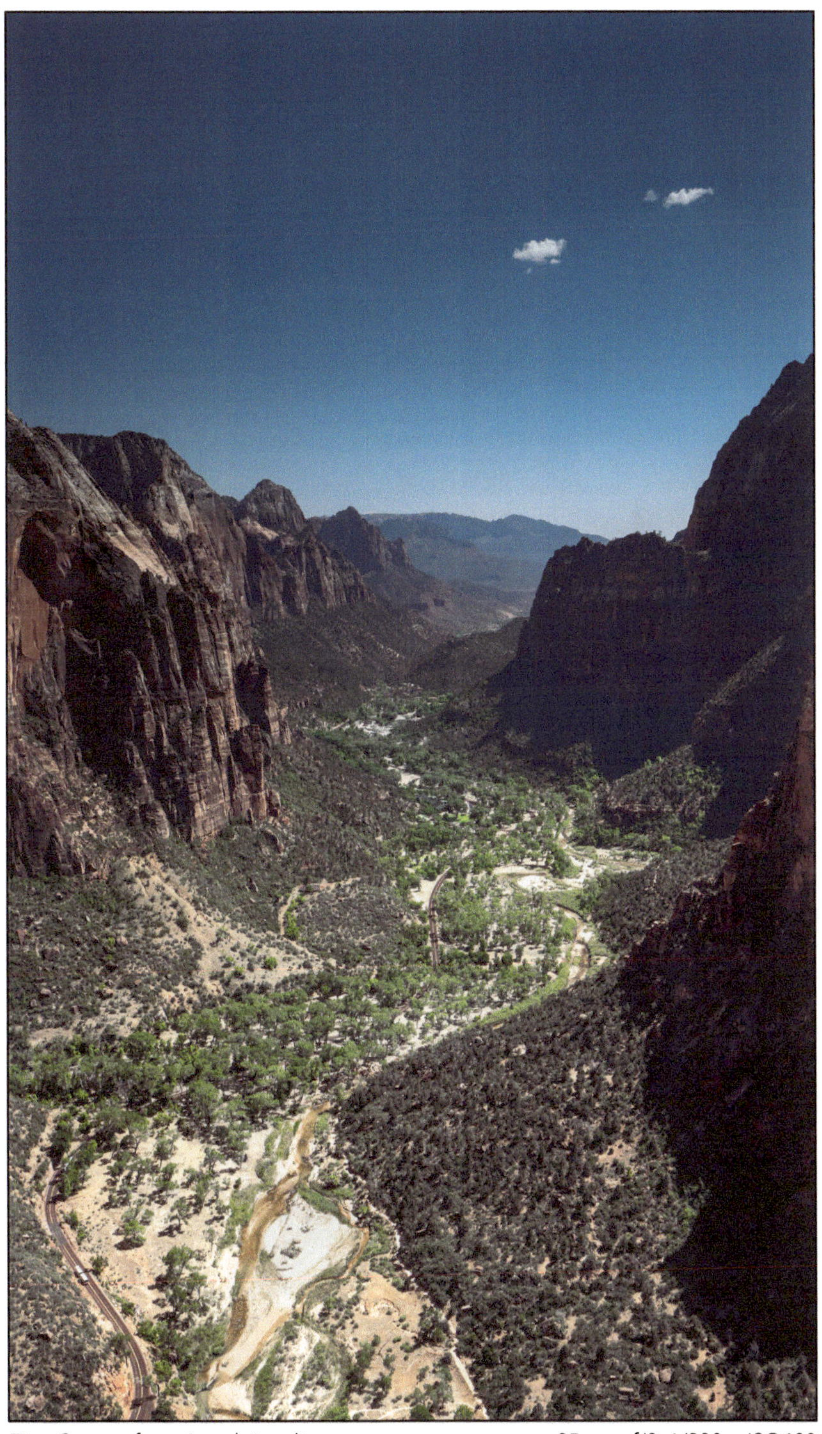

Zion Canyon from Angels Landing   35mm f/8 1/320s ISO400

Time	Best / Good		Reward	
Budget	30-45 min	Type	Out & Back	Effort
RT Distance	~0.4 mi	Δ Elev.	~100 ft	Zoom	Wide, Tele

Weeping Rock is a popular stop in the Zion Canyon, and requires minimal effort and not a lot of time to experience.

The destination is an alcove where water regularly "weeps" through the stone, supplies hydration for hanging gardens, and drips in many places from above a visitors' viewing platform. The water is from rainfall 1,200 years ago, as it has slowly permeated through the above sandstone to its freedom here.

And while this geology is quite fascinating, the truth that is this alcove isn't nearly as interesting as the one at Emerald Pools, as a photography subject if framing it as a whole.

Still, it's worth trying. So, bring a wide angle lens, but also a telephoto, because framing the delicate flora on the walls' surfaces generates photos not easily seen elsewhere in the park.

Lighting can become challenging here. Early morning arrival is a must, and also your best bet at dodging the large crowds of people.

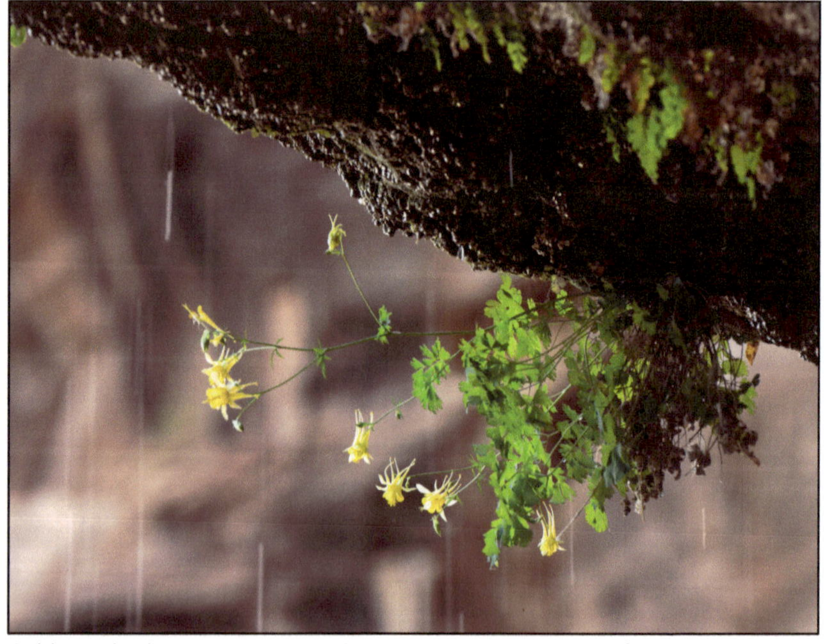

Golden Columbine at Weeping Rock   300mm f/5.6 1/20s ISO800

The short walk up is along a paved trail, but it is semi-steep and often slippery. Be cautious on your way up and down.

See the next section, Hidden Canyon (11), for a bird's eye view of the Weeping Rock alcove.

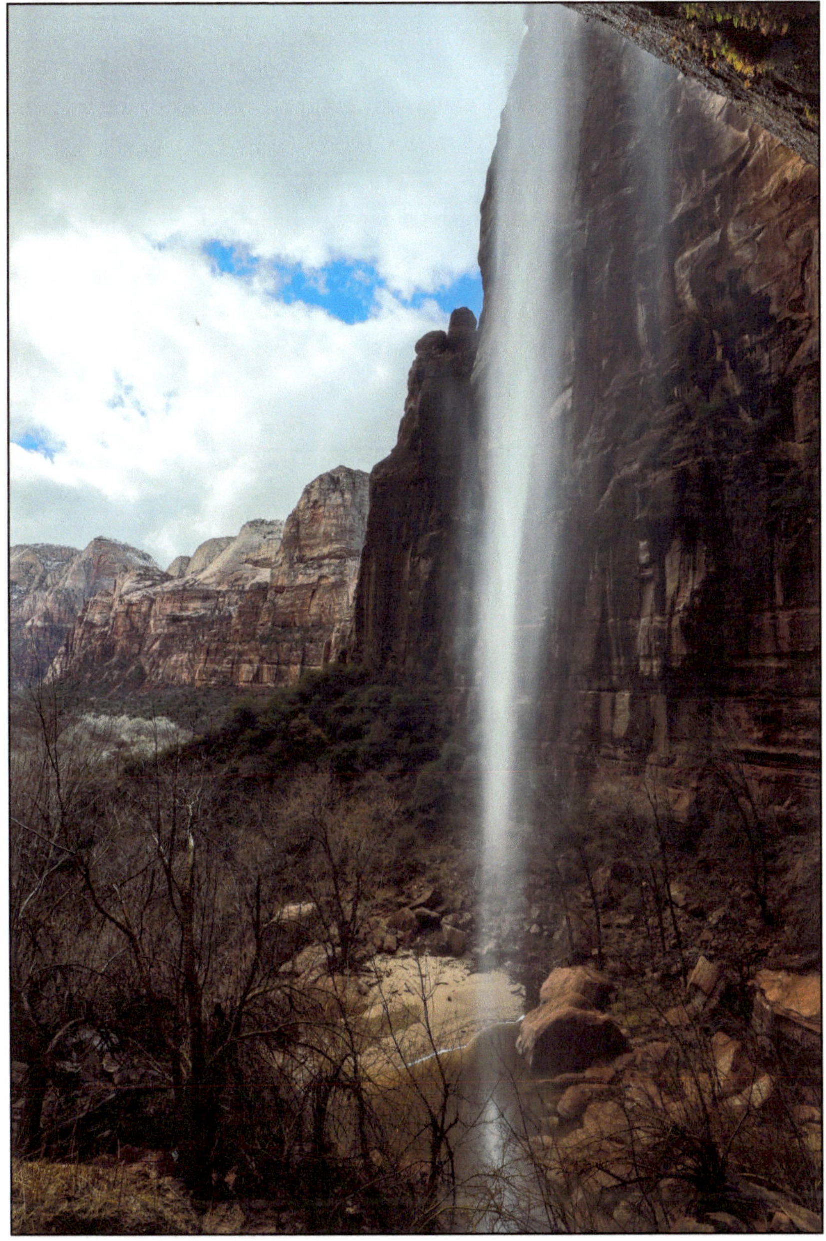

Wintertime Waterfall at Weeping Rock   16mm f/22 1/4s ISO100

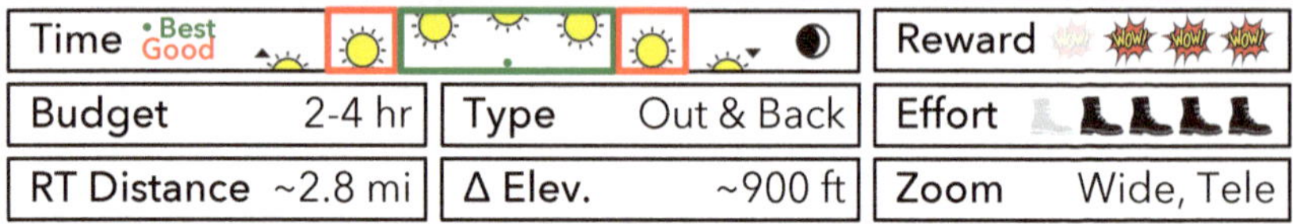

Time	Best Good		Reward
Budget	2-4 hr	Type	Out & Back	Effort
RT Distance ~2.8 mi	Δ Elev.	~900 ft	Zoom	Wide, Tele

The Hidden Canyon Trail is a gem. It offers a bird's eye view of Weeping Rock, the Virgin River and canyon floor below, an interesting hike, a cool canyon with interesting pools of water near its entrance, and a beautiful arch at its end. That's a lot to offer on a hike in under 4 hours!

This hike includes 3 distinguishable sections... First a switchback ascent, next an exciting traverse towards the mouth of the canyon (excitement thanks to some hand chains in places to hold on to), and finally the hike into Hidden Canyon. ...The section with hand chains, while not as extreme as the hike to Angels Landing, does require mental and physical aptitude. Though, its difficulty is far less than that required of Angels Landing.

The trailhead is adjacent to Weeping Rock. This trailhead serves two destinations – one to Hidden Canyon, and the other to Observation Point. Begin with the switchbacks, quickly gaining elevation. Along the way, you will have good views of Weeping Rock below. A sign, after about 20 minutes of walking, directs you towards Hidden Canyon. (The other route is towards Observation Point.)

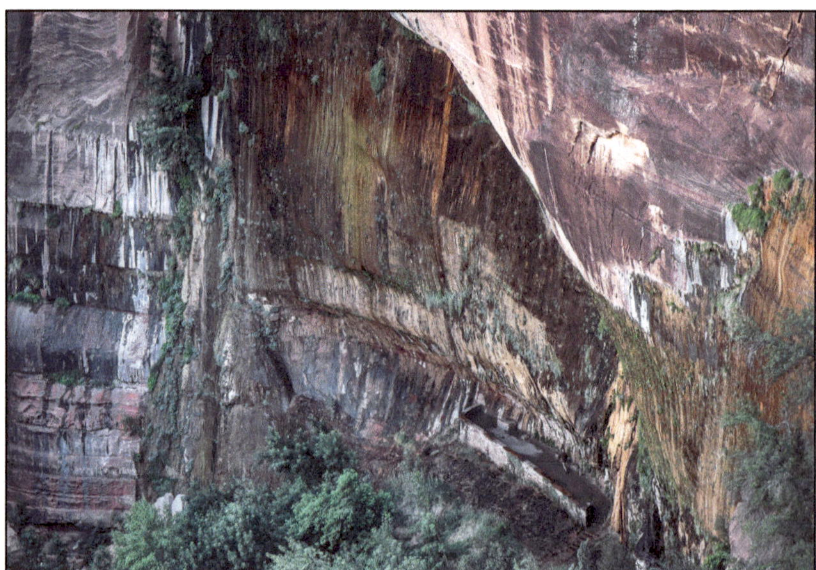

Weeping Rock from Hidden Canyon Trail   200mm f/5.6 1/400s ISO800

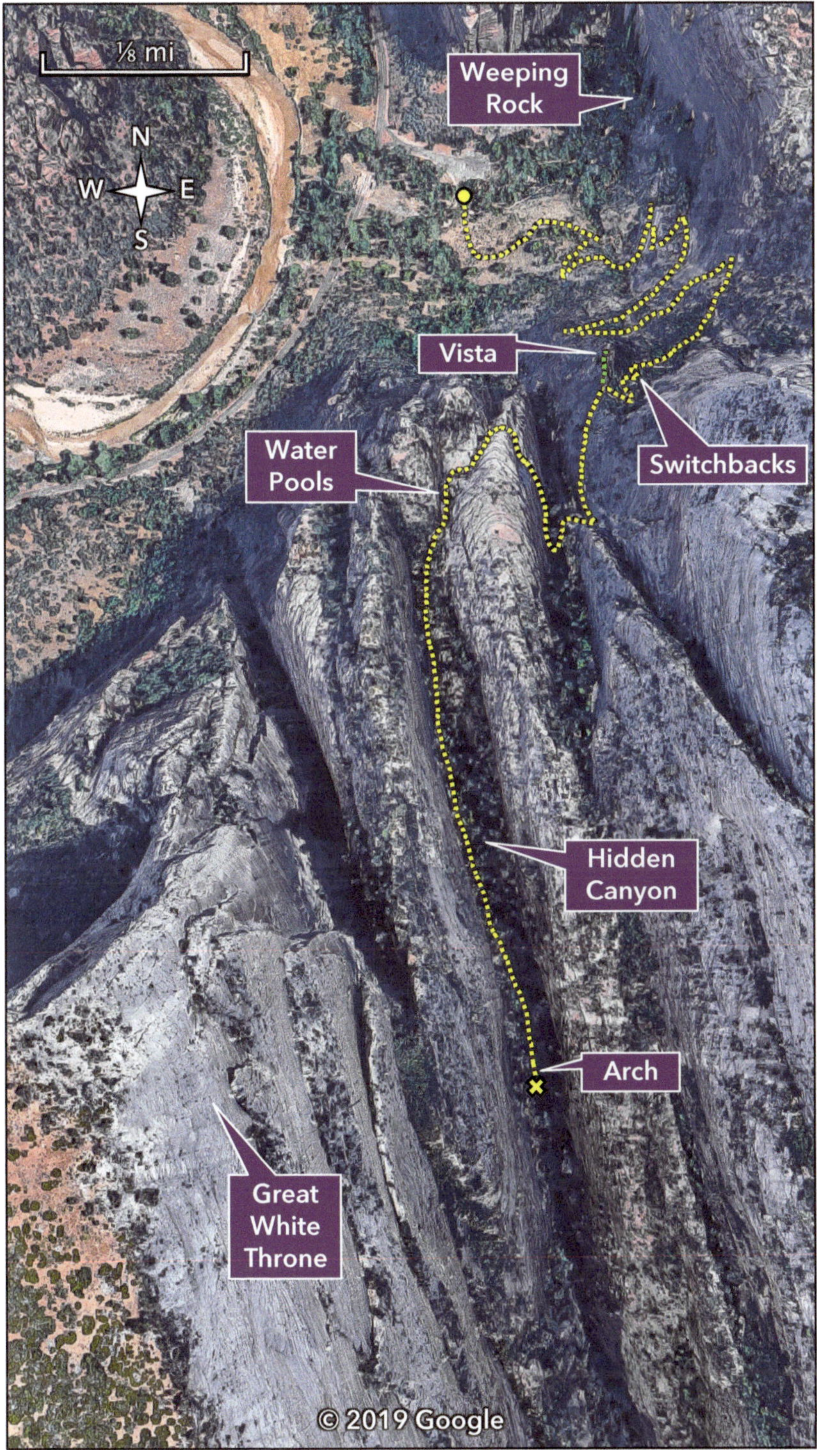

⅛ mi
N
W
E
S
Weeping Rock
Vista
Switchbacks
Water Pools
Hidden Canyon
Arch
Great White Throne
© 2019 Google

After this split in the trail, you will continue up on even more switchbacks, but on a more narrow path and changing direction more frequently. At the top of the final switchback, you may notice an unmarked path to your right... This is a good, very short detour to a spectacular vista. I recommend taking it either on your ascent or descent, as it's a great place for a break and some photos. (If you miss it on the ascent, it is easier to spot on your way back down.)

Next up are multiple traverses along canyon walls and the afore-mentioned hand chains. Take your time here. This is undoubtedly the most "exciting" part of the hike!

And finally – Hidden Canyon. You are hiking *behind* the Great White Throne. How cool is that? Some rock and log scrambling is required here. I recommend your target destination be the free-standing arch. Not far beyond the arch is a mass of rocks that becomes arguably impassable, for casual hikers. Otherwise, enjoy the cool temperature in the canyon and the multitude of textures and colors, quite suitable for great photography!

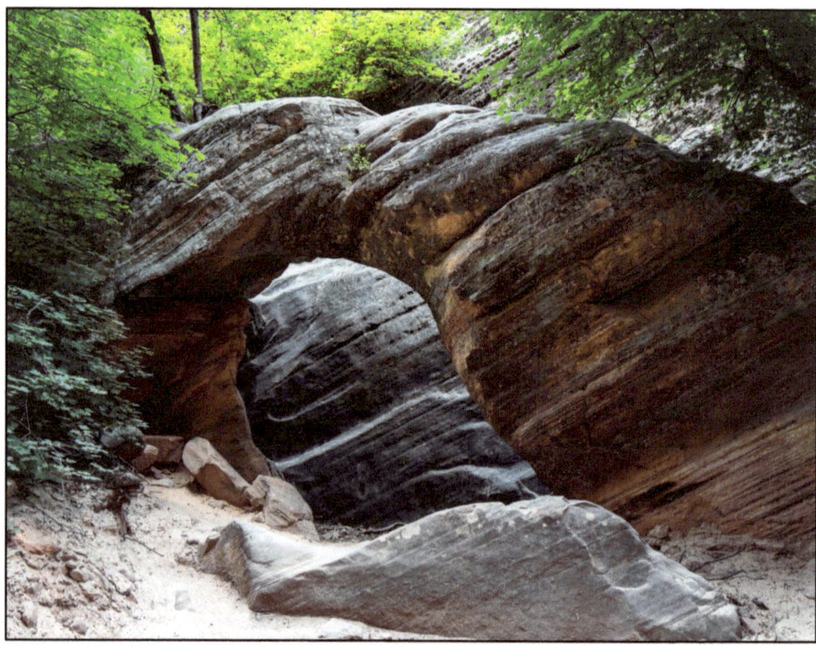

Free-standing Arch   24mm f/8 1/15s ISO800

Once finished, retrace your steps back down.

Truth be told, I purposefully left some really fun photographic features out of this narrative... I want you to be delightfully surprised when you reach them!

As I'm sure you have already surmised, Zion Canyon has many vistas to its valley below. A fun technique to employ, if your camera has this feature (and many do), is its "miniature effect" filter.

This filter simulates the use of a perspective control lens, also known as a tilt-shift lens.

This effect creates sort of an optical illusion. With a narrow plane of focus, and all above and below that plane severely out of focus, it gives the impression of looking at a toy or scale model of your composed scene.

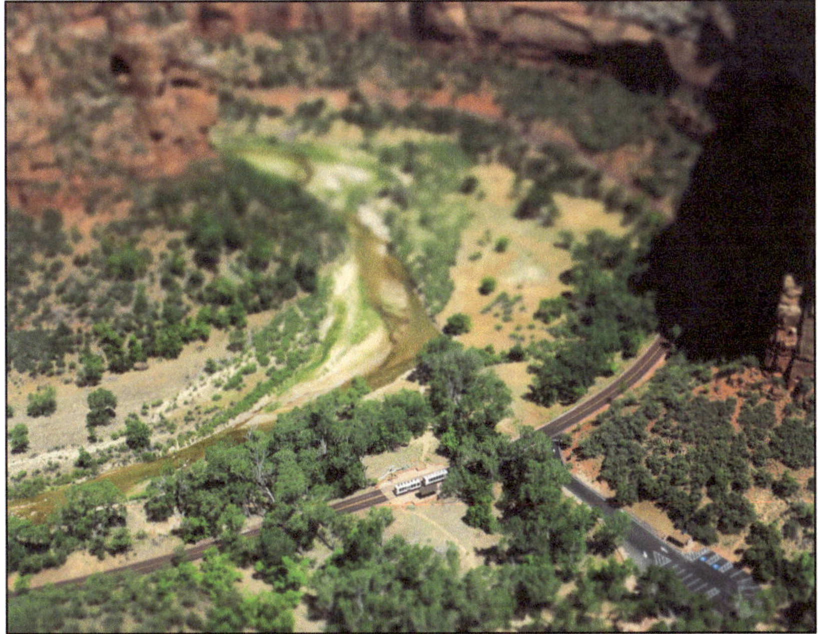

"Miniature" Version of Weeping Rock Shuttle Stop   35mm "f/5.6" 1/400s ISO200

For those of you with actual perspective control or tilt-shift lenses, set tilt to maximum and see the results. Some experimentation here may be required.

In the photograph here, I am still on the Hidden Canyon Trail, looking down at the Weeping Rock Shuttle Bus Stop. Isn't it neat how it makes the buses and road look? ...Fellow photographers may not be in awe, but I guarantee non-photographer family and friends will be.

One final hint: Since this is intended to look like a scale model, applying extra saturation helps to convey the look even more so.

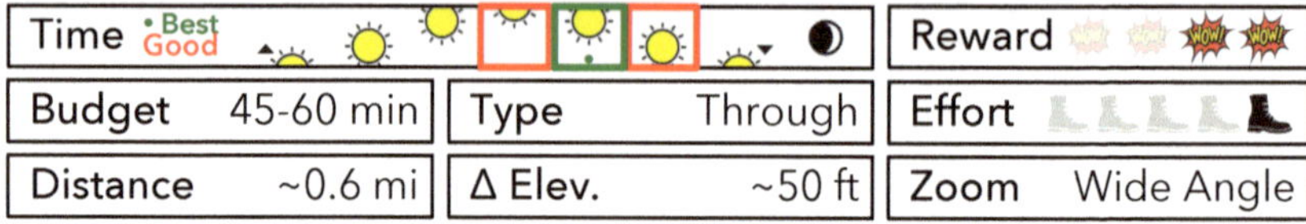

Time	Best Good		Reward				
Budget	45-60 min	Type	Through	Effort			
Distance	~0.6 mi	Δ Elev.	~50 ft	Zoom	Wide Angle		

About halfway in between the Weeping Rock and Big Bend Shuttle Stops on the Virgin River side of the Zion Canyon Scenic Drive is a rarely-visited exhibit known as the Great White Throne Viewpoint. The distance listed above is between these two shuttle stops.

Walking just down from the pullout is a wonderful, old painted and very weathered metal plaque uniquely catering to visiting photographers. In so many words, it states "you make the picture," while philosophizing about just how difficult it may be to do so! Ha!

While this exhibit's focus is clearly on the Great White Throne, its placement allows for a more interesting composition of the Great White Throne, The Organ, Angels Landing, and the Virgin River.

The plaque is right – lighting can be extremely challenging here. Overcast days help with this a lot. Regardless, it is such an easy stop to make and quite enjoyable to read the plaque, I recommend it if you have time. ...And if you are traveling this stretch in your personal vehicle in the winter, pull in and park. It will only require 10 minutes.

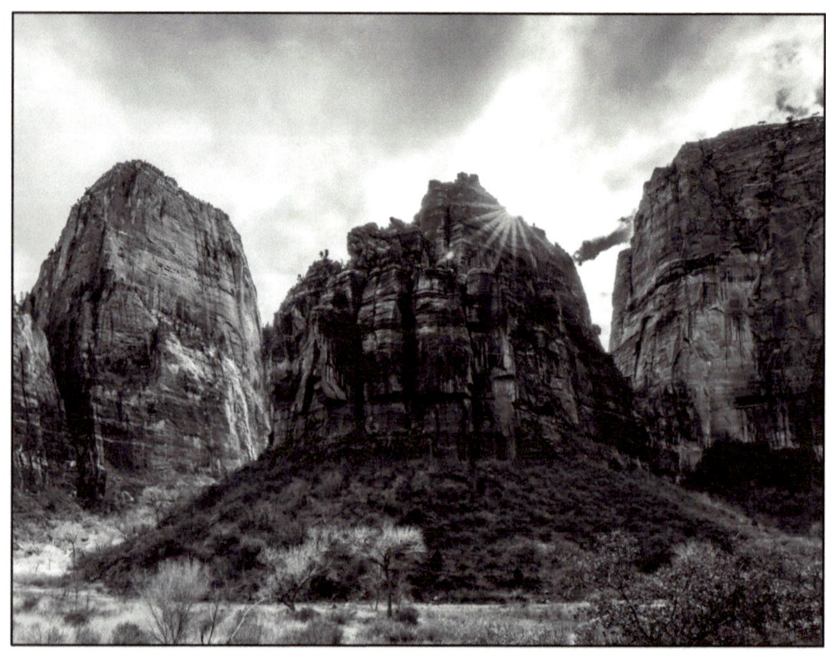

Great White Throne, The Organ, and Angels Landing   24mm f/22 1/30s ISO200

Time	•Best •Good	☀ ☀ ☀ ☀ ◑	Reward	💥 💥 💥 **WOW**
Budget	10-20 min	**Type** Meandering	**Effort**	👢👢👢👢 👢
RT Distance <800 ft	**Δ Elev.** <60 ft	**Zoom** Norm, Tele		

Big Bend is a *Jack of All Trades* for photographers. And because most of what there is to see is within a stone's throw from the shuttle stop, it takes very little time to do so. You could expect to hop off one bus, take some pictures, and hop on the next one.

While the potential compositions here aren't all that sensational, there are many possible, and they may be made quickly. So take a mental break, and just snap a variety of different pics!

One of my favorites is the draw works on top of Cable Mountain. Look almost due east... Cable Mountain is to the left of Great White Throne. A telephoto lens is required, and the longer the better. (Be friendly, and point this out to others at the shuttle stop – I've found others enjoy seeing it too.)

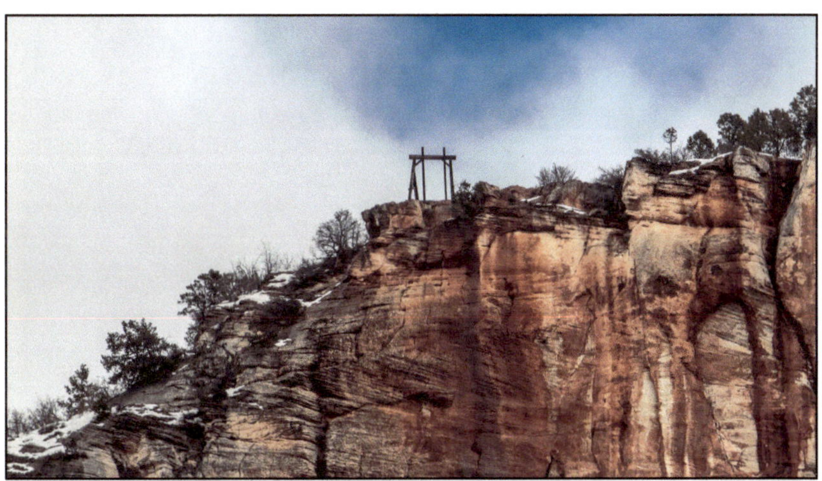

Cable Mountain Draw Works   300mm   f/5.6   1/640s   ISO200   (then 2:1 digital crop)

With your telephoto still mounted, now turn around and see hikers making their way to Angels Landing. The silhouettes are interesting.

Now for some wider-angle work, try different compositions around this same area. The sunlight will strike the canyon walls very differently all around you, so concentrate on where the lighting is agreeable.

Lastly, if you're interested, wander on down to the Virgin River and seek compositions there, with the abundance of large riverside trees.

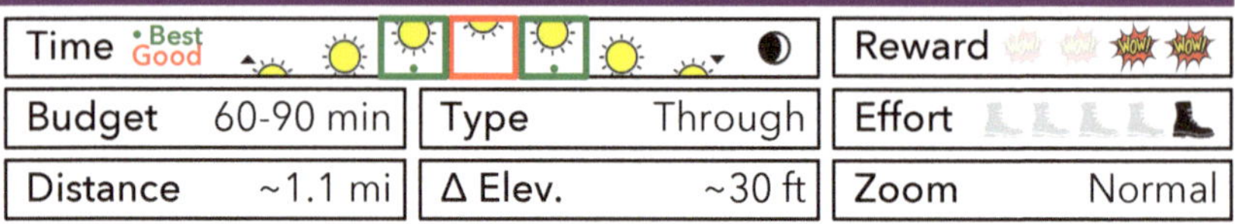

Time	•Best •Good	☼	☼	☼	☼	☼	◑	Reward	💥 💥 💥 💥
Budget	60-90 min	**Type**			Through			**Effort**	👢
Distance	~1.1 mi	**Δ Elev.**			~30 ft			**Zoom**	Normal

Another regularly-overlooked site along the north end of the Zion Canyon Scenic Drive, Menu Falls is a delightful little waterfall at the end of a short and well-maintained boardwalk.

It is located on the east side of the road, between the Big Bend and Temple of Sinawava Shuttle Stops. From Big Bend, it is 0.5-mile; from Temple of Sinawava it is 0.6-mile. The very short walk along the boardwalk includes stairs to a viewing platform.

As the story goes, this little waterfall got its name after it graced the cover of the Zion Lodge dining menu. How about that!

Menu Falls is not a "must do," but it does add a bit of variety if you've explored many of the usual sites already in Zion Canyon.

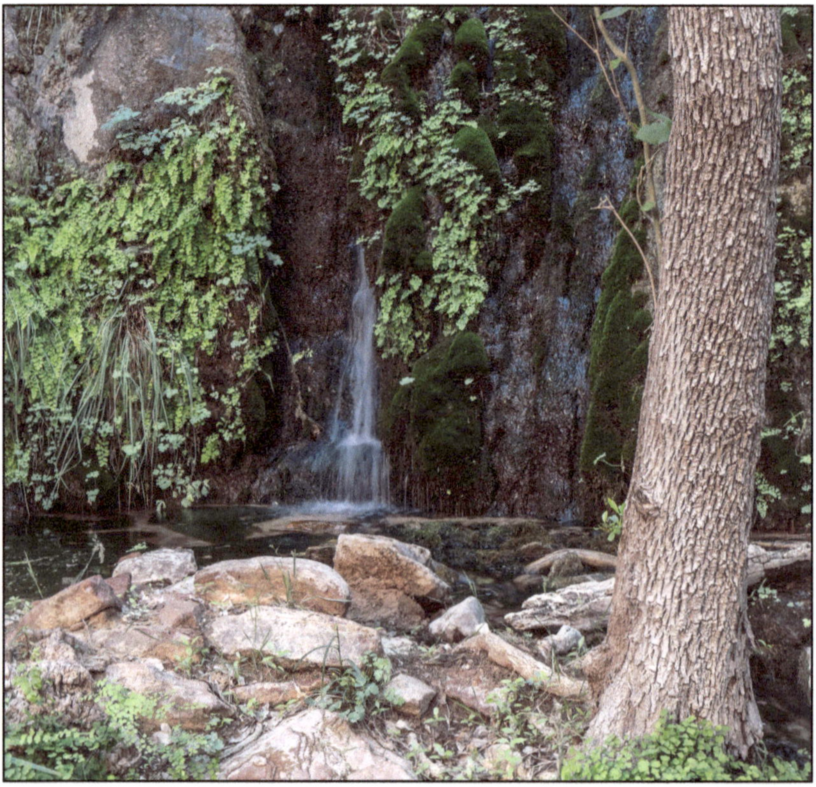

Menu Falls   35mm f/16 1/4s ISO400

Time	Best / Good		Reward	WOW! WOW! WOW!
Budget	30-45 min	Type	Out & Back	Effort
RT Distance	~0.5 mi	Δ Elev.	~20 ft	Zoom	Normal

The centerpiece of the Temple of Sinawava, the best view is from the southeast, along a long, sandy area adjacent to the road. A 10-minute walk from the shuttle stop is required, following the river as it makes its broad curve. Bonus if you are in the area following a storm – a tall and slender waterfall can be seen on the canyon wall behind it.

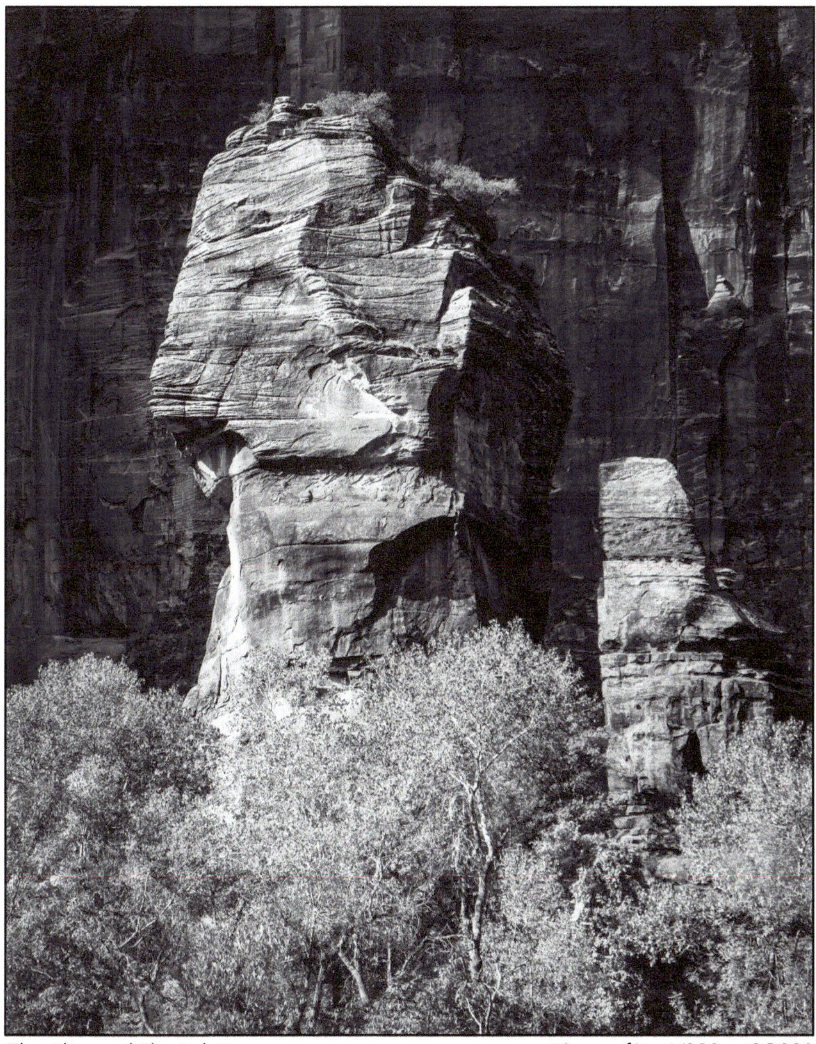

The Altar and The Pulpit   50mm f/4 1/320s ISO200

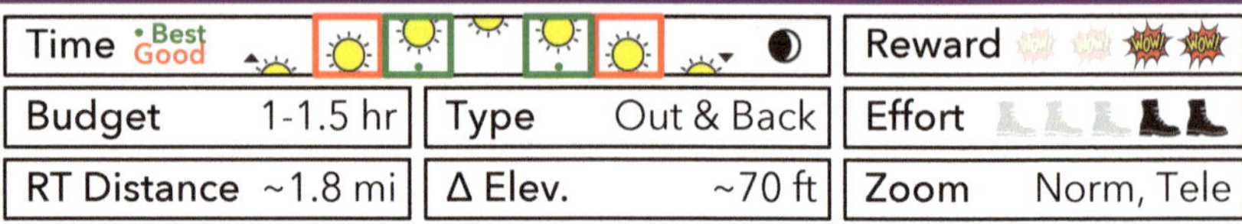

Time	Best / Good		Reward	
Budget	1-1.5 hr	**Type**	Out & Back	**Effort**
RT Distance	~1.8 mi	**Δ Elev.**	~70 ft	**Zoom** Norm, Tele

Riverside Walk is aptly named – it is a paved, mostly level path along the east bank of the Virgin River, as canyon walls close in on the approach to the entrance of The Narrows. It begins at the Temple of Sinawava Shuttle Stop and ends at a paved and stone platform where steps lead down to the river. Trekking any further north in Zion Canyon will require walking in the river. (Covered on the next site narrative.)

The best photography along this route is near its end, where many informal routes over sand and rocks take you to the river's edge. There are multiple cascades of water here over boulders within the river. Follow your ears – they will help guide you towards the rushing water.

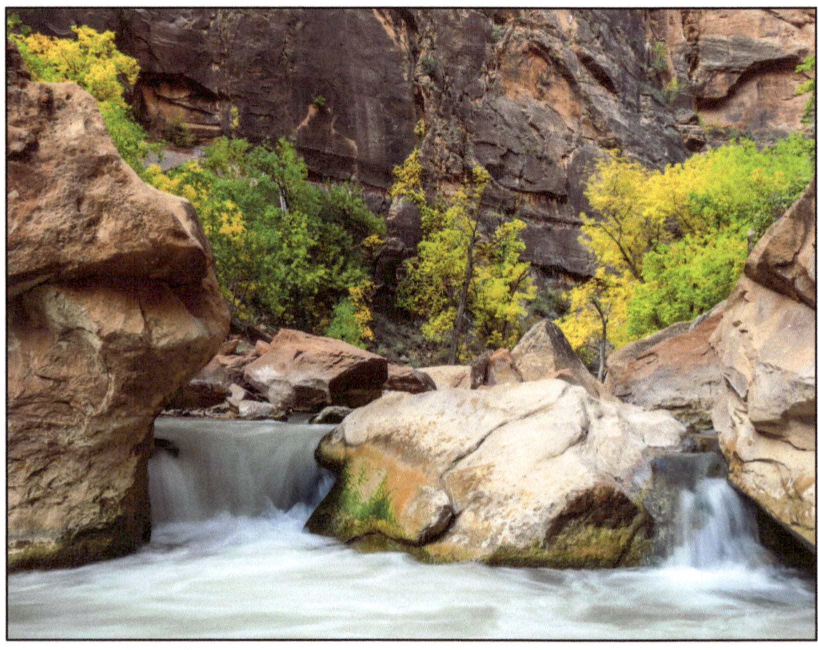

Virgin River Cascade   28mm f/16 0.5s ISO100

Wild turkey and deer also frequent the riverbanks along this walk. Fortunately, neither seem to ever move too swiftly, so if you see one you'll likely have time to ready your telephoto lens and better your position for a shot.

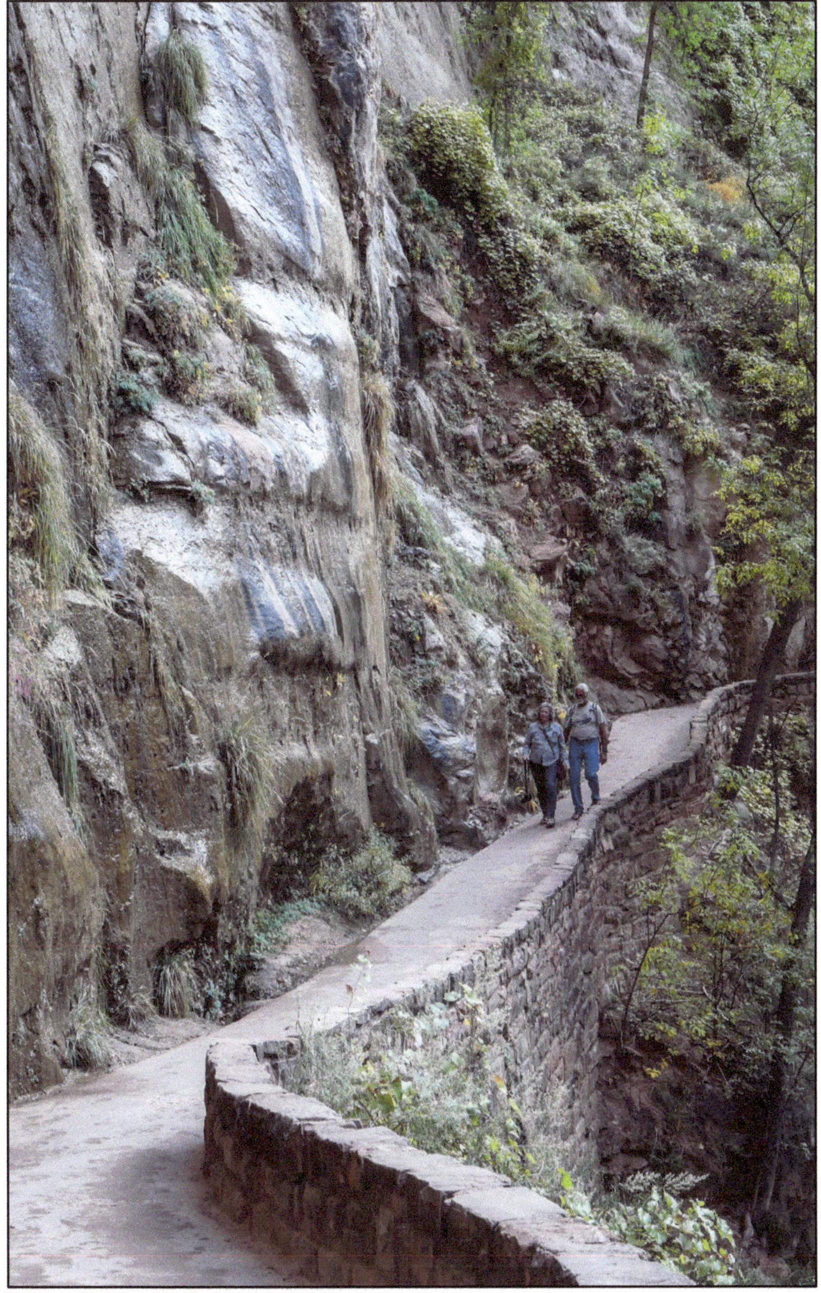

Along the Riverside Walk   50mm f/8 1/60s ISO800

At the end, take a break and enjoy seeing visitors enter and exit the water. And those who may be contemplating doing so! People-watching here is among the best in the park.

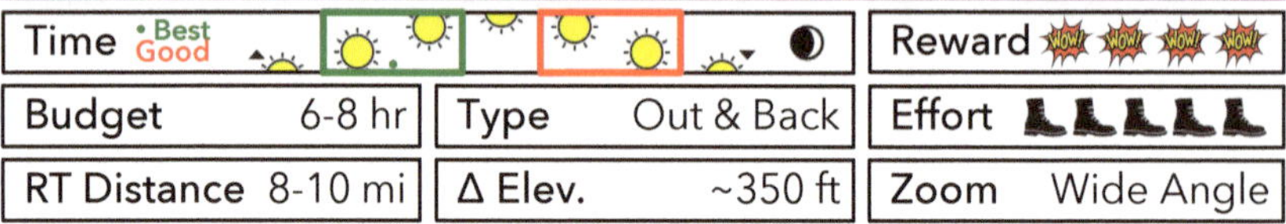

Time	Best Good	☀ ☀ ☀	☀ ☀	🌓	Reward	💥 💥 💥 💥
Budget	6-8 hr	**Type**	Out & Back		**Effort**	🥾🥾🥾🥾🥾
RT Distance	8-10 mi	**Δ Elev.**	~350 ft		**Zoom**	Wide Angle

It wasn't until my third visit to Zion National Park that I explored The Narrows. In a way, I'm glad that it took me some time to do so. Why? Because The Narrows is that awesome. Dare I say that the Zion I had already explored would have been subdued by this amazing and unique experience. So... I encourage you to explore elsewhere in Zion first too. Then, proceed to The Narrows!

The Narrows mostly is a hike in and through water (the Virgin River) atop slippery, round river rocks under your feet. Occasionally there are sandy and rock-strewn beaches to traverse, but they are few. Expect to be in water nearly the entire time.

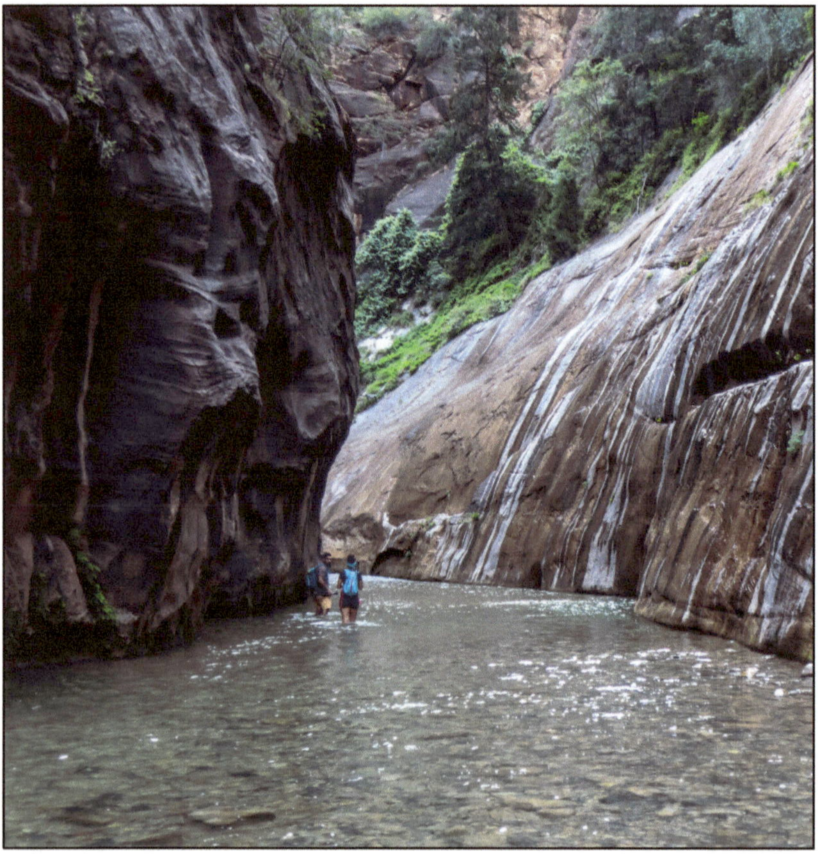

Early in the Walk Upriver   40mm f/5.6 1/60s ISO800

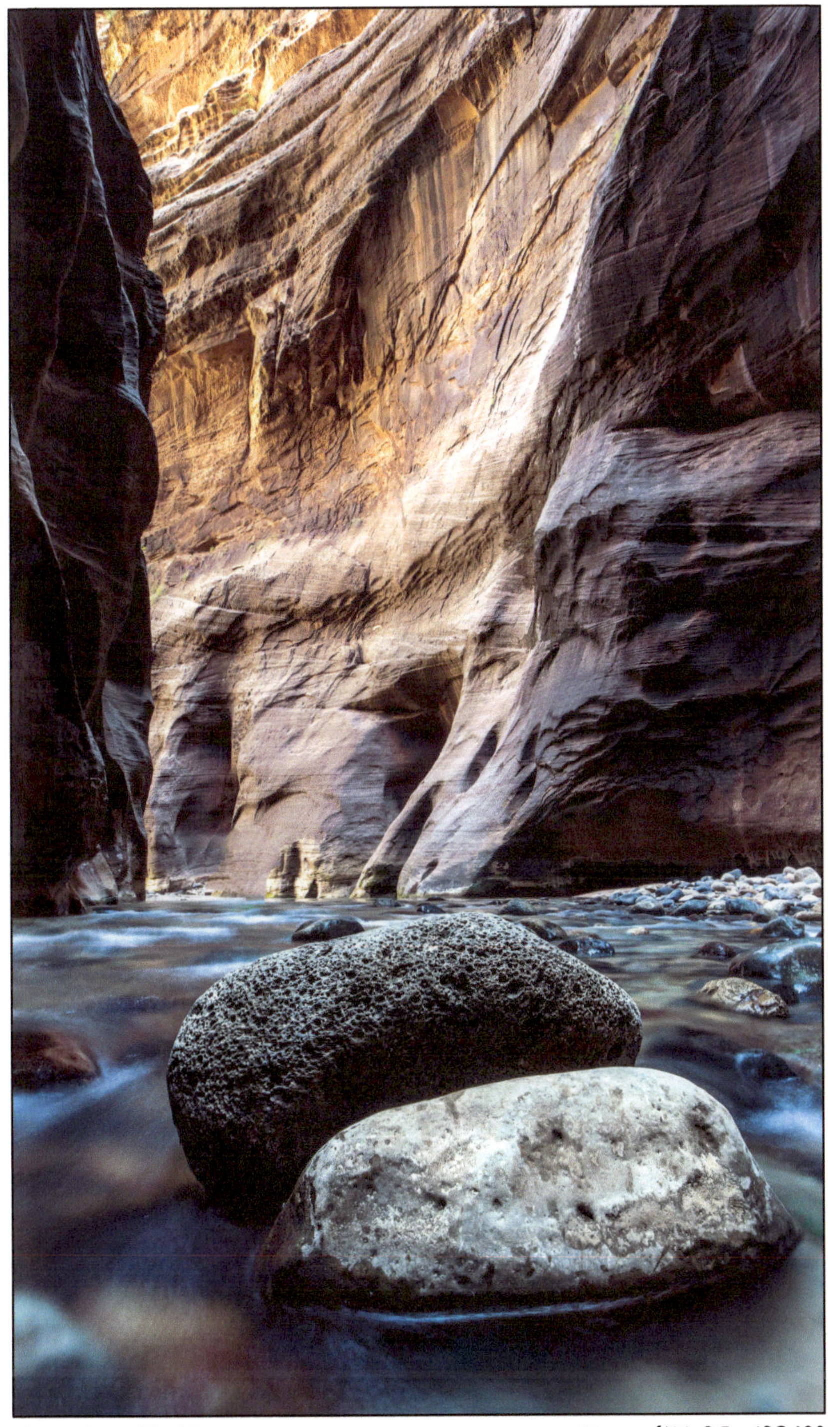

Tranquility in The Narrows

16mm f/16 2.5s ISO400

While I attempt to adequately prepare you on all hikes in this book, seeking an outfitters' advice and guidance is mandatory for The Narrows. (The other hike being The Subway [31].) Also, check with the National Park Service on current conditions and weather forecasts. I have utilized rental gear and have obtained detailed maps from Zion Adventure Company in Springdale. I recommend them, without hesitation. They provide a video with hiking guidelines specific to The Narrows.

My experience on The Narrows has been in relatively shallow water (that is, relatively low water flow). This is typical late spring through early fall; however, conditions can change rapidly, so again – seek guidance from your outfitter and the National Park Service for hiking suitability and safety.

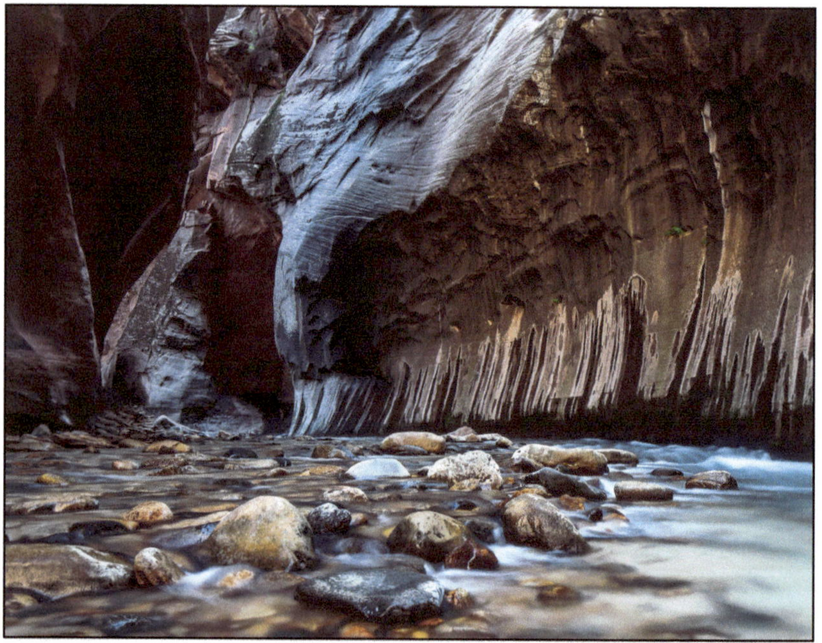

Wall Street   24mm f/22 3s ISO400

Under these conditions, I was equipped with a pair of rental boots, typical for this service, and also a wooden hiking staff. For novice "river hikers," a staff is essential. While it steadies you, from time to time it will literally be helping your unsteady feet and body stay erect and out of the water. The transverse load your body will occasionally apply to the staff is great – too great for traditional trekking poles. You will likely bend or break a composite or aluminum trekking pole in this application. Rent or buy a wooden staff.

I have to admit, my threshold for voluntarily getting wet has been not any higher than my waist. Perhaps your interest is different! With this "self-imposed" restriction on myself, I have been able to hike nearly all of The Narrows that's allowable without a permit. There are some pools that are deep enough for my boundary to be challenged, so do realize that the entire journey is not only always to the knees and below. Sometimes it gets deeper, briefly.

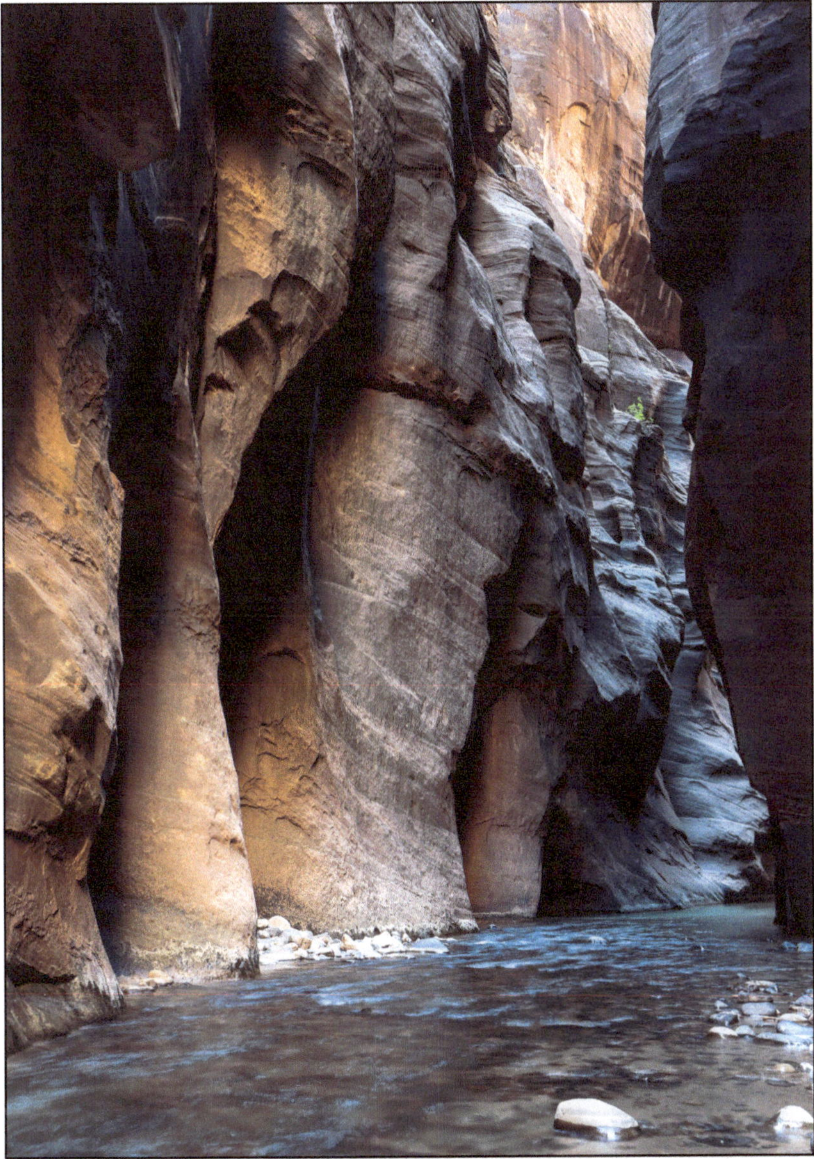

Golden Light and Shadows   35mm f/5.6 1s ISO200

My setup has been a backpack with any and all items that cannot withstand an accidental submersion in dry bags. For the slow shutter speeds necessary to capture light and sinuous water flow, a tripod is arguably a must for sharp photos. Do yourself and your equipment a favor... Practice deploying and repacking your tripod and camera in your room ahead of time. Make adjustments, as necessary.

Regarding the hike... It can get awfully crowded with people mid-morning through mid-afternoon. Your goal should be to be on the first shuttle bus heading up canyon for the day. This is your best chance to have adequately, uninterrupted photography work within The Narrows. The first shuttle bus' arrival to Temple of Sinawava, plus Riverside Walk, will have you in the water at about 7am. I've been able to trek to the end of this non-permit route, double-back and then explore Orderville Canyon, and finally back to the end of Riverside Walk usually between 1-2pm. These 6-8 hours allow for a satisfying amount of photography, a break or two, plus a lunch stop.

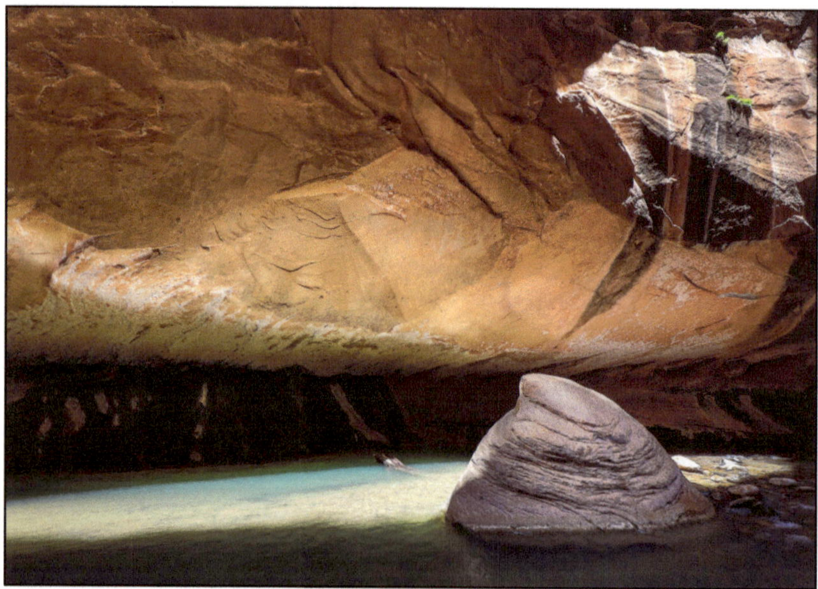

Reflection of Light   17mm f/8 1/25s ISO100

Regarding the photography... While not "dark," the light within The Narrows is dim in places. This dim lighting is also soft – a best friend to photographers. Be on the lookout for drastic color and texture changes. Look for interesting water features, including stones interrupting the water's flow. A post-processing tip: experiment with applying color saturation to your captured photos, or perhaps more than you are accustomed to. While in this soft light, the camera doesn't seem to translate quite what the eyes see in this space.

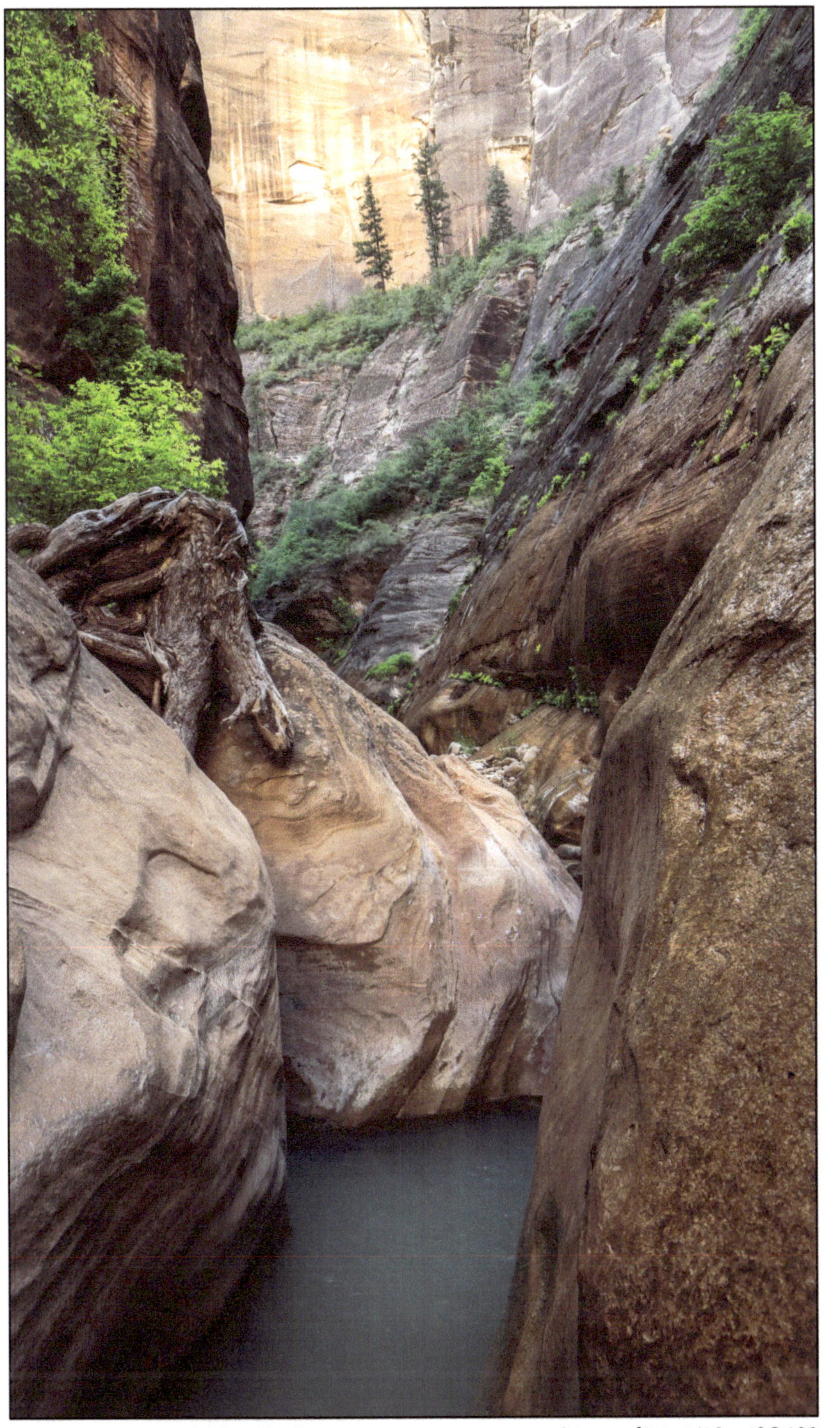

Narrow Passage in Orderville Canyon

24mm f/11 1/10s ISO400

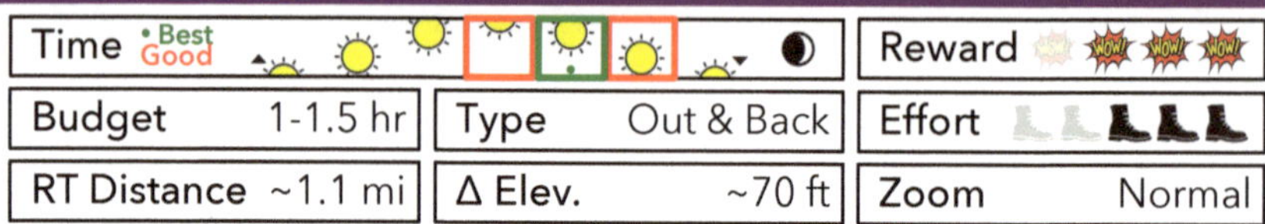

This is a sweet little hike to a nice little waterfall. (An emphasis here obviously on *little*.) At just over 1 mile round trip, and almost no elevation gain, this one is definitely suitable for families, although there are some boulders to traverse, so be sure to help the *little* members of your family navigate them.

The trail begins at the first switchback, if you are driving away from Canyon Junction and upwards toward the Zion-Mount Carmel Tunnel. Parking can sometimes be a challenge in this area, especially mid-morning through early afternoon. Usually by mid-afternoon, spaces more regularly become available. And that's a good thing, because this is a great spot to shed-off some summer heat and wet your feet in the pool at the end.

There are a few forks in the trail along the way. In my experience, they all eventually re-intersect, and ultimately get you to the right place. Just stay more-or-less alongside Lower Pine Creek. If you find a route that has you gaining elevation, then you're off-track.

Consider taking a towel with you, to dry off your feet and legs before heading back.

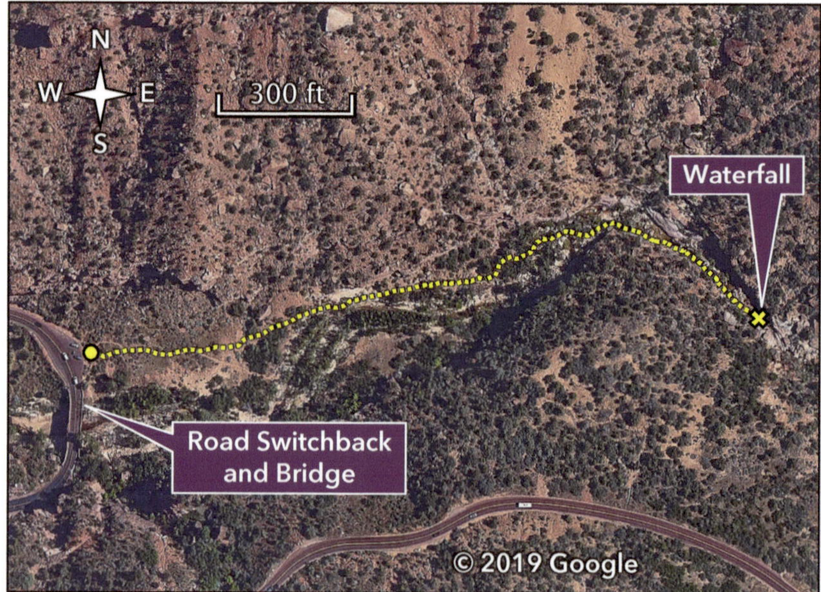

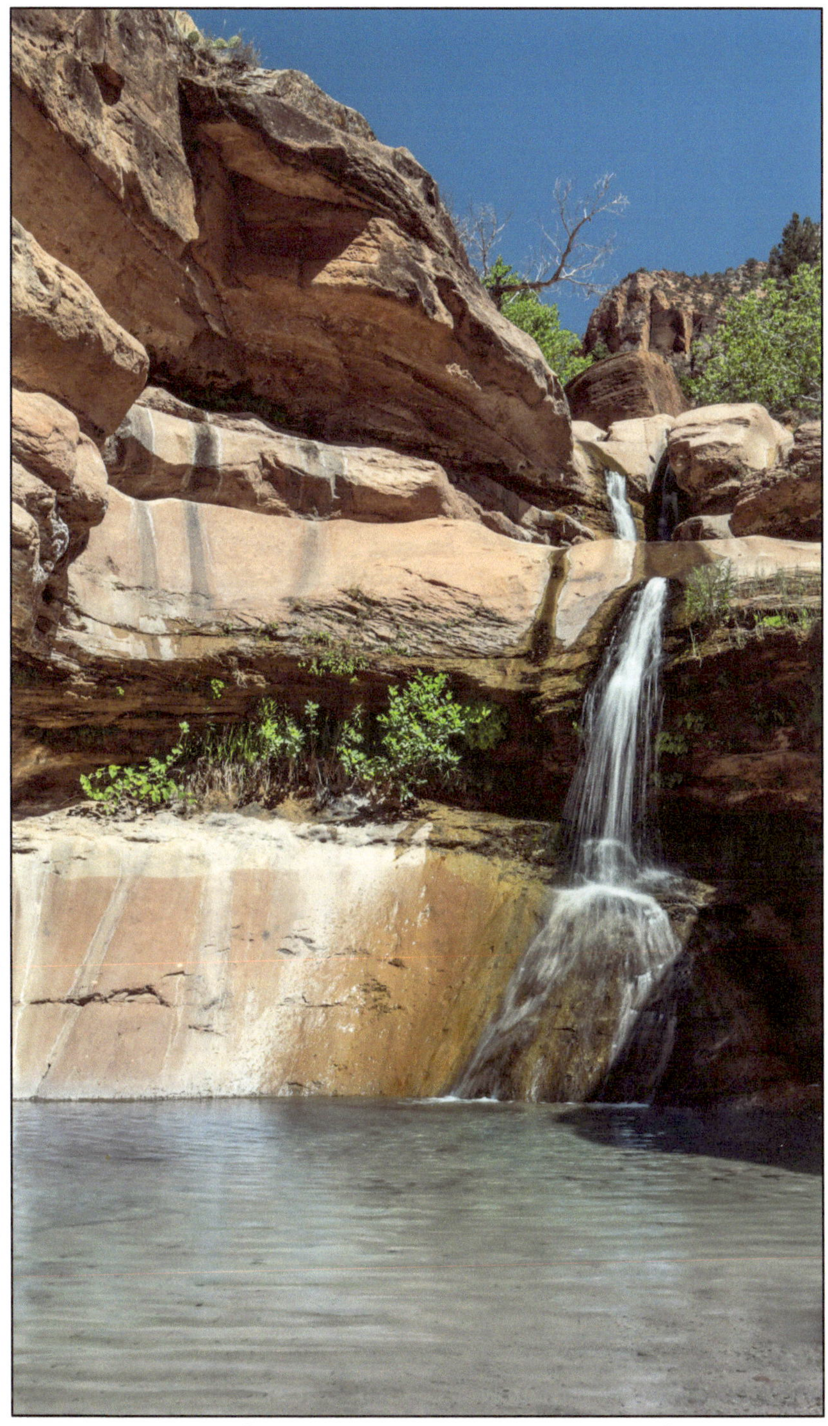

Lower Pine Creek Waterfall

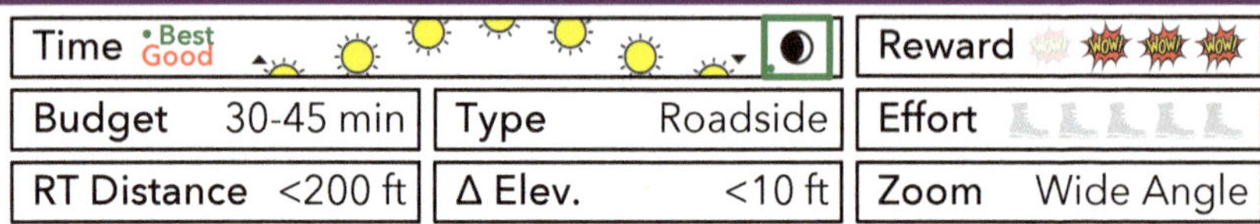

Time	• Best Good								Reward			
Budget	30-45 min	Type	Roadside	Effort
RT Distance	<200 ft	Δ Elev.	<10 ft	Zoom	Wide Angle

I think these are always fun – to look at, and to photograph – and I usually seek-out places in national parks where the effect translates well within a photo.

Here, we have a pretty unique topic, so I'll lay-out an abundance of pointers specific to this activity.

But let's address the "where" question first. My rule of thumb is that you're composing for 3 key features at minimum here – a car's tail light "trails," the starry night sky, and then something interesting that captures "where you are." For the shot on the following page, I selected the switchback drive up to the Zion-Mount Carmel Tunnel. This is facing uphill at the final, easterly switchback, adjacent to a roadside exhibit sign. (A lot of space is available to work here.)

There are arguably better spots within Zion National Park, but this is a spot that I have enjoyed. It's kind of mesmerizing seeing and hearing the vehicles make their way up and down the switchbacks at night. That, and since you have a lot of time to sense their approach, timing the shot is straightforward too.

Some other spots that would also work... Along the road near the Zion Human History Museum, with a silhouette of The Watchman and night sky. Around Big Bend, if transportation allows. Almost anywhere on the east side!

OK, so now that we have a few location options at your disposal, let's tackle the technical how-to, from primary setup to final camera adjustments. (All photographers know the one truth about "rules" in photography are that they're meant to be broken, so please think of all the following as guidelines or starting points. Experimentation is encouraged!)

Assuming you are roadside (to your subject vehicle or vehicles), work in the direction that permits capturing the passing car's tail lights. The issue with headlights, is that from this vantage, the bright light will illuminate the inside of your lens and in essence totally wash-out your exposure. Plus, the passing car will aid in your overall light capture by "painting" the roadway (and roadside features) with light.

Some sort of rigid camera support is mandatory. I recommend a tripod. A headlamp or flashlight also helps immensely.

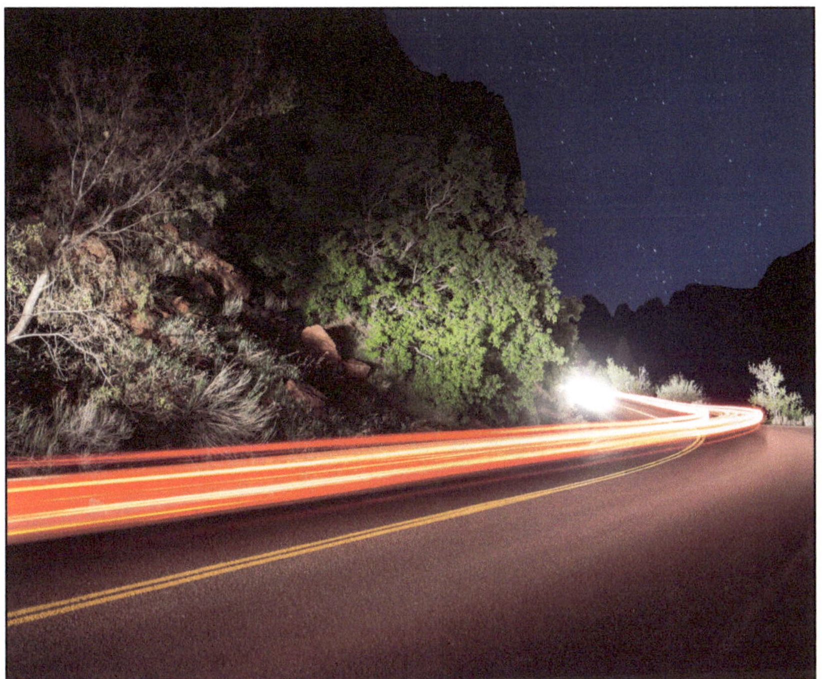

Stars and Lights on Zion's Red Asphalt   28mm f/2.8 30s ISO400

Lens selection... If you have the option, a fast wide angle is best. By "fast," I mean f/1.4-f/2.8. And by wide angle, 35mm or wider. You can use a slower lens, it just means there will be some compromises to ISO and shutter speed. And lenses with longer reach than 35mm will begin to struggle with depth of field and capturing the whole scene. This is all a bit subjective, so if you have multiple lens options, try each of them out, and learn their strengths and weaknesses for this work.

Here, perhaps, is the hardest part... You're going to need to manually focus your lens to infinity and leave it there. Leaving autofocus turned on is the best way to a very frustrating evening. It just won't work. So, illuminate something in the distance, lock-in focus, and leave it there. (Hopefully your lens has a focus window, and if it does check the lens' setting occasionally, to ensure it hasn't moved.) Warning!: If you are using a zoom lens for this, you cannot zoom in or out after you have set focus. Focus is only set for a particular focal length. So if you're using a zoom, be careful of this as well.

Alright, we're getting close... Compose your shot, as best you can. (This can be difficult sometimes, depending on how dark it is.) If after you take some shots, you can make some alignment and positioning adjustments.

Set your camera body to Manual mode, and now we need a starting point... The following table lists some options.

Aperture	f/1.4	f/1.8 or f/2	f/2.8	f/3.5 or f/4
ISO	100	200	400	800
Shutter Speed	15 sec	15 sec	15 sec	15 sec

You're ready to go. Now, using either a timer or a remote shutter release, listen for an approaching car, begin your exposure, and wait to see what happens! Take a look at your screen, and adjust accordingly.

Generally, you want to keep your ISO as low as possible, to minimize noise. Those of you with faster lenses (f/1.4 to f/2, for example), may find that you need to stop down to f/2.8 for depth of field (focus throughout your frame). Adjust the shutter speed (8 to 30 seconds) to suit your needs.

That's basically it. Be careful, good luck, and have fun!

Oh wait, there's more good news! This same technique works well for photographing the Milky Way. Utilize a "Planisphere" (a portable star-finder), or use any number of popular online tools or mobile applications to forecast its orientation in the sky. Below is our Prominent Pinyon Pine (28) "painted" by a passing car's headlights.

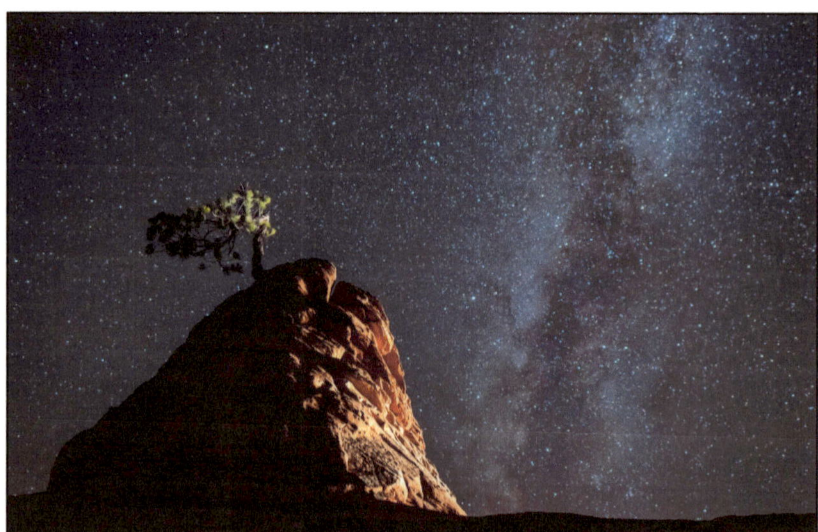

Painting Stone with Light and The Milky Way   24mm f/2 20s ISO1600

Time	Best Good	Budget	5-10 min	Type	Roadside	Reward		Effort	

Budget	5-10 min	Type	Roadside	Effort	
RT Distance	<200 ft	Δ Elev.	<10 ft	Zoom	Normal

This one is a bit of a no-brainer. I mean, while the Great Arch does not necessarily get a lot of press, once you see it (whether I made mention of it here or not) you're going to be compelled to photograph it. But I felt the need to include it for a couple of reasons. So let's get to it...

The location is straightforward enough. It is best photographed from the final easterly switchback on the way up to the Zion-Mount Carmel Tunnel. (Or the first left switchback if you are making your way down.) Parking here is ample, so this should not be an issue.

This can be a *superb* spot for a portrait with your travel companions. I have been asked by many people here to take their picture, and have always obliged. It's apparently the thing to do at this spot. And rightfully so – it's a nice backdrop.

But alas, there is a gotcha. The lighting here can be extremely harsh with dark canyon shadows. The fix? Well, if you're like me, you may find yourself making this traverse between Zion Canyon and the east side many times. Take a look each time you pass – you may find that *this* time is the right time to stop and take a shot.

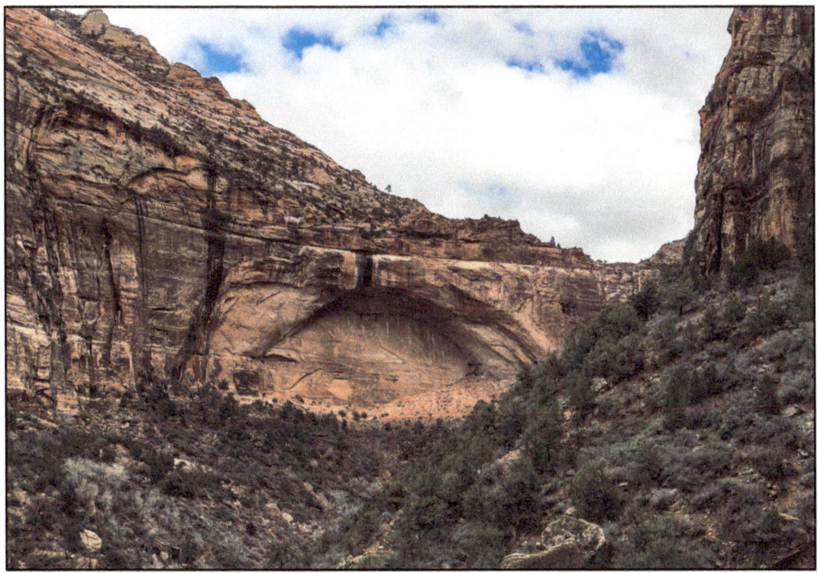

The Great Arch   50mm   f/8   1/200s   ISO200

Very many days in Zion have boring skies without clouds. I have not masked this fact with the photos in this book. Using black and white, you can redirect your viewer's eyes to your main subject. Here's an example while at The Three Patriarchs (4).

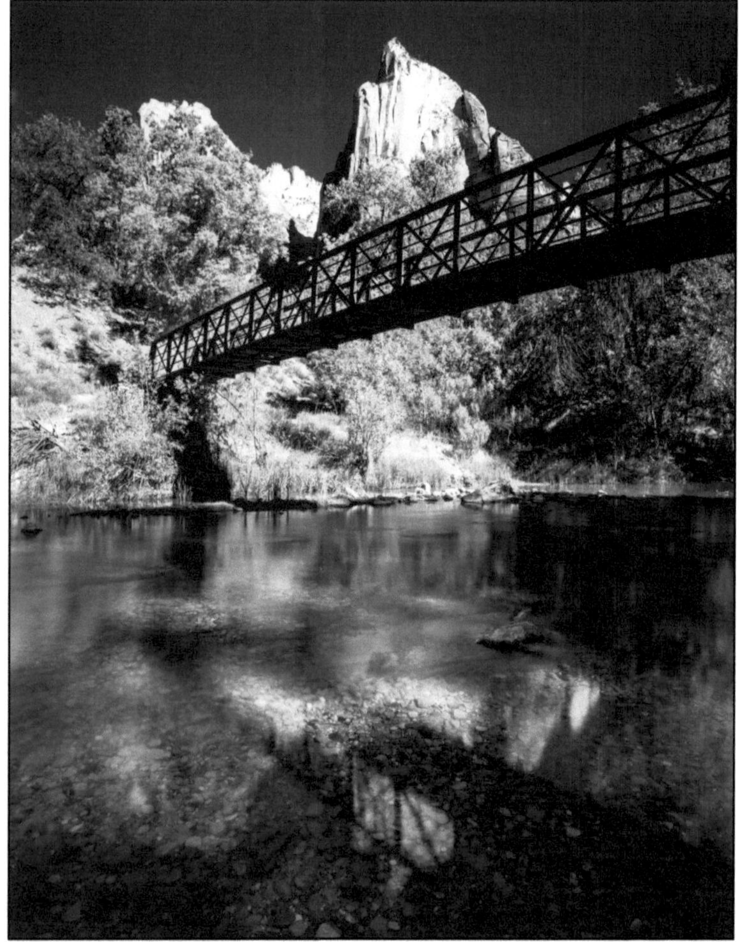

Isaac and The Virgin River   16mm f/22 4s ISO50

What I have found helpful (though some purists may argue that I'm bending the rules) is to grab my mirrorless digital camera with an electronic viewfinder and with the camera in monochrome mode, be able to see the composition in black and white before I take the shot. This can also be accomplished using a camera's rear screen, but sometimes glare from the sunlight challenges this method a bit.

East (ZMC Highway)

Zion-Mount Carmel Tunnel to East Entrance

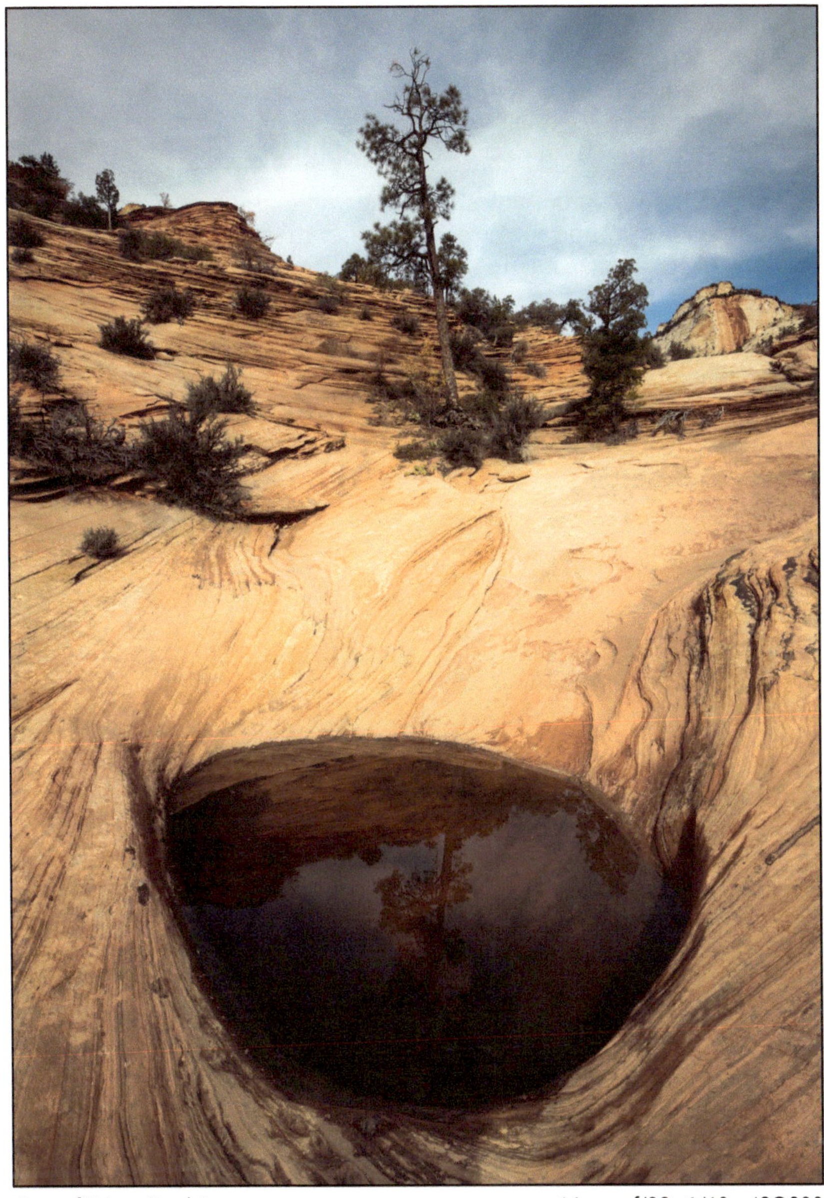

One of "Many Pools"

16mm f/22 1/60s ISO200

Time	Best Good							Reward				
Budget	~5 min		Type			Through		Effort				
Distance	~1.1 mi		Δ Elev.			~300 ft		Zoom				Normal

The Zion-Mount Carmel Tunnel is a heck of an engineering feat. Completed in 1930 at just over 1 mile long, it meanders underground while gaining elevation towards the East Entrance of Zion National Park. What I find most remarkable are the windows cut into the canyon walls for passing views of the remarkable landscape you're stealthily meandering past.

So... In order to capture any shots from within the tunnel, you'll need a chauffer. Do not attempt to take these shots while driving. (And stopping your vehicle inside the tunnel is strictly prohibited.)

The recipe for taking an in-motion shot is to preset your camera as much as possible before entering the tunnel. A fast (f/1.4-f/2.8) 24-35mm lens is ideal (24-28mm is arguably best). I recommend to set your camera to 1/500s, a wide open aperture, focus preset to infinity, and use Auto ISO. Now the camera's onboard computer only has to "think" on one variable – ISO.

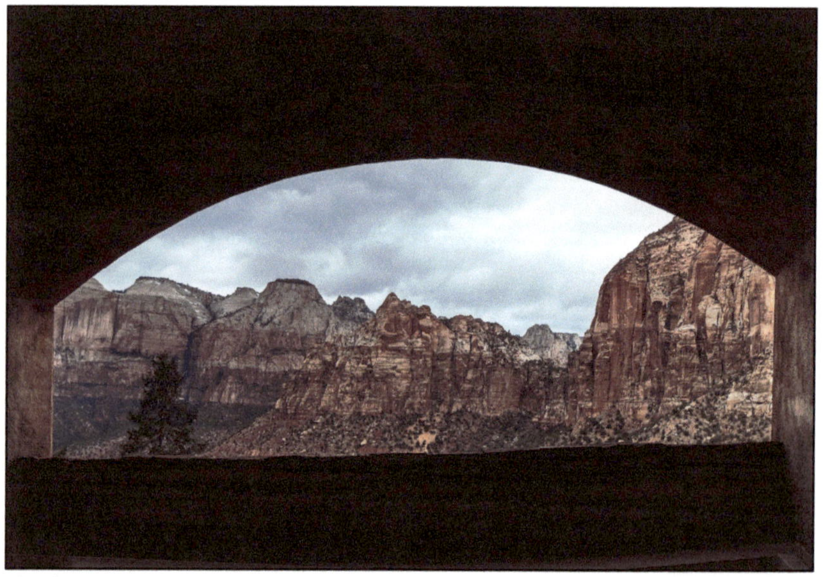

Window View   24mm f/2.8 1/500s ISO1000

Alternatively, photos of exterior features may be taken without a driver. (Of course!) See these windows from the outside, where you photograph the Great Arch (20) and also from Canyon Overlook (22).

Time	Best / Good		Reward	WOW! WOW! WOW! WOW!
Budget	60-90 min	**Type** Out & Back	**Effort**	
RT Distance ~0.9 mi	**Δ Elev.**	~180 ft	**Zoom**	Whole Kit!

-Winner of-
Best Short Hike
Zion National Park

There was no contest. As in literally – *there was no contest.* There aren't any other categories in this imaginary contest either. It's just that every time I hike the Canyon Overlook Trail, I feel like it deserves some sort of a prize. So I've given it one.

It begins near the east entrance of the Zion-Mount Carmel Tunnel. Unfortunately, due to this hike's popularity, parking can at times be challenging – especially midday. Though if you're early, for a sunrise shot, you shouldn't have a problem.

The trail ascends immediately, up stone steps, then to a more level route. A great view of the east tunnel entrance becomes visible. Between the tunnel entrance and your trail is the Pine Creek canyoneering route... Yet another photographic candidate. Soon you will come to a short, cantilevered metal-and-wood walkway. Watch your head! Under a low-headroom alcove, you exit to now a meandering path towards the lookout atop the Great Arch. The route is not well-marked near the end, and there are many dry rain-water beds tempting your choice in direction. Study the sand for heavy traffic – this is where you want to follow (due west).

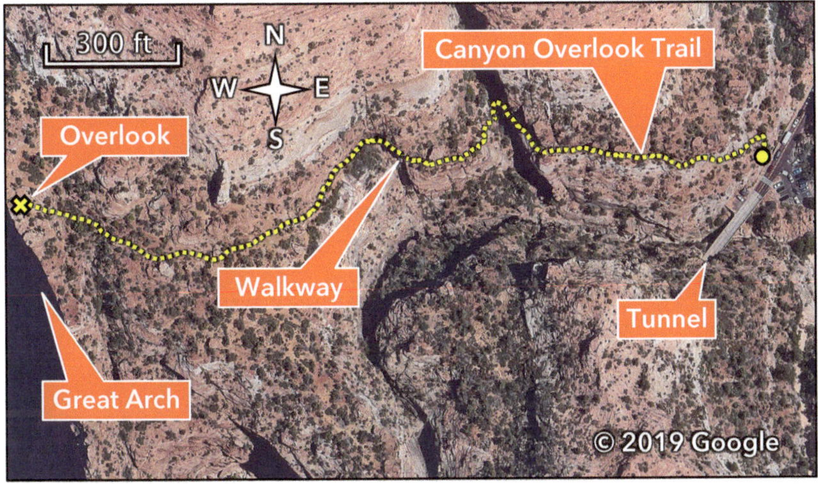

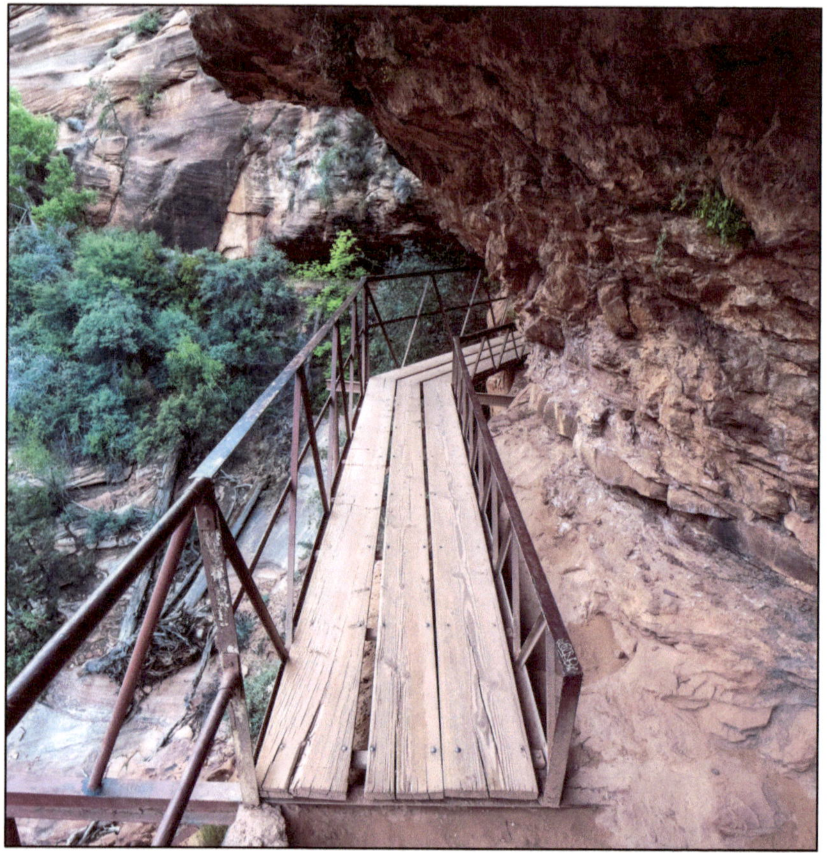

Cantilevered Walkway   16mm f/11 1/30s ISO1600

While there are some very interesting photo op's along the way, the real prize is at the end... The panoramic view into Zion Canyon, including the Towers of the Virgin in the distance.

I have experimented with various times of day, and I have learned the following:

> Sunrise: The desire is to capture the elusive filtered light on Towers of the Virgin. However, to expose them correctly, the canyon floor below will be too dark, so a zoom is required to isolate them. Also, the route to the overlook can be difficult to follow in the dark. The more efficient way to capture this similar shot is from the Zion Human History Museum (2).

> Mid-morning to Midday: Great for a traditional panorama.

> Sunset: While tempting, I have found the lighting contrast again too extreme to capture the canyon floor below. Only attempt this if abundant clouds are present to help filter the direct light.

Also while at the viewing area, look to your left and spot one of the several Zion-Mount Carmel Tunnel windows. While not singularly that interesting, on the early morning or evening visits, you can use a telephoto and a tripod to capture passing car lights from within it. (This is a fun way to pass the time while waiting for the sun to appear or disappear.)

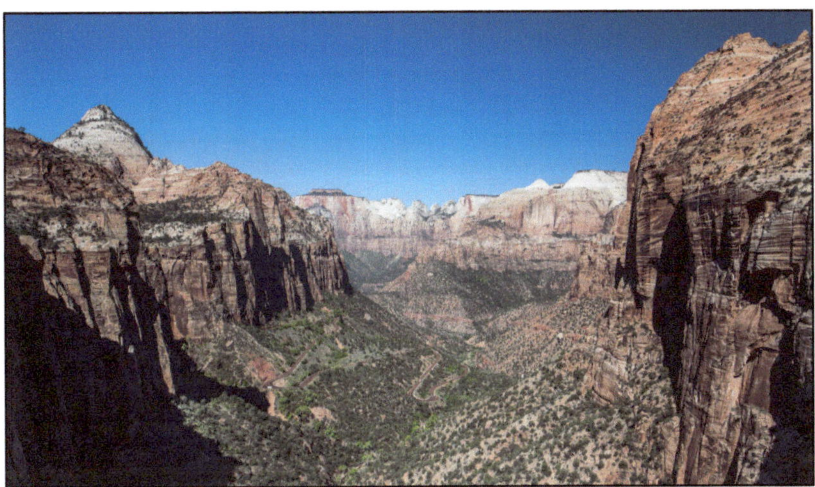

Mid-morning atop Canyon Overlook   24mm f/5.6 1/200s ISO100

My favorite Towers of the Virgin landmark – The Altar of Sacrifice. What an eerie name for this stone monument!

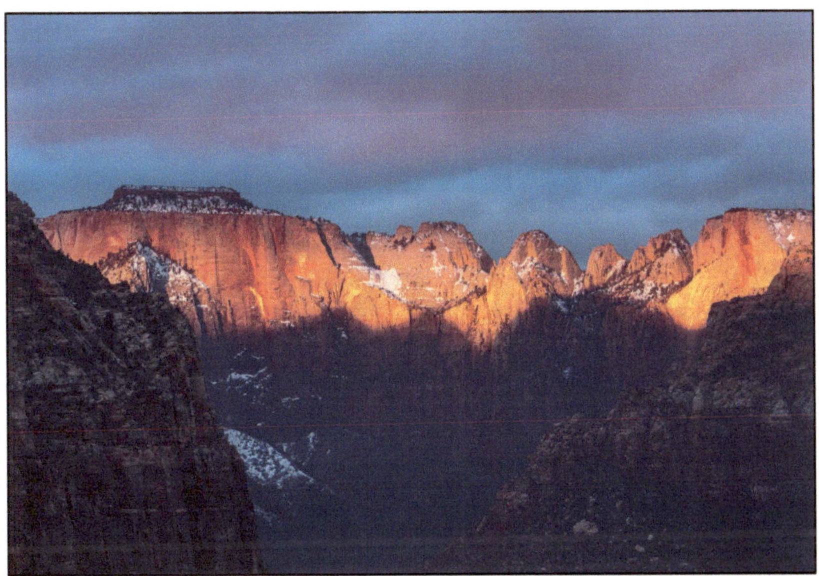

First Light on the Temples of the Virgin   100mm   f/11   0.8s ISO400

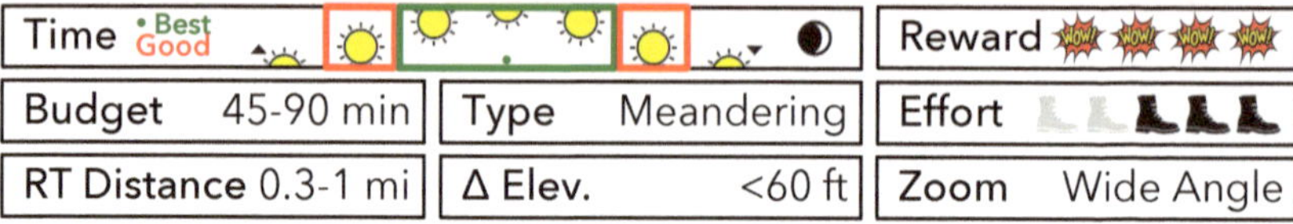

Pine Creek's source is runoff from a plateau on the east side of Deertrap Mountain, nearly two miles north of the Zion-Mount Carmel Highway through Zion's East Side. (This plateau is about ¾ mile east of Zion Lodge.) Pine Creek flows south, then is routed under ZMC Highway, before making a bit of a zig-zag path west towards its feed into the Virgin River. So we have an "Upper Pine Creek" – the section north of ZMC Highway, "Pine Creek" – the section around ZMC Highway, finally to "Lower Pine Creek" which is adjacent to the switchbacks on ZMC Highway between the tunnel's exit and Canyon Junction. The area we are interested in here is from where it sneaks below ZMC Highway to where it runs again below the road, at the overpass to the east tunnel entrance.

Some of this area is within narrow, inescapable slot canyons. Do not enter if water is flowing. Do not enter if any threat of flash flooding is present. Do not attempt to wade through standing water, as the subsurface sand and rocks may be dangerous.

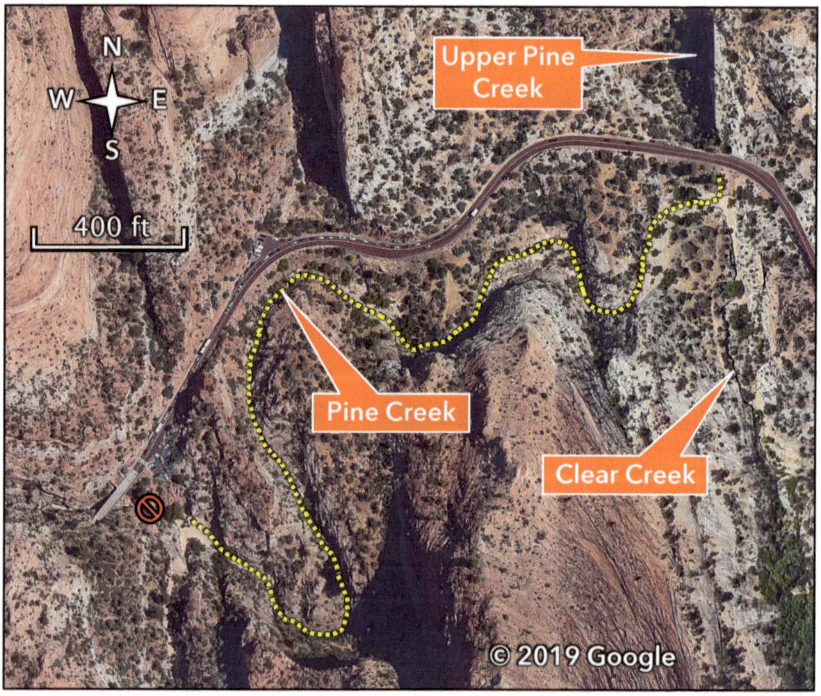

Depending on seasonal rainfall, some sections of this route may have standing water. If you encounter standing water and want to explore further, backtrack and enter elsewhere to find where again the route is passable.

Access is possible at multiple locations. Where you park may help determine this. Be careful of your footing while making your way down to the creek bed.

A lot of warnings, I know. But I want you to be careful and remain safe. The photography opportunities are interesting and definitely warrant a visit. Just be mindful of where you parked, your path, and your footing.

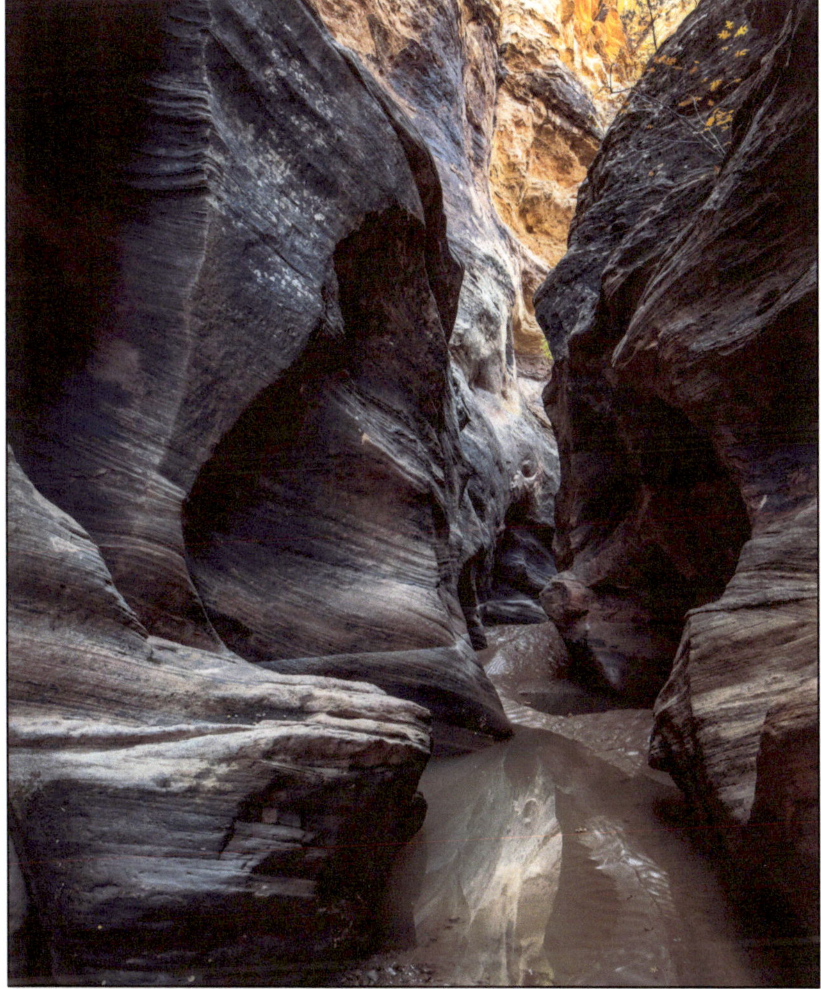

Pine Creek   20mm f/11 1/25s ISO1600

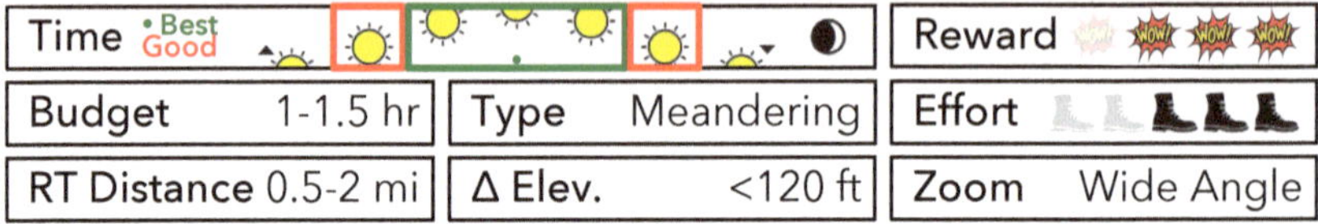

Time	•Best Good		Reward
Budget	1-1.5 hr	Type	Meandering	Effort
RT Distance	0.5-2 mi	Δ Elev.	<120 ft	Zoom	Wide Angle

Clear Creek is most times a dry creek bed, meandering along the entire length of the Zion's East Side, adjacent to the Zion-Mount Carmel Highway. It begins well northeast of the park's East Entrance and feeds into Pine Creek.

The very end of Clear Creek is within a narrow, inescapable slot canyon, so the same guidelines apply as mentioned in the section on Pine Creek (23), yet should be observed over the entire length of Clear Creek... Do not enter if water is flowing. Do not enter if any threat of flash flooding is present. Do not attempt to wade through standing water, as the subsurface sand and rocks may be dangerous.

Clear Creek may be hiked in its entirety along the ZMC Highway, or you can elect to visit sections of it. Along stretches, photography interest is limited. As such, I have highlighted below the 4 areas that I believe are of most interest. (Two miles covers what is highlighted.)

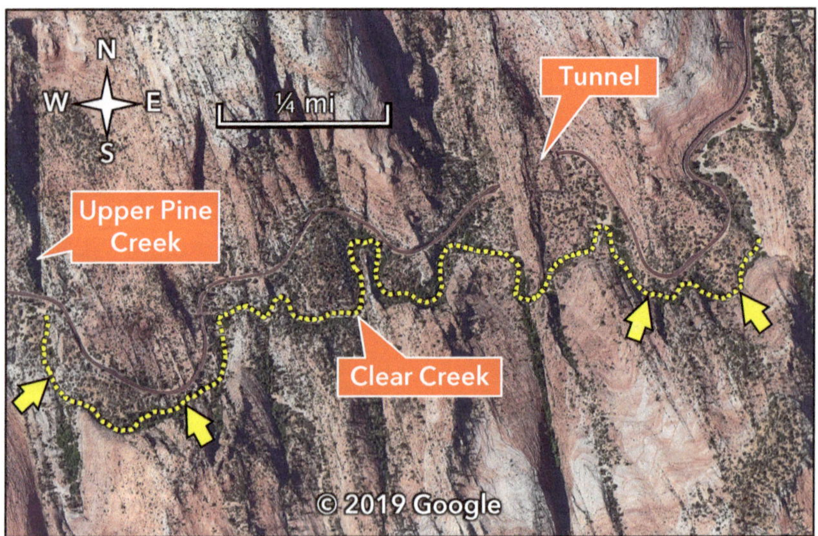

A lot of Clear Creek tends to be sandy, rocky, wide, and with a lot of brush along its sides. Still, trees flourish along this creek bed, and sometimes within it, making for very gracious subjects adjacent to the vertical canyon walls. Seek contrasting colors and textures. Many varying compositions are possible along these sections.

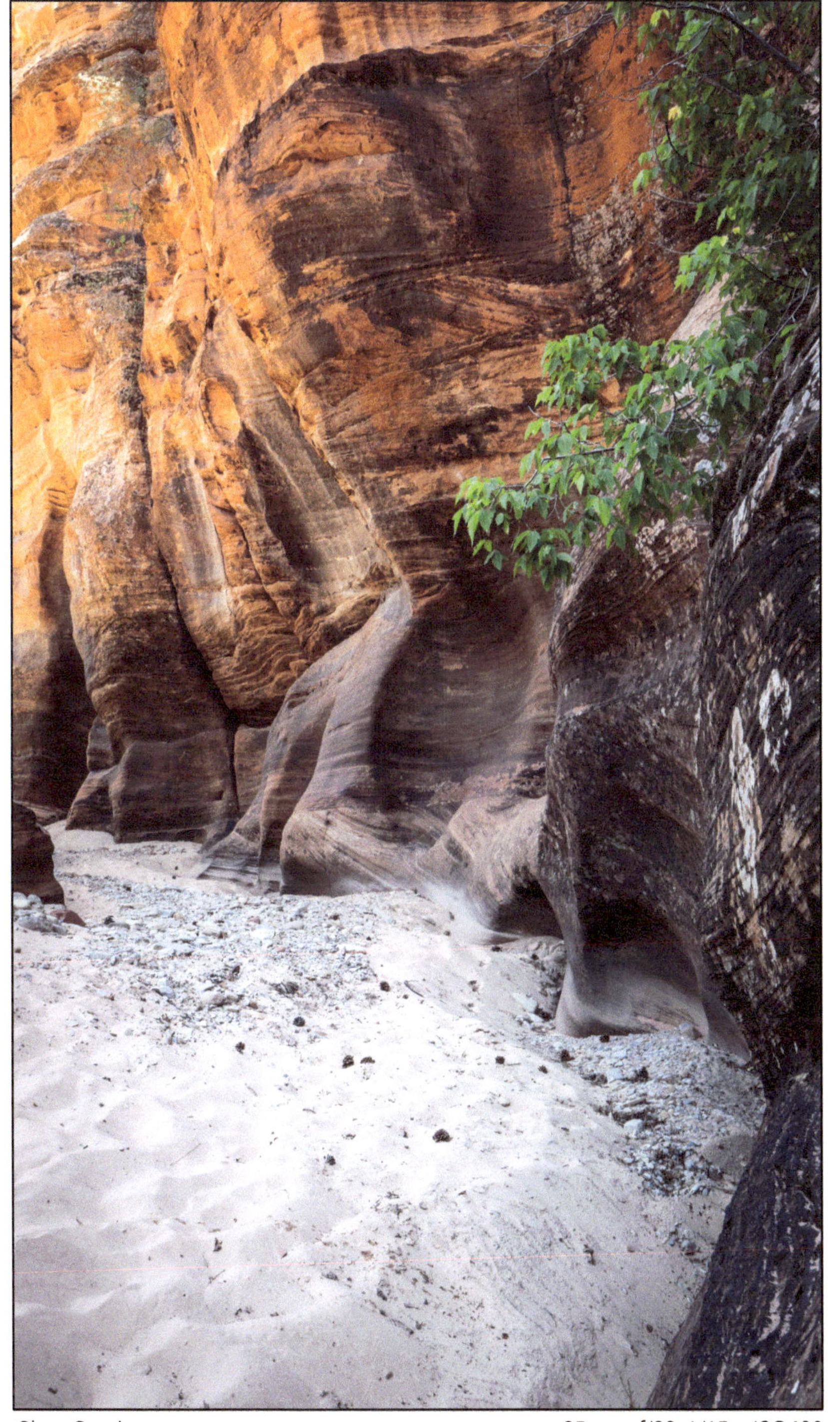

Clear Creek

35mm f/22 1/15s ISO400

Time	Best / Good		Reward	
Budget	45-75 min	**Type**	Out & Back	**Effort**
RT Distance	~0.8 mi	**Δ Elev.**	<200 ft	**Zoom** Wide Angle

Many Pools is a rainwater runoff with *many* small *pools* of standing water. (Clever, right?) Sometimes the best things are simple too.

There is one major gotcha on this one though. This hike and the photographs you want from it are all about the pools of water. And unfortunately, many times of the year there is no water. So here is my sincere "good luck" to you, for standing water during for your visit!

Ultra-wide angle seems to be the way to go photographing these pools. The wider focal lengths let you get up and personal with the water and the reflections, as well as capturing the adjacent slickrock.

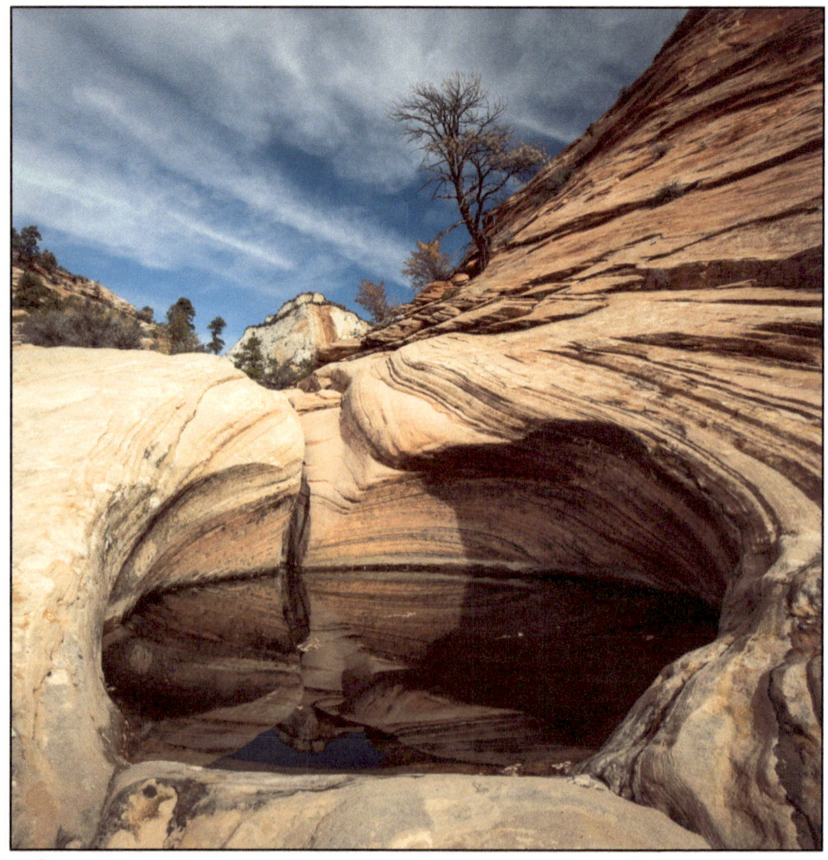

Reflections   16mm f/22 1/15s ISO100

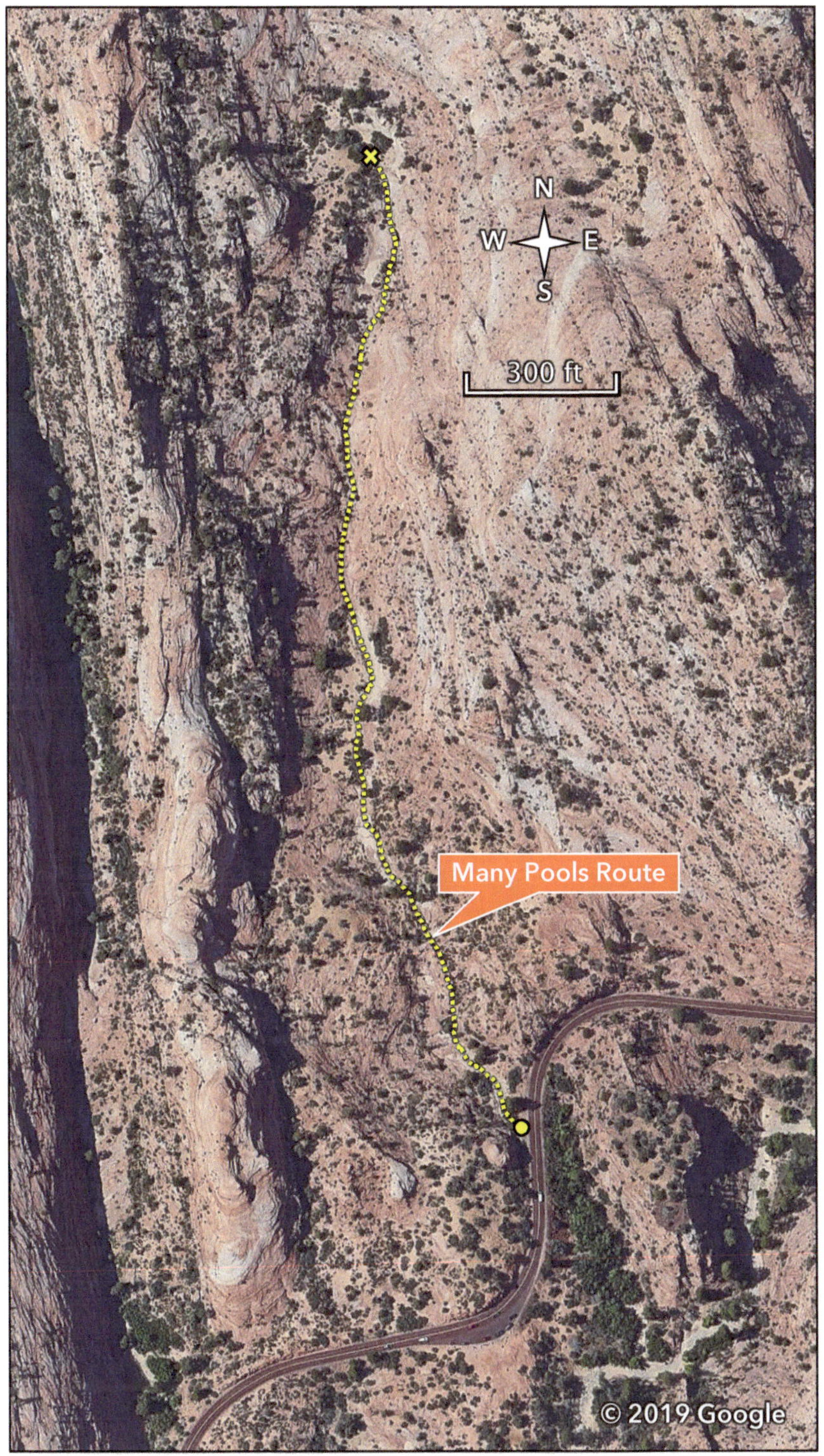

N
W
E
S
300 ft
Many Pools Route
© 2019 Google

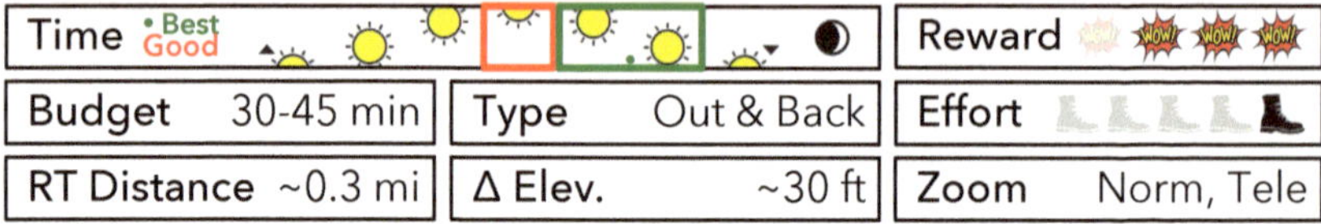

Time **• Best Good**		Reward
Budget	30-45 min	Type	Out & Back	Effort
RT Distance ~0.3 mi	Δ Elev. ~30 ft	Zoom	Norm, Tele

An easy-to-reach, wonderful set of petroglyphs awaits your discovery.

A National Park Service sign reads, "Humans have occupied the Zion area for perhaps 7,000 years. Past inhabitants include Archaic groups, Ancestral Puebloans (Anasazi/Fremont), and ancestors of the Southern Paiute. Any or all of these groups may have contributed petroglyphs (pecked, scratched, or incised) images to this site..."

Visiting this rock art in person is a truly sensational experience.

Uniquely, the parking area for this site is the only one along this stretch of the Zion-Mount Carmel Highway with a split rail wooden fence alongside it. (This fence provides a convenient waypoint.)

Walk across the road, and drop down into the rainwater runoff, heading north. Look for a trail to your left, just after a large tree almost in the middle of the dry runoff. The trail leads to two viewing areas.

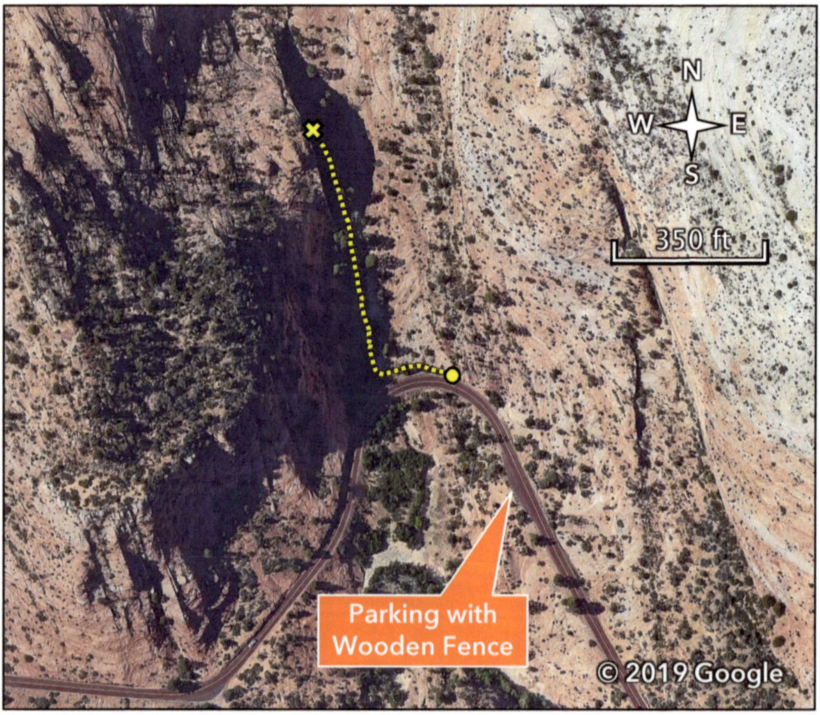

The best time to visit is in late morning or into the afternoon, so as to eliminate harsh shadows across the face of the wall where the petroglyphs reside.

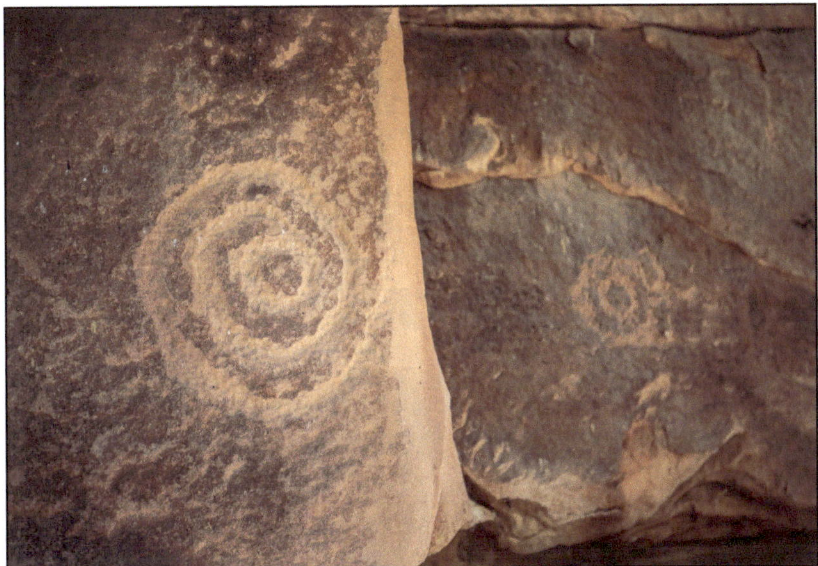

Spiral
35mm f/4 1/50s ISO200

You can only get so close, as there are wooden fences protecting the art. Exercise use of both normal and telephoto focal lengths.

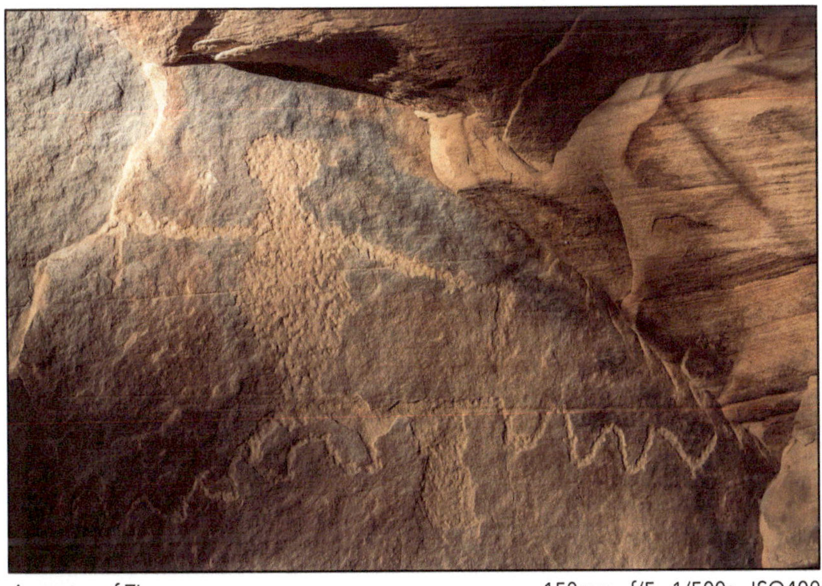

Ancestor of Zion
150mm f/5 1/500s ISO400

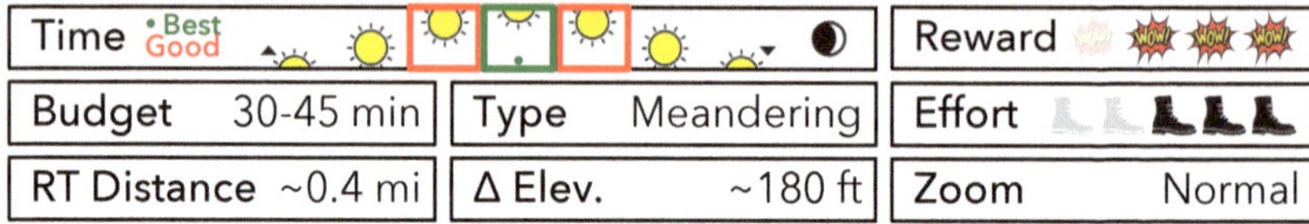

Time	Best Good	Reward
Budget	30-45 min	Type	Meandering	Effort
RT Distance	~0.4 mi	Δ Elev.	~180 ft	Zoom	Normal

At some point (I do not remember when exactly) while exploring Zion's east side I realized that I wanted a shot with the sinuous lines of the slickrock seemingly flowing away from me, and towards the bright blue sky. So the search began, but I found the concept difficult to execute. The landscape has so many ups and downs... But I could not rid the composition of a nearby hoodoo or hillside. I started to look towards higher elevations, and then became even more greedy – I wanted the white-colored slickrock and not the widely-present orange variety. One sunny day in June, I found it!

I'm excited to share this site with you. Accessing it does require climbing and subsequent descent. You must gauge your ability to safely navigate this terrain and elevation change. **Do not attempt this when the ground it wet – it can be deceptively slippery.** Wear shoes with good grip and affixed tightly to your feet. Gloves can be helpful, as the slickrock is rough (which aids traction, but can be abrasive to bare skin). Take your time.

The route below is for reference only... Find a path along and up the slickrock, with as-necessary turns along the way so as to provide adequate traction.

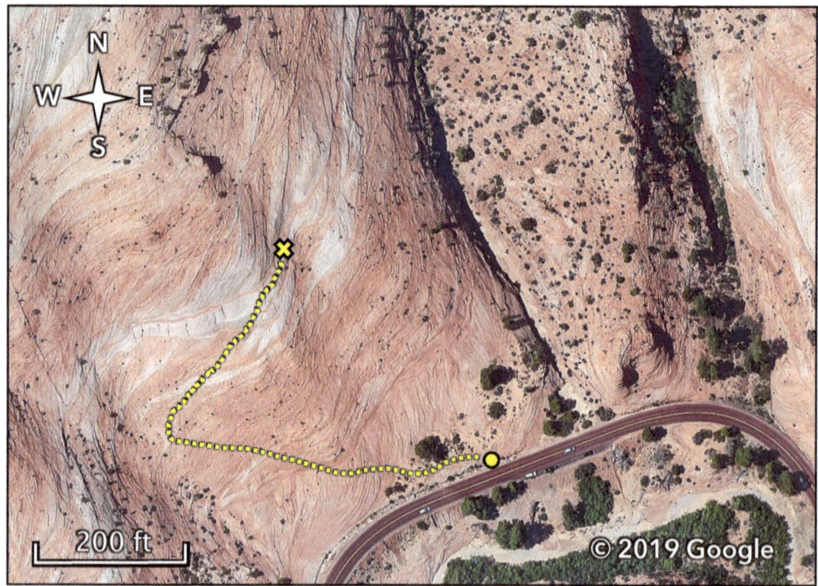

From the roadside, you will be able to see strips of white among the otherwise orange slope. In these bands of white are also hues of apricot and yellow. Head in this direction.

The shot is straightforward – position your camera low to the ground and stop-down your aperture for sufficient depth of field. The sky is to the north.

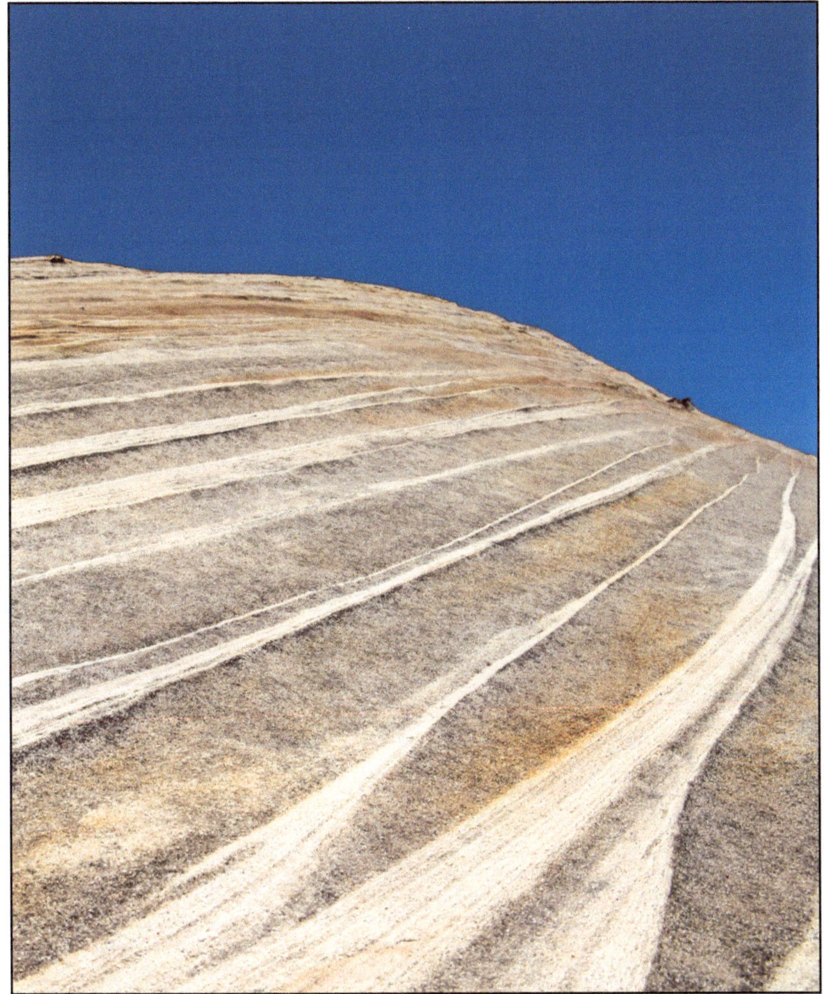

Waves of Bright Colors   24mm f/16 1/320s ISO100

Whether it be in Zion National Park, or where ever your landscape photography takes you, consider a composition that you would like to discover and photograph. This exercise in creativity and the resulting exploration are rewarding, regardless of whether you find "the shot" or not.

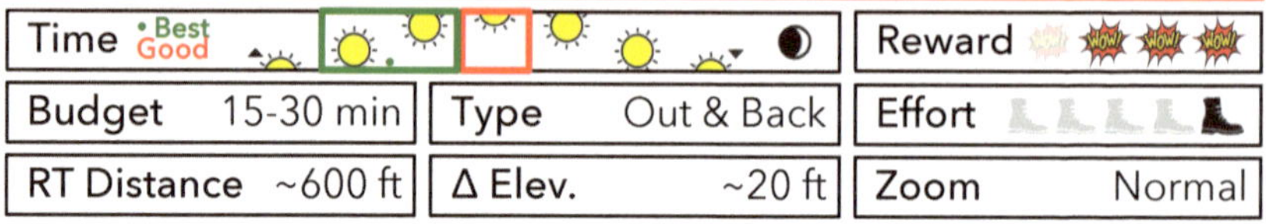

Time Best Good		Reward
Budget	15-30 min	Type	Out & Back	Effort
RT Distance	~600 ft	Δ Elev.	~20 ft	Zoom	Normal

This may be the most photogenic tree in Zion National Park!

It's an obvious and easy composition. And bonus – it's easy to reach as well!

Now that's not to say that you won't find yourself spending a bit of time on-site. Due to the tree's unique shape and its position on this lone hoodoo, if you're like me you'll find yourself sampling many perspectives of it, and with varying focal lengths. It's hard to go wrong, as its simplicity makes it remarkably photogenic from many angles and with many different focal lengths.

On page 88, because of its easy access and uninterrupted background, I utilized it for a late-night shot of the Milky Way.

The only downside is that the parking pullout is short and not wide. At best, only two vehicles can fit here simultaneously. Though, I have yet to find the area crowded... If so, try one of the two adjacent parking strips, or instead visit another nearby site, and return later. (People don't tend to stay long.)

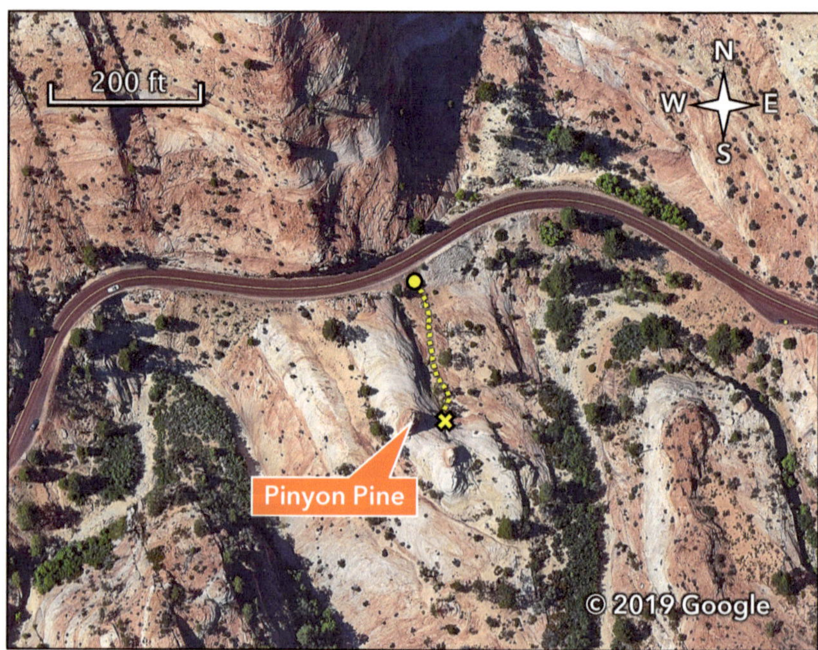

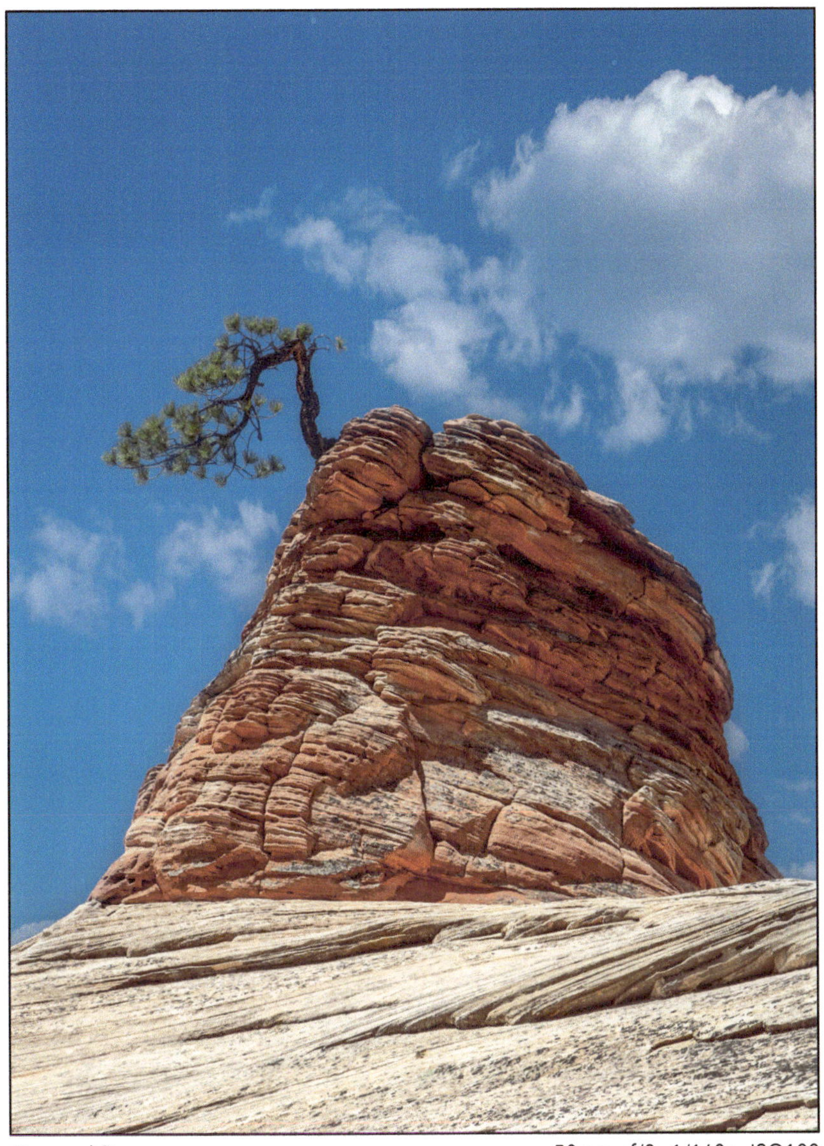

Pine and Stone

50mm f/8 1/160s ISO100

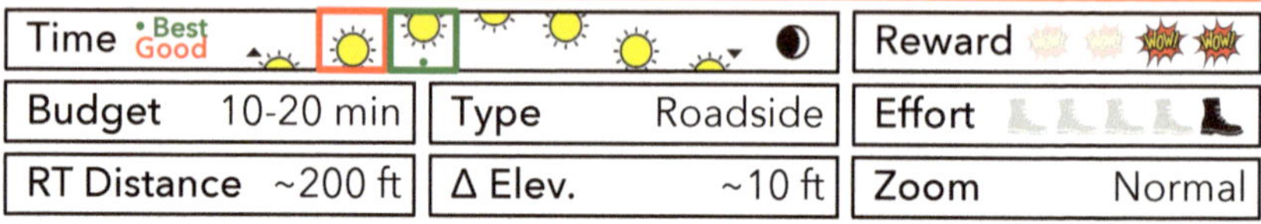

Time	Best Good		Reward	
Budget	10-20 min	Type	Roadside	Effort
RT Distance	~200 ft	Δ Elev.	~10 ft	Zoom	Normal

Checkerboard Mesa has a fantastic, geometric pattern and is a photographers' favorite. It is well-marked both from its west and east, so there is no missing it.

There is a pullout directly across the road from its base, if you want to explore it up close. Too close though, and the broad, square-shaped pattern seems to be a bit subdued. Still, I have had fun working along its northeast side, focusing on its interesting lines.

There is a formal, and very large pullout between the East Entrance and it. This makes for an OK shot, but with so many trees in the foreground, it's hard to frame it adequately.

My recommendation is to park at this large pullout, and find across the road a very short (albeit rocky) climb of about 10 feet higher up. Others have apparently done the same, as the soil is more loose and disturbed than adjacent areas. Take this short climb, experiment with varying positions, and take the shot. I just hope you are graced with more interesting skies than I have always been!

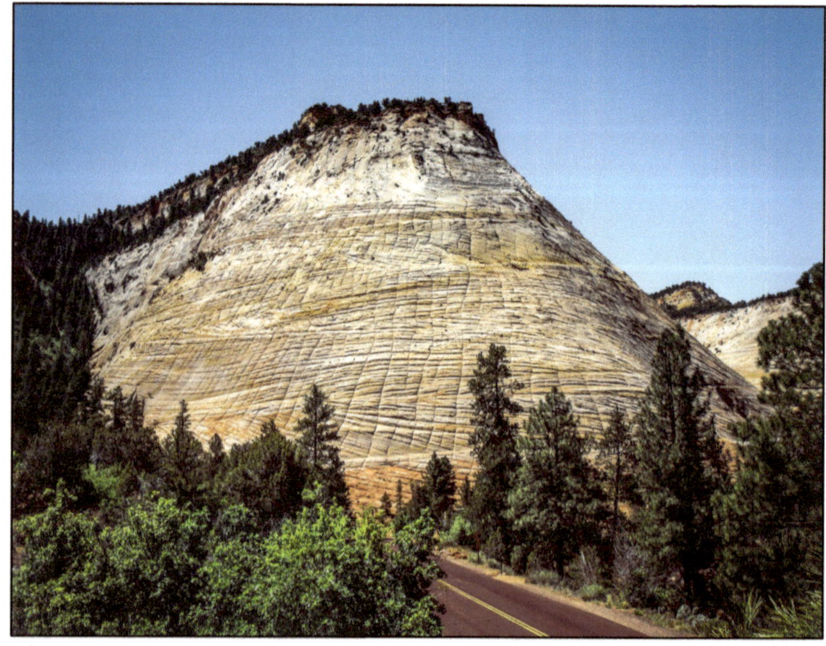

Checkerboard Mesa   24mm f/8 1/320s ISO100

Kolob Terrace

Kolob Terrace Entrance to Kolob Reservoir

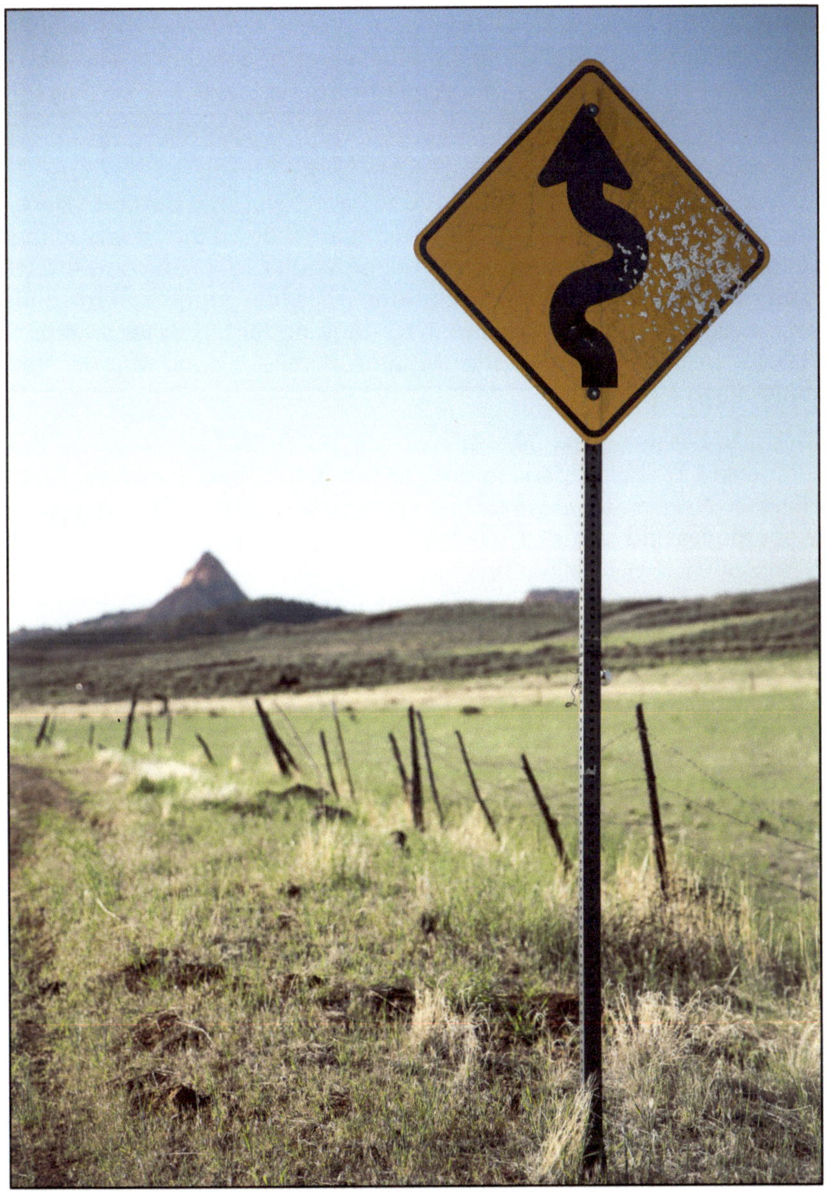

Winding-up the Kolob Terrace Road

70mm f/2.8 1/400s ISO100

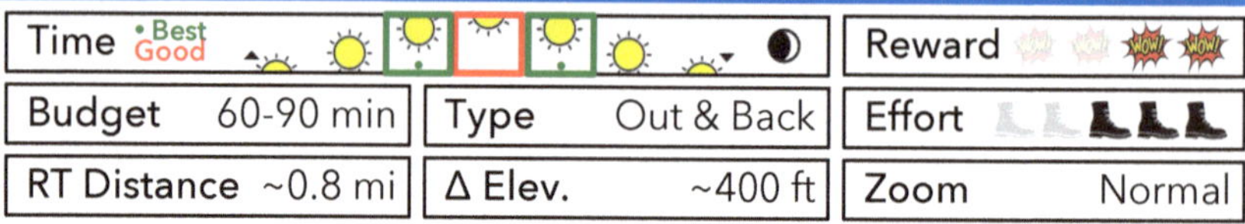

Time **Best Good**	Reward
Budget 60-90 min	Type Out & Back	Effort
RT Distance ~0.8 mi	Δ Elev. ~400 ft	Zoom Normal

I am going to cut to the chase on the Grapevine Trail. It's best reserved for visitors who have spent time exploring the Kolob Terrace and have 60-90 minutes to spare, or for those who have already seen the majority of the rest of the park and are looking for something new and different.

The "greater" Grapevine Trail makes its way north, all the way to Grapevine Spring. This narrative does not cover that portion. Here, we are simply trekking from the parking area, down the ravine, to the immediate, lush area of the Left Fork of North Creek. (If you were to continue north to Grapevine Spring, while the creek's route only covers about ½ mile, expect your zig-zagging feet to cover an entire mile. So you would expect to add 2 miles round trip to this condensed hike.)

This hike has three unique sections... First, a rather plain trek from the Grapevine Trailhead parking area to the basalt (black, volcanic rock) decline. Next, a *very loose* descent down the basalt trail. **I urge you to wear gloves and pants!** Then finally the approach to the creek (still at a decline, but not as steep or loose).

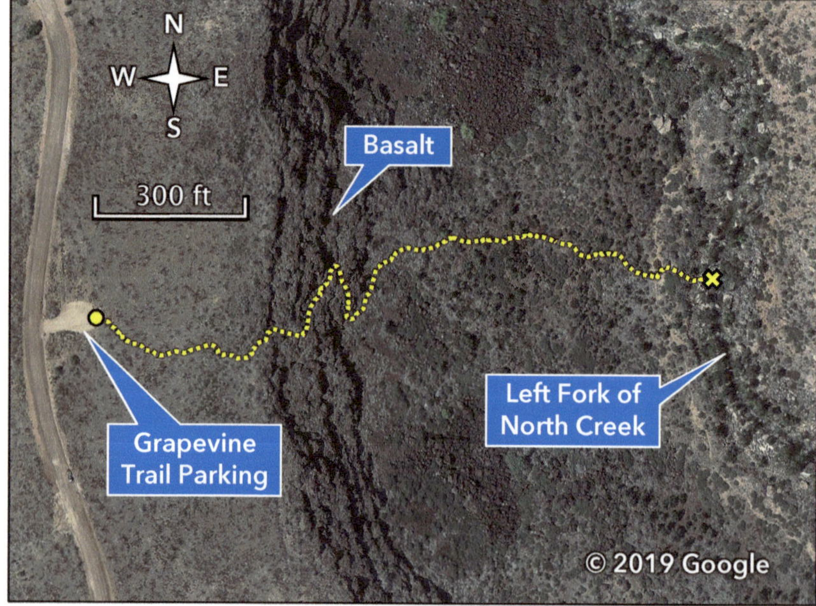

Once at the creek, make note of your position and the trail location to exit. Explore the areas just north and south, on both sides of the creek. (It is possible to cross when the water level is low, and it usually is.)

Lighting can be challenging. This may be a good scene to experiment with your camera's onboard HDR feature, if so equipped.

Enjoy this small desert oasis, and when ready head on back up!

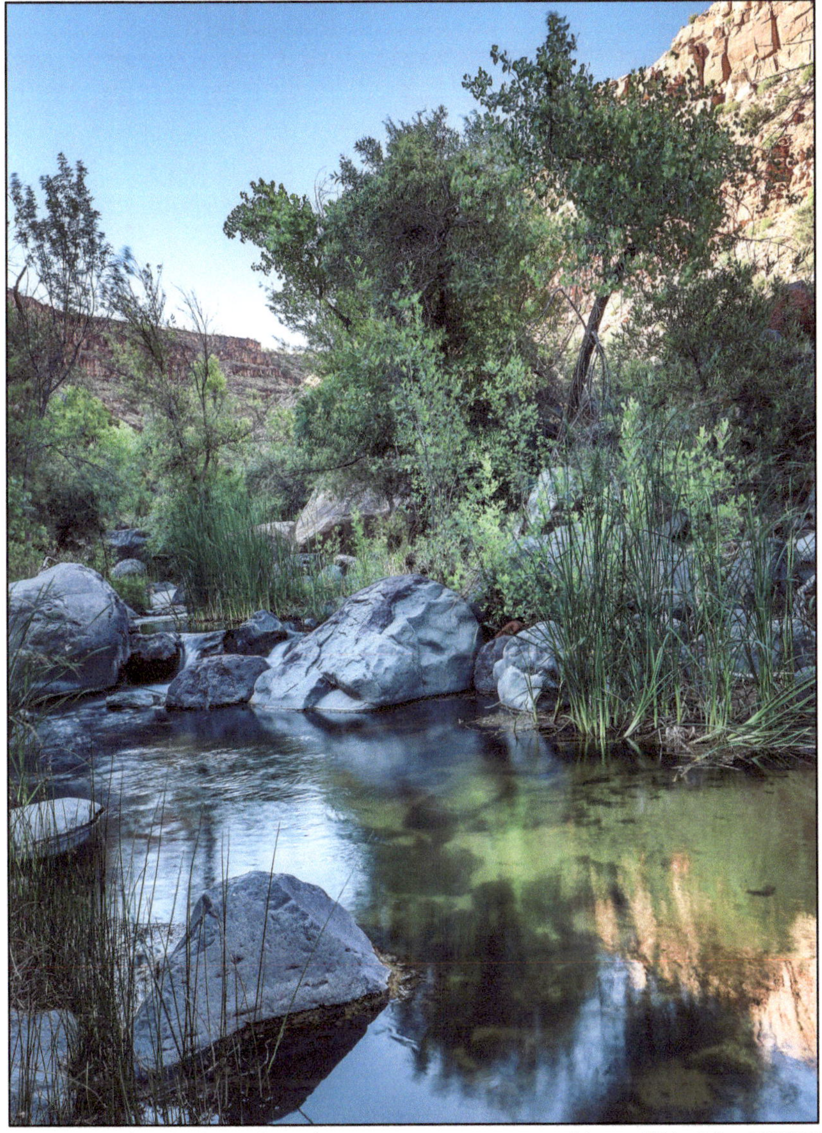

An Oasis in the Shadows of Sandstone   24mm   f/16   0.3s   ISO200

Time	Best · Good	Reward	WOW! WOW! WOW! WOW!
Budget	7-9 hr	Type	Out & Back	Effort	(5 boots)
RT Distance	~9 mi	Δ Elev.	~500 ft	Zoom	Wide, Norm

Before ever visiting Zion National Park, on my earliest research I kept coming across pictures of The Subway and the nearby Archangel Falls. "Wow," I thought – any national park that hosts these two photography treasures must have a lot to offer. And while my hypothesis proved correct for the park as a whole, I was naive to think that either The Subway or Archangel Falls would be easy to access. Quite simply, they are not.

The Subway is a short stretch of a slot canyon with walls so rounded that from within it feels as though you're in an underground subway (railway) tunnel. There is no "ceiling" (it is open to the air above), but from certain angles it feels enclosed. This is *the* milestone location along the Left Fork of North Creek accessed from the Kolob Terrace. Canyoneering routes exist, for approaches from the north, but the route in this book is the traditional non-canyoneering ("non-technical") day hike "from the bottom-up" route. For the bottom-up route, The Subway feature is the end point. Beyond it, canyoneering is required.

This hike has two other fantastic photographic subjects. Archangel Falls, as mentioned, is one. The other is a crack in the creek bed with water flowing within it, know aptly as "The Crack." (How apropos.)

Now back to my potentially discouraging final comment in the opening paragraph...

First, while there are many other more challenging hikes within Zion National Park, this one is the most challenging and most strenuous in this book. The mileage circulated among many sources is as though you are tracking exactly as the Left Fork of North Creek flows. You are not. You will be route finding and zig-zagging so much that your real world mileage is about 25% greater than the elsewhere-advertised 7 mile RT. Plus there are many sizable boulders you will have to scramble over. It is quite technical for the casual hiker. (I fit squarely in this category.)

Second, a Wilderness Permit is required for this hike. The National Park Service, at time of writing, only permits 80 visitors per day. That is not a lot, and during peak months the number of visitors interested far exceeds this limitation. If this hike is on your bucket list, as it was mine, consider a December, January or

February trip. These are the three slowest months for permits, and although nothing is a sure bet, these months are darn close. One of my visits was in January, and I loved it. There only is some lack of foliage around Archangel Falls, but the site is still sensational!   Visit The Subway permitting system for more information and to apply online.

www.nps.gov/zion/planyourvisit/subwaypermits.htm

Like The Narrows (17), it would not be prudent for me to guide you step-by-step on this hike. Seeking an outfitters' advice and guidance is mandatory for The Subway. Also, check with the National Park Service on current conditions and weather forecasts. I have utilized rental gear and have obtained detailed maps from Zion Adventure Company in Springdale. I recommend them, without hesitation.

Plan to begin your hike at first light to allow yourself plenty of time.

The hike begins at the Left Fork Trailhead along the Kolob Terrace Road. Near the parking area is the trailhead sign. The trail begins adjacent to this sign. As you begin, the trail weaves back and forth a bit, but stays mostly straight. Do not make the mistake that I did and make a hard right onto an obsidian stone-cluttered rainwater runoff to the right. That's a dead end! In other words, you may cross over or through some of these black rocks, but it should only be momentarily. Your trail remains the more narrow, orange sand route.

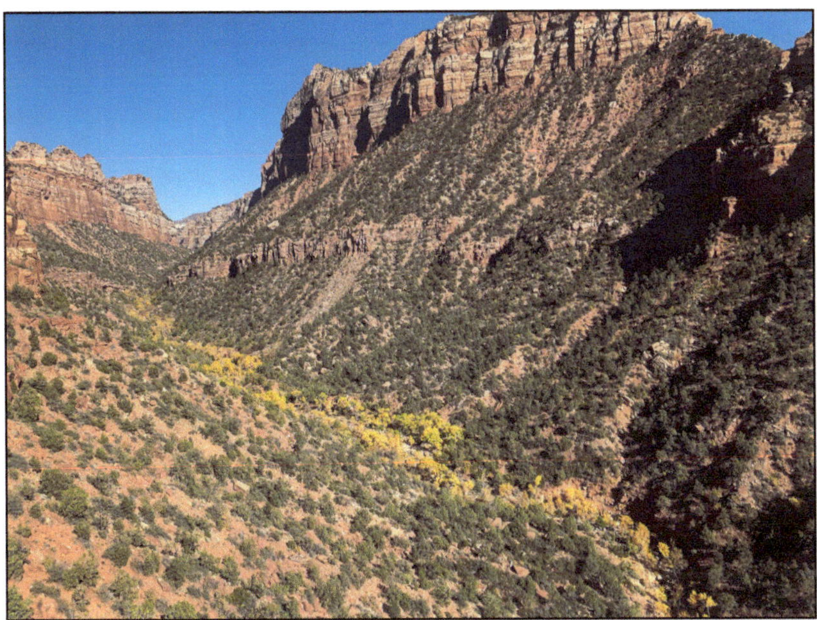

Autumn Glow of Trees along the Left Fork of North Creek 28mm   f/8 1/640s ISO100

After ½ mile it gets more interesting. You make a 400 foot descent to the Left Fork of North Creek over some very rocky and loose terrain. The prescribed route can be difficult to select at times. Take your time and use good judgment. **Once at the bottom, study the topography you just descended from carefully. Many people miss the exit on their return.**

Your hike up-creek begins. This is not a well-marked route. The best advice that I can provide is to seek footprints left behind from fellow hikers, as well as the sand left behind from their boots on top of rocks in or adjacent to the creek. If you reach an obstacle that seems unsafe or impractical to conquer, it may be that you missed another, more straightforward route option. You will double-back from time to time. (This is where the mileage adds up, but it is just the way it is.)

At about the halfway mark on the north side (left side) of the creek next to the trail is a pair of large, bright white boulders with dinosaur footprints! Be on the lookout. And if you miss it on the way up, be again on the lookout during your return trip.

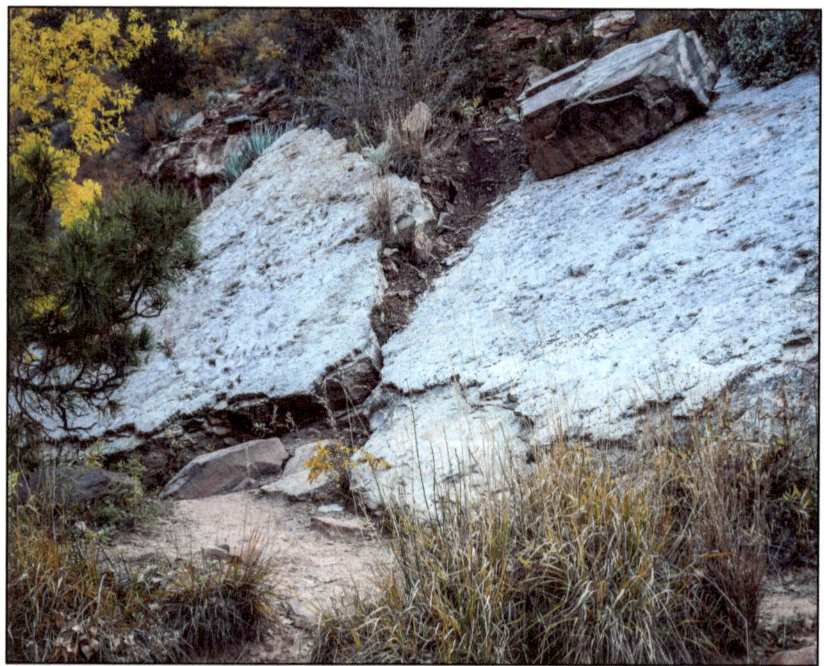

Boulders with Prehistoric Footprints   24mm f/4 1/80s ISO400

Continuing on, the canyon walls begin to close in. There is an early Archangel Falls imposter. (Ha!) Though still a bit away, Archangel Falls is the first major photographic site you will reach. And you will know it when you get there. It's spectacular.

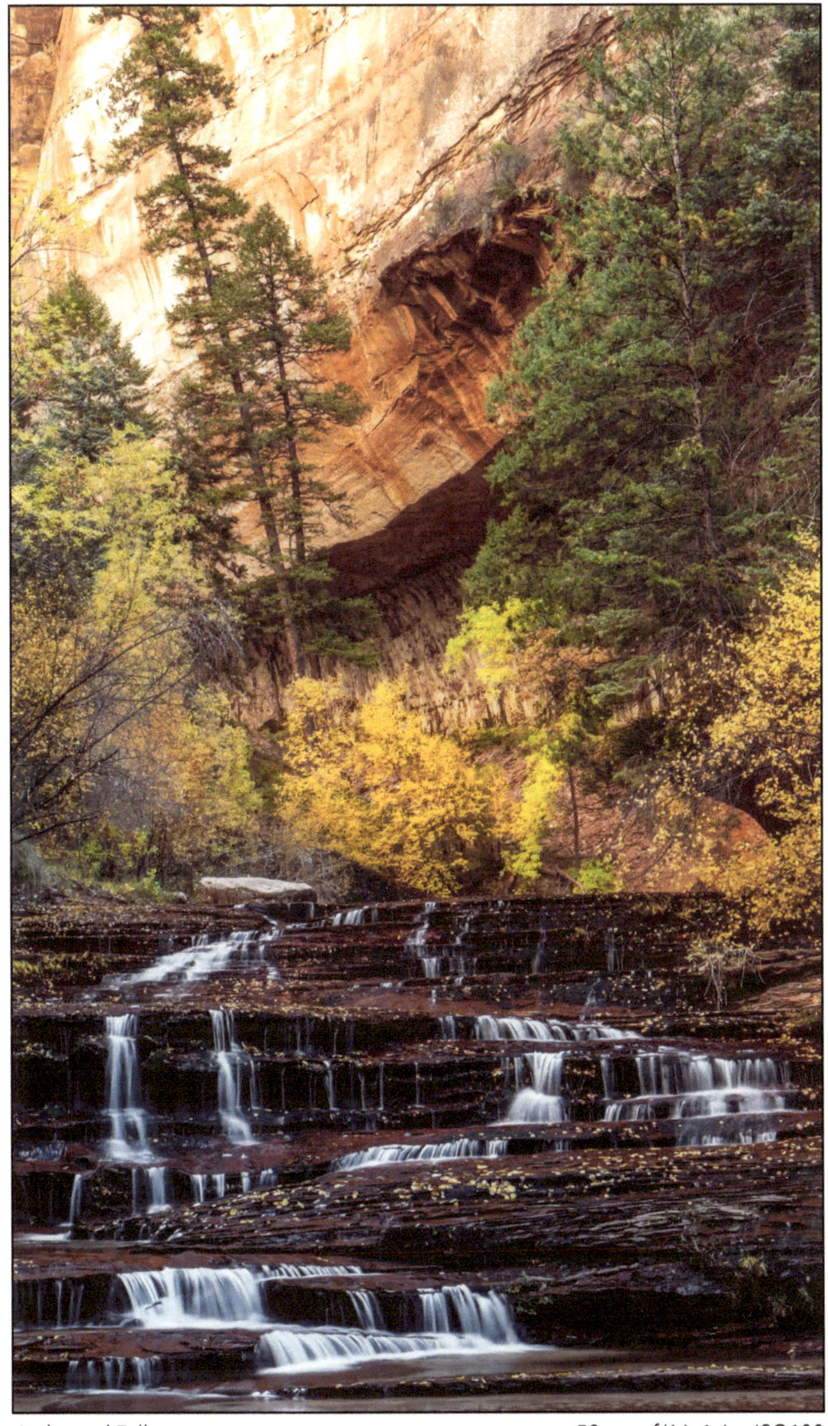

Archangel Falls

50mm f/16 1.6s ISO100

Not far beyond Archangel Falls is The Crack and The Subway. Your first sighting of The Subway is a truly unforgettable experience.

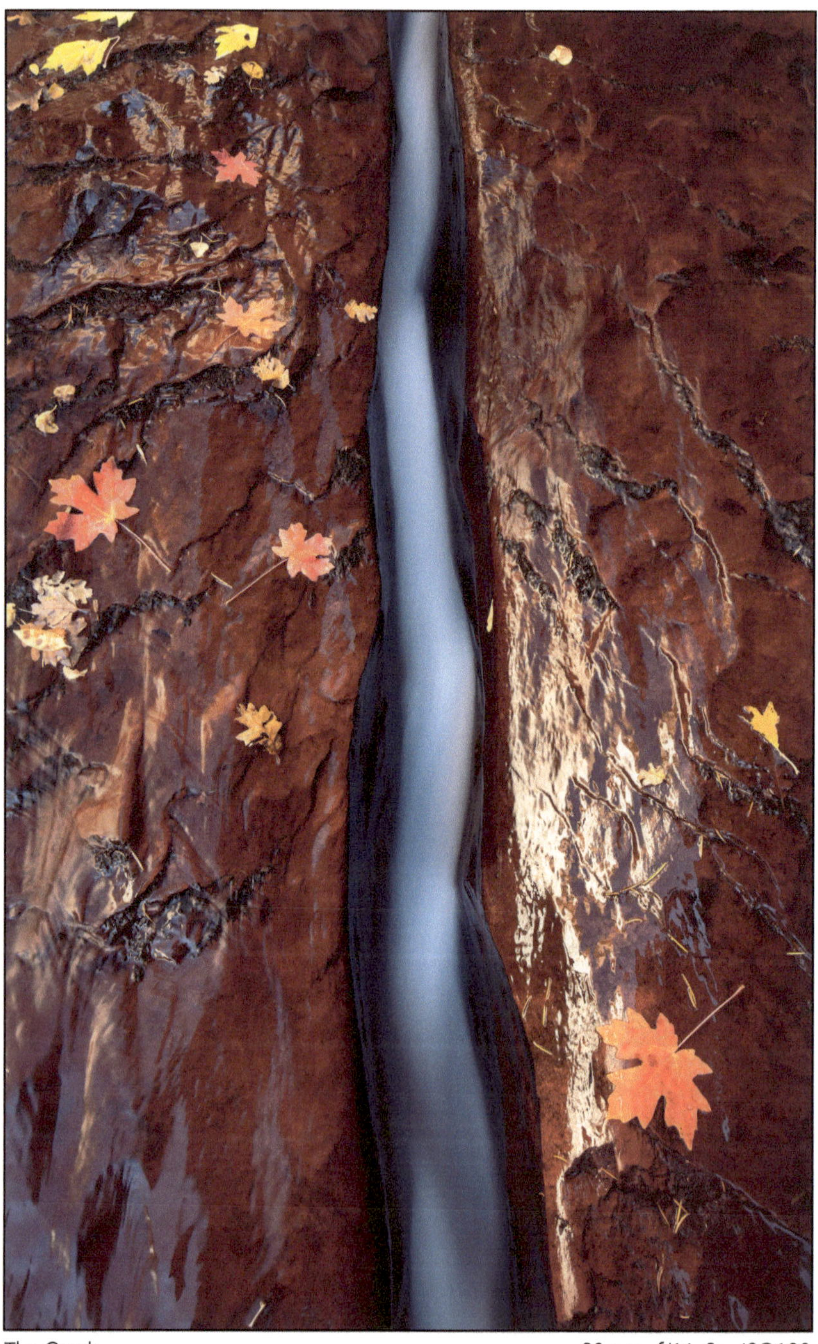

The Crack

20mm f/16 2s ISO100

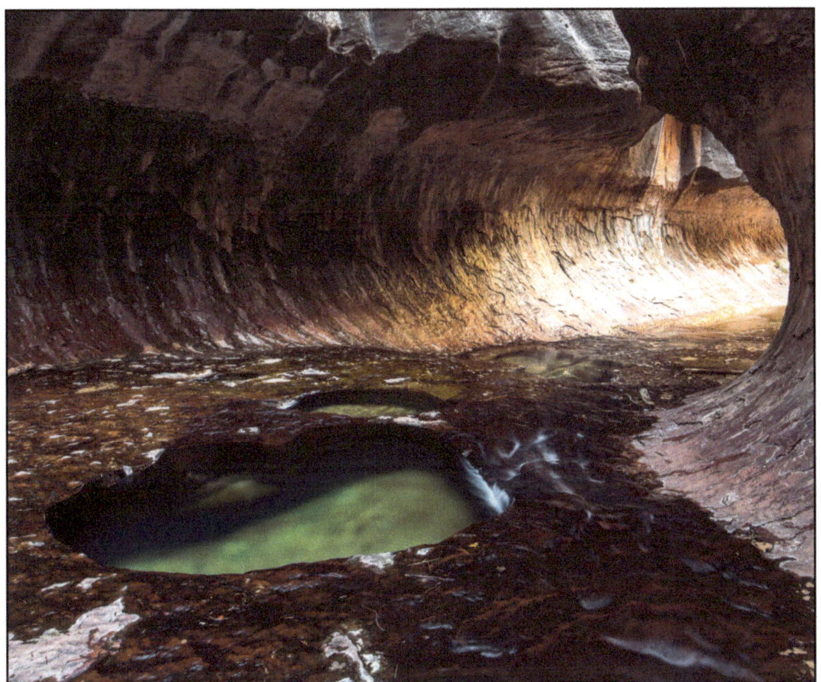

The Subway with Midday Light   24mm f/16 6s ISO50

Walking in water is mandatory at times, but it is not like walking The Narrows. It is more shallow along this hike, and I would argue that a good pair of traditional waterproof boots would be adequate (though each time I have hiked this route I have worn rented boots). **One caution – the wet surfaces can be extremely slippery, so a sole with a rubber compound suitable for improved underwater traction is advisable.**

With your early start, you should have a lot of time to experiment with different compositions and techniques at The Subway. Once finished, head on back the same way you came. Keep an eye out for that exit, and reserve energy for the 400 foot climb out!

I've touched on boots. Trekking poles (or a single pole) could be helpful, but with the many boulders you will be scrambling over or around, you will find yourself stowing the pole(s) very regularly. I highly recommend gloves, to protect your hands on these scrambles, and of course for warmth too. While on warmth, the temperature along this hike can change drastically. Dress in layers. Near the end or when in direct sunlight, it can be hot in many months. However, while in The Subway, the temperature can be very cold. Hand warmers may be helpful in between operating your camera.

"Do your best to carry less" while on this long hike. Take a tripod.
You actually could do with only a wide angle zoom. Leave the
telephoto lenses and their weight behind.

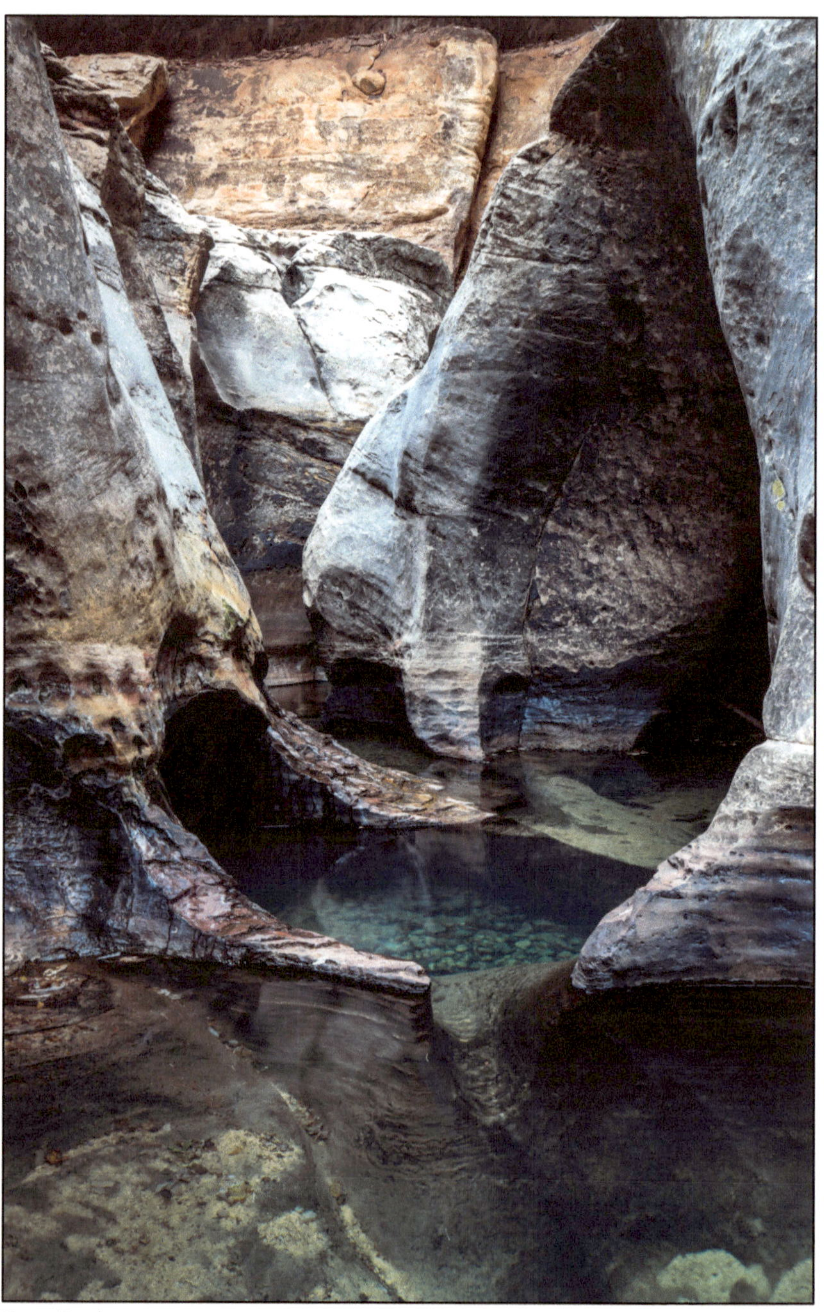

Deep Pools   35mm f/11 3s ISO100

I'll wrap with some photography advice... (Most of this text has been on the hike itself!)

Archangel Falls

Here, you have a lot of room with which to work. In fact, where to begin may be the only challenge!   I have included a photograph here using a focal length of 50mm, where I was set back a bit from the lowest cascade. I included this shot, because most shots you will see utilize an ultra-wide angle lens (14-18mm), with the camera positioned right up next to this same lowest cascade. It's hard to go wrong. Work close, work far away, work higher, work lower. Here, like inside The Subway, my governing recommendation is to experiment.

The Crack

This one is the most straightforward of the bunch. You will want to arrange your tripod so that it straddles The Crack, and so that your camera is pointed more-or-less down at it. Widening your focal length essentially compresses the gap's apparent width.

The Subway

It is slippery in The Subway. Be careful and watch every step! For the traditional composition, you will shoot at about a 20mm focal length. 24mm seems too narrow, and 16-18mm captures too much of the opening at the top, plus it tends to distance the curved walls too far away in your image. Try various angles. In order to draw the pools of water right up into the bottom of your image frame, typically you will shoot very close to the ground.

I sincerely hope that you can make it, and that you enjoy your time in this amazing place.

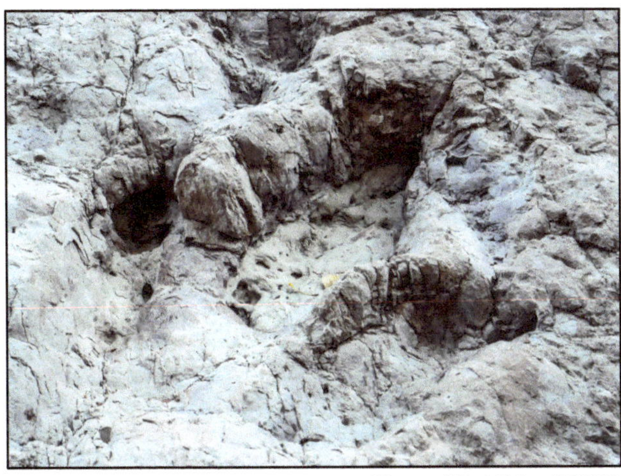

Dinosaur Footprint   50mm f/8 1/60s ISO800

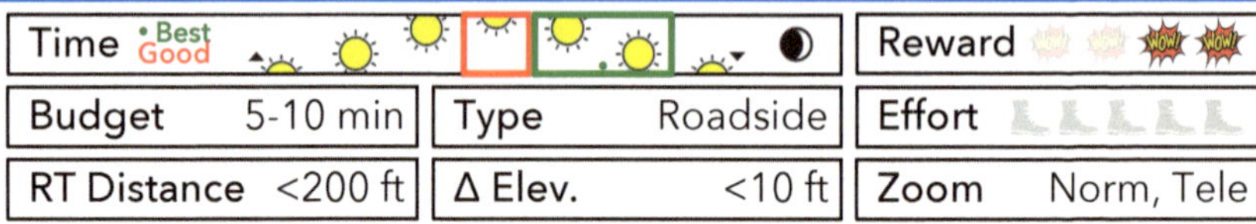

Time	Best Good			Reward	
Budget	5-10 min	Type	Roadside	Effort	
RT Distance	<200 ft	Δ Elev.	<10 ft	Zoom	Norm, Tele

Cave Knoll is aptly named – here we have a hill (a.k.a. knoll) with a vertical, just-aboveground cave in its side. But if we were to name the photograph, it would be "Cave Knoll and Meadow." In the spring and summer the grass between the road and Cave Knoll is stunning. Unfortunately, because it is used for grazing cattle, fall and winter are *not* stunning. If your itinerary falls in the latter, then explore the cave as best you can with a telephoto lens!

Along this section of the Kolob Terrace Road, you are actually outside the Zion National Park boundary. However, Cave Knoll (itself) is within the park boundary! So, the panorama would include the private property adjacent to the road, as well as Cave Knoll within the park. (Kind of interesting – or at least makes for a conversation piece with friends.)

Spotting the cave on your first visit or in harsh lighting can be a bit of a challenge. In fact, identifying which hillside to photograph in this area can also be a challenge! The best advice that I can provide is to locate the road sign pictured on page 109, just south of the 90 degree bend in the road near Spendlove Knoll. This spot next to the sign is a good start for your composition. There is a 1-2 car pullout for your use on the opposite side of the road from the sign. Walk south to further adjust your framing, as desired.

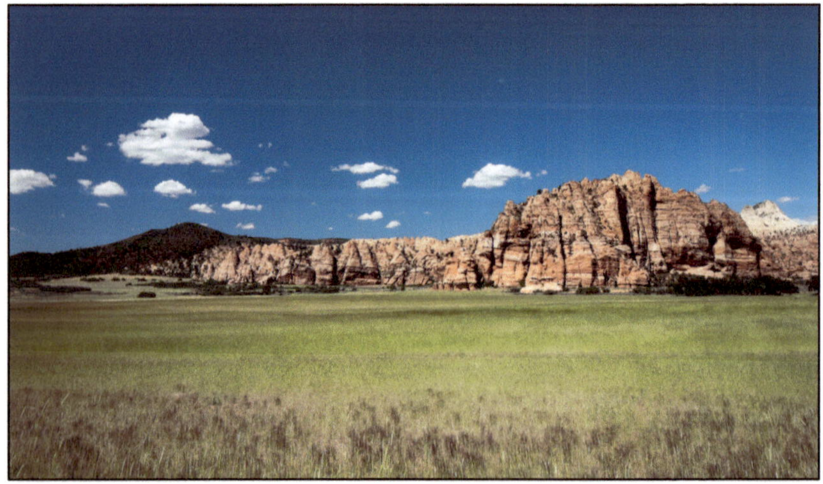

Cave Knoll and Meadow   24mm f/22 1/50s ISO200

Time	Best / Good 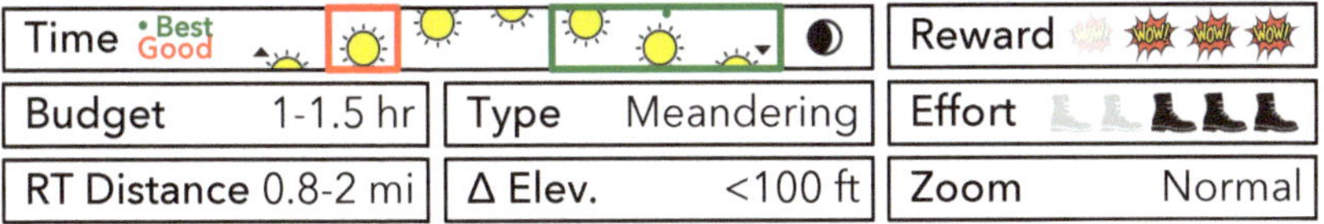	Reward	WOW! WOW! WOW! WOW!
Budget	1-1.5 hr	Type	Meandering	Effort	👢👢👢👢👢
RT Distance	0.8-2 mi	Δ Elev.	<100 ft	Zoom	Normal

Dare I say, this cluster of hoodoos is impossible to miss while driving up the Kolob Terrace Road. Though, from the road, they appear difficult to access... There are two routes. One easier, but longer. The other more challenging, but also more direct.

The longer "Route 1" is via the Hop Valley Trailhead. Ample parking is also available here. You begin on the Hop Valley Trail, then at a rainwater runoff turn right and follow it around to the backside of this hill.

The more direct "Route 2" begins at an informal pullout, sized for about two vehicles. (It's an easy pullout to miss.) From here, you zig-zag down and then back up, directly to the east side of the hoodoos. This pullout, and the vista near it, are superb to take in the setting sun. More on this later.

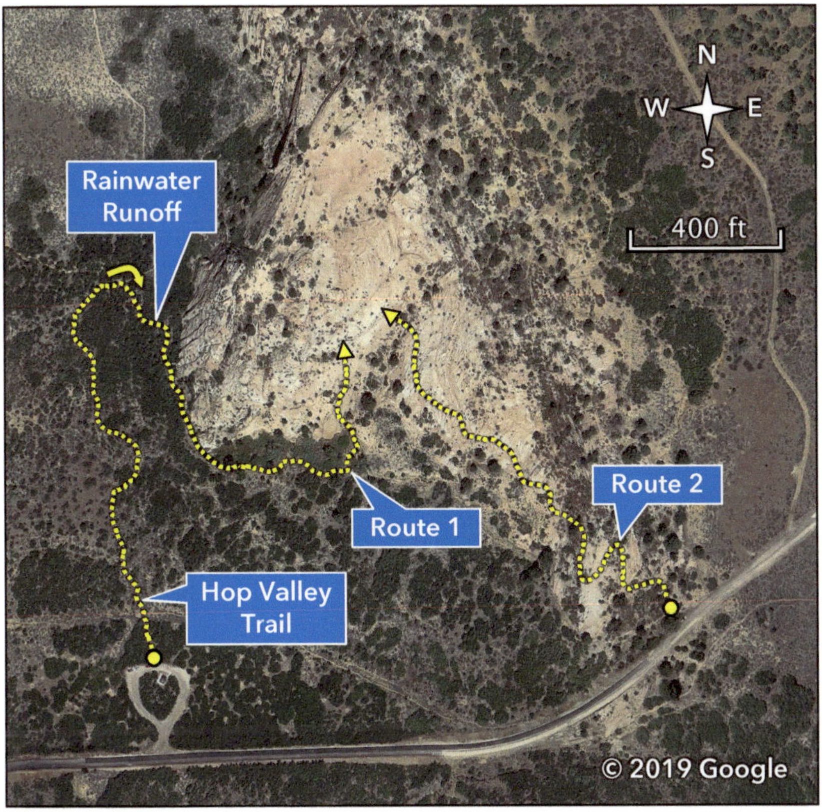

Before you embark on foot, I do recommend to take some shots from along the Kolob Terrace Road. (Or do so after your up-close encounter.) If your experience resembles mine, while they are fun to explore up close, the view from a distance with a telephoto lens is great as well.

Now while on foot... There is an abundance of possible compositions here. The more time you have to spend, the more you will find. Not only are the hoodoos of interest, but other eroded features as well (along the ground).

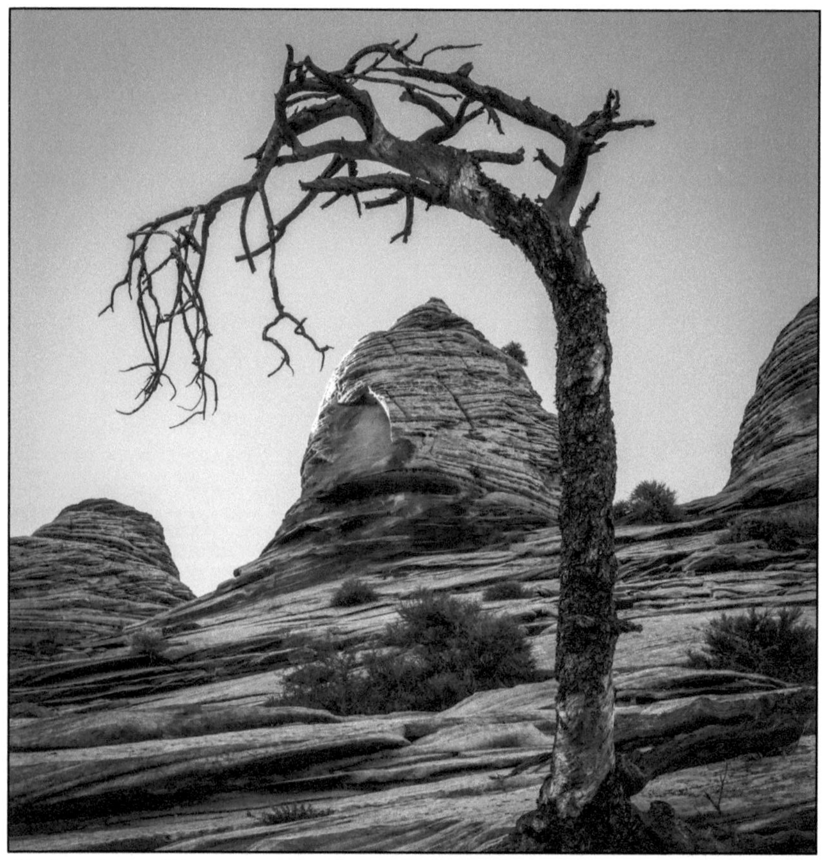

Kiln Hoodoo and Tree   50mm f/11 1/60s ISO400

Do be careful! When along the top of this hill, it is a very steep drop from its west side.

I mentioned sunset. Late afternoon at the hoodoos and to their east (in the direction of the small, roadside pullout) produce some really fantastic shadows. So while really anytime of day works for this location, it's at its prime in the late afternoon. Thus, after making the

122

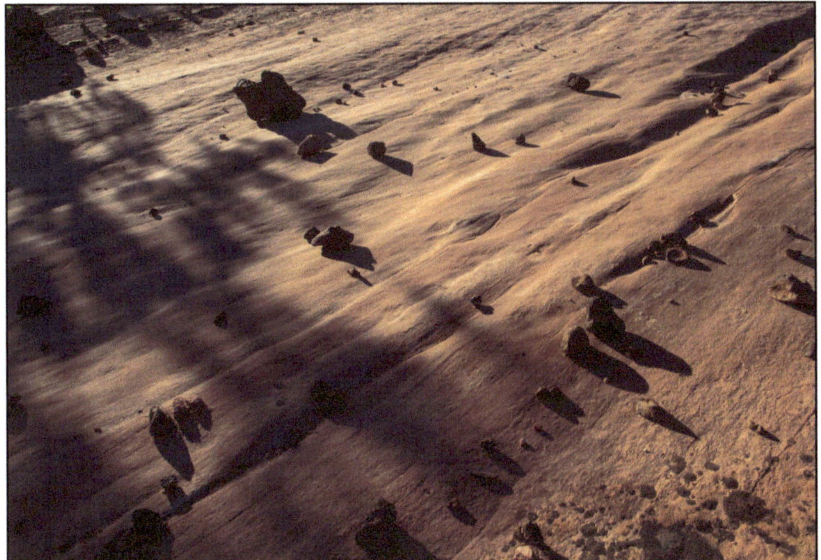

Stones and Shadows   24mm f/11 1/100s ISO100

rounds in the late afternoon (up close with the hoodoos), make your way back or on over to the roadside pullout and await the setting sun. From the road, you will need to walk down just a bit – 100 feet in distance at most.

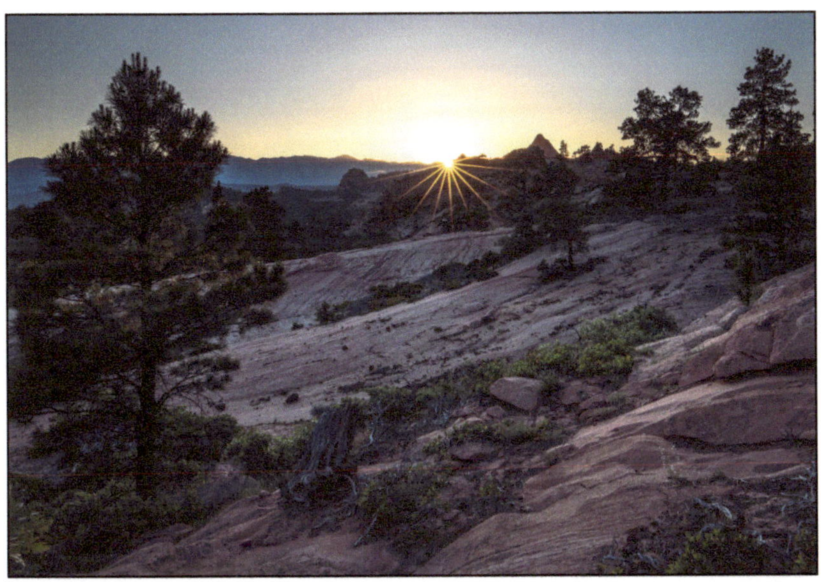

Sunset at Hoodoo Hill   24mm f/22 1/13s ISO200

In the above, I stopped-down to "create" the sun's rays for my image.

Time	•Best Good		Reward
Budget	15-30 min	Type	Roadside	Effort
RT Distance	<200 ft	Δ Elev.	<10 ft	Zoom	Norm, Tele

It is no secret, Rocky Mountain National Park is *the* place to photograph Aspens in the fall. They're seemingly everywhere there. The colorful trees are gorgeous and a real treat for photographers.

I was ecstatic to find some here also, in this area. However... The more dense groves are not within the Zion National Park boundary. They are on private property, so it is best to simply capture their splendor roadside.

When do they change color? That is the million-dollar question. There may be signs the last week of September, but I think this is just a bit early to catch the majority in transition. (Still, it is worth a look if you are there!) Better to expect abundant color the first and second weeks in October. By the end of October and into November, only a more-dull yellow remains – albeit still magnificent – though trees at some elevations will have already dropped their leaves.

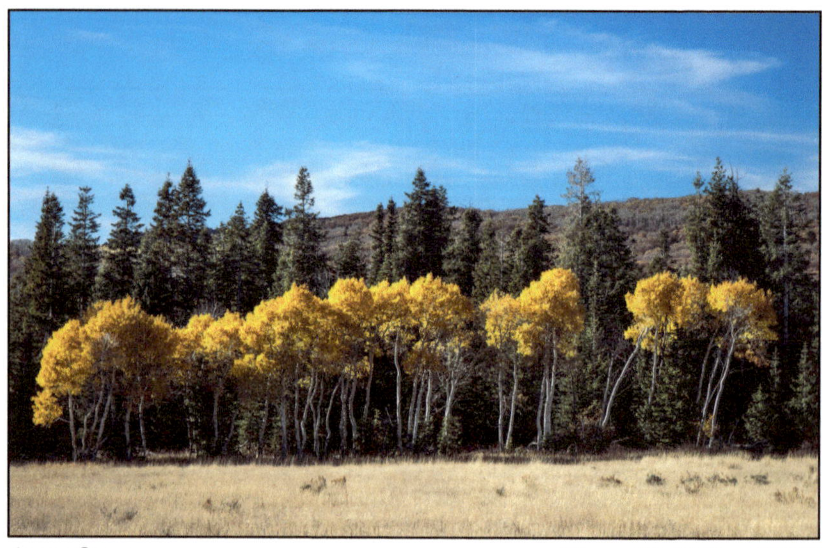

Aspen Grove   70mm f/8 1/100s ISO100

As you drive up the Kolob Terrace Road, after the switchbacks and the turnoff for the Wildcat Canyon Trailhead, Aspens begin to appear. Continue towards Lava Point Road, and as you near it, scan side-to-side, on the lookout for groves of trees. Just beyond the turnoff to Lava Point Road are additional roadside groves to explore.

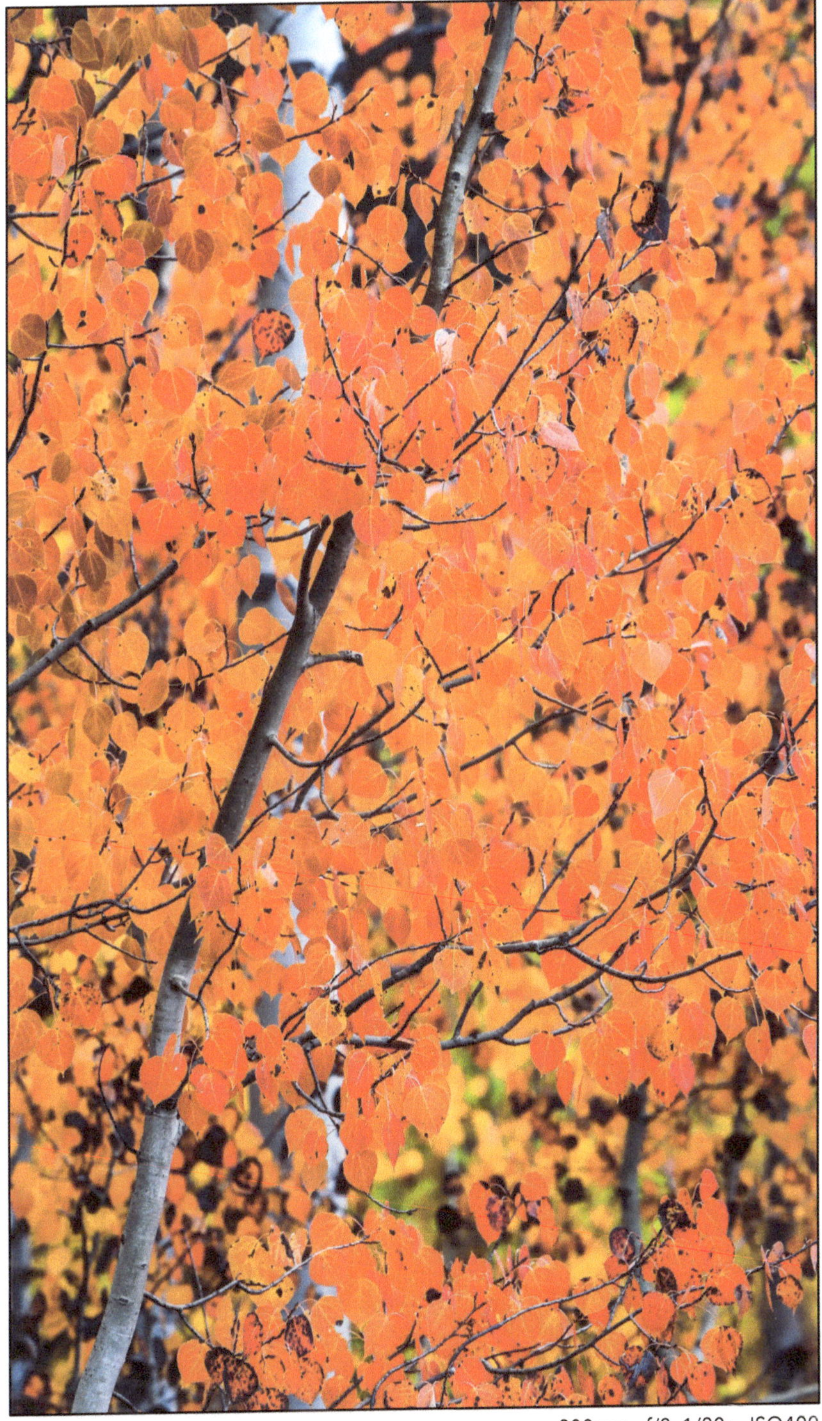

Vivid Color

200mm f/8 1/80s ISO400

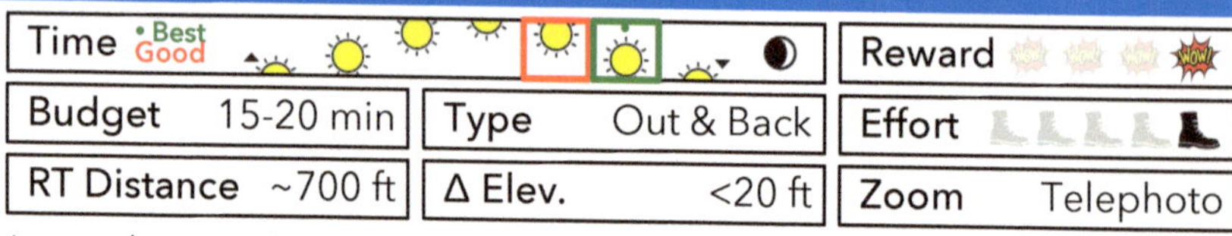

Time	•Best •Good ☀☀☀☀☀☀●	Reward ✳✳✳ 💥
Budget 15-20 min	Type Out & Back	Effort 👢👢👢👢👢
RT Distance ~700 ft	Δ Elev. <20 ft	Zoom Telephoto

I may have a better reason for you to visit Lava Point than for the vista! One afternoon in June I turned off of Highway 9 onto the Kolob Terrace Road in Virgin... The temperature was 95 degrees. Making my way to the Upper Kolob Plateau, I watched the temperature gauge in my car slowly descend. Once I parked at Lava Point and hopped out, it read 78! That's what climbing over 4,000 feet can do! A very welcome break from the summer heat.

The Lava Point Overlook makes for a better "end of the Kolob Terrace" destination than for a remarkable photograph. It's simple, and marvelous to experience in person, but the interesting subject (the features of the distant Zion canyons) are so far away that in the end the photograph isn't very glamorous. Do not be deterred – if you have time to make the journey, it is worth it.

Once on Lava Point Road, follow the signs to the overlook, not the campground. Knowing this, it is easy to find.

A final note – as mentioned on pages 23-24, though you may be tempted, I discourage travel to the Kolob Reservoir. Not only is it further than it appears on the map (in driving time), but the views are not at all interesting. You are better off using your time elsewhere.

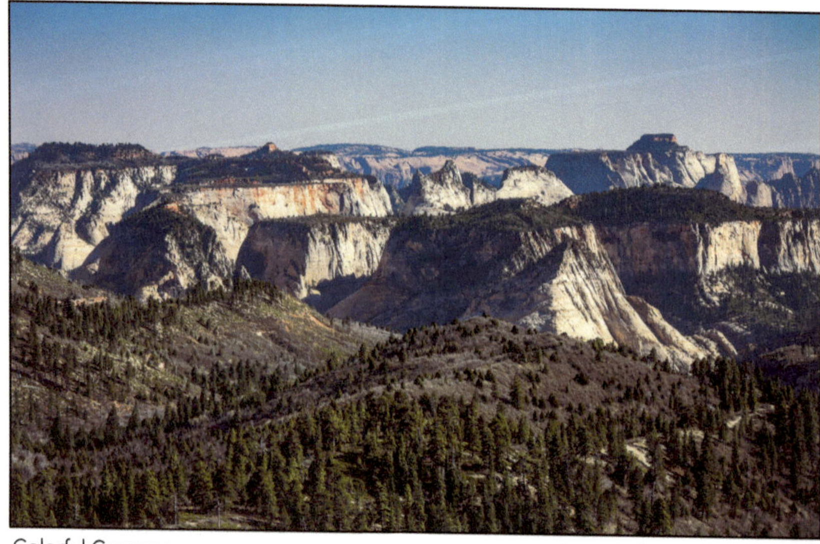

Colorful Canyons

135mm f/4 1/320s ISO100

Kolob Canyons

Kolob Canyons Entrance to Kolob Canyons Viewpoint

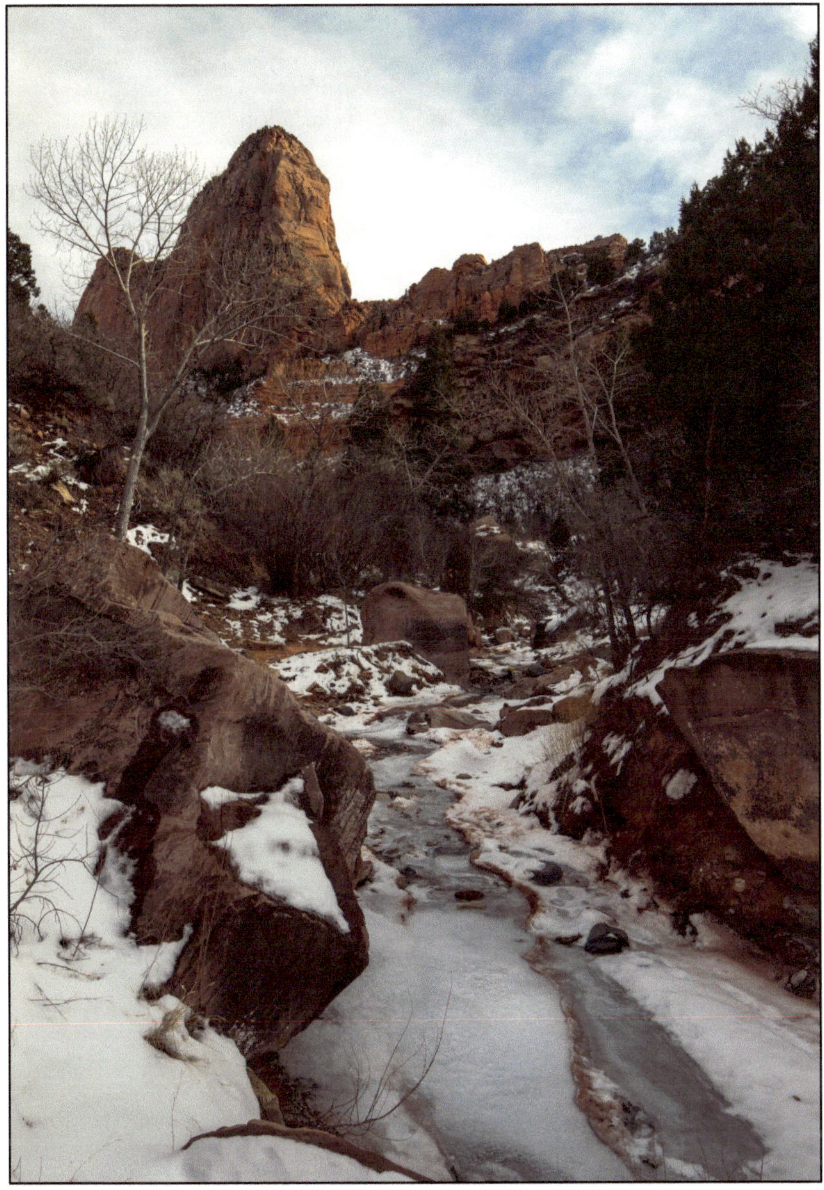

Paria Point above Taylor Creek 24mm f/11 1/60s ISO100

Time	•Best Good						Reward	
Budget	2.5-3.5 hr	Type		Out & Back		Effort		
RT Distance	~5.0 mi	Δ Elev.		~450 ft		Zoom		Wide Angle

The Taylor Creek Trail provides 4 noteworthy subjects for your portfolio – a pleasant view along Taylor Creek with Paria Point in sight (see the prior page), two abandoned cabins, and the Double Arch Alcove (the gem of the lot). For the non-thrill seekers among us, it's a straightforward hike with a gentle gain in elevation over its length.

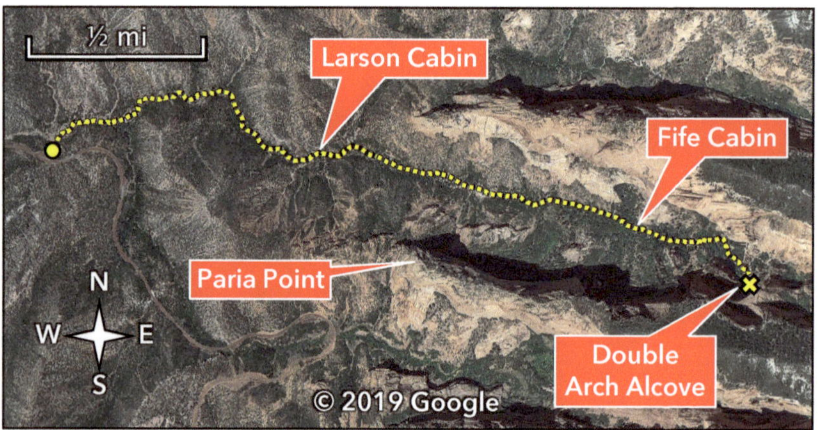

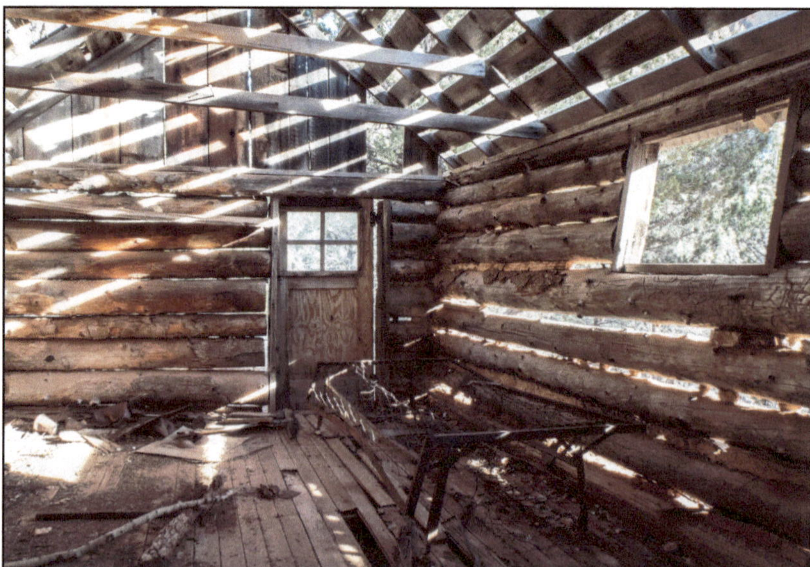

Larson Cabin   24mm f/11 1/15s ISO800

There are very many creek crossings during this hike. Waterproof shoes or boots are highly recommended. How wet your footwear will get is dependent on the creek's water level.

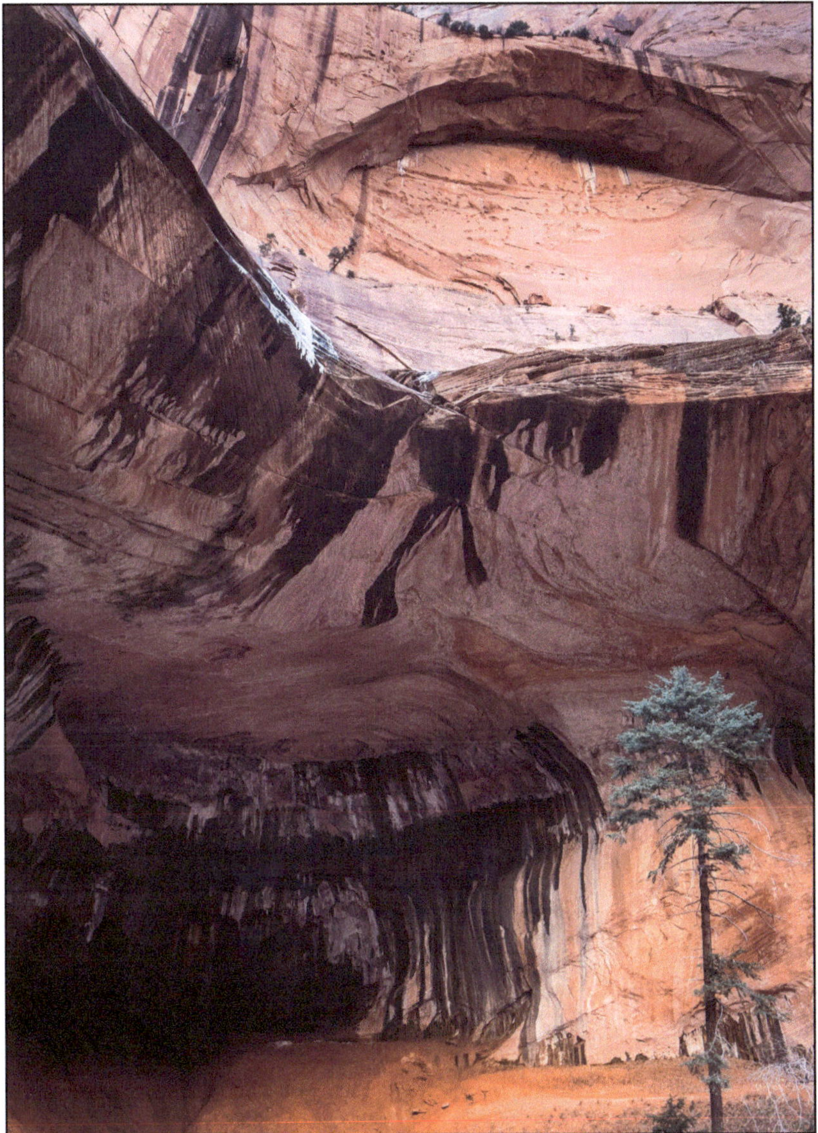

Abundant Color in the Double Arch Alcove   16mm f/8 1/40s ISO400

For the Double Arch Alcove, take your time and experiment with different compositions and focal lengths. Be careful of any bright sky above – it may throw your camera's auto-exposure off a bit. (It may be best to simply eliminate the sky altogether, as I have done here.)

Time	Best Good								Reward			
Budget	45-60 min		**Type**		Out & Back		**Effort**					
RT Distance	~1.0 mi		**Δ Elev.**		~100 ft		**Zoom**		Wide Angle			

At the end of the Kolob Canyons Road is the Kolob Canyons Viewpoint. The parking lot has an exhibit, outlining the Kolob Canyon's multiple peaks. This is a superb place to take a photo, especially focusing on the interestingly-shaped Shuntavi Butte.

Next to the parking lot lies the Timber Creek Overlook Trail. Despite this trail's short length and minimal grade, there is some uneven terrain on the way up, hence the "2-boot" rating on effort. The trail heads due south, to an enjoyable panoramic viewpoint.

Ideal light on the Kolob Canyons is late in the afternoon, approaching sunset. The colors really light up. Though for the shot to continue to work into sunset, clouds are key.

The viewing area at the end of the trail is expansive, providing many angles to shoot from, as well as many options with various rocks and short trees for use as a foreground.

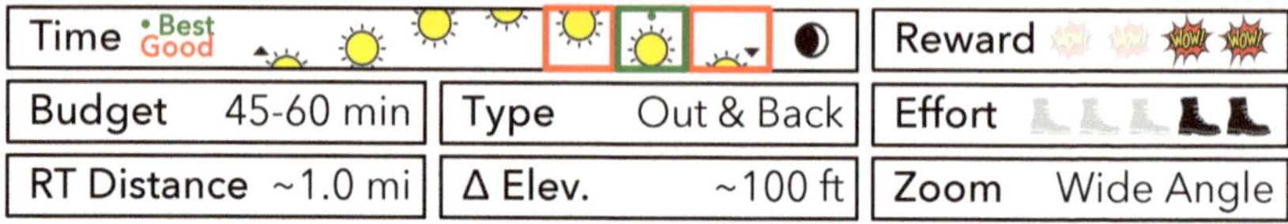

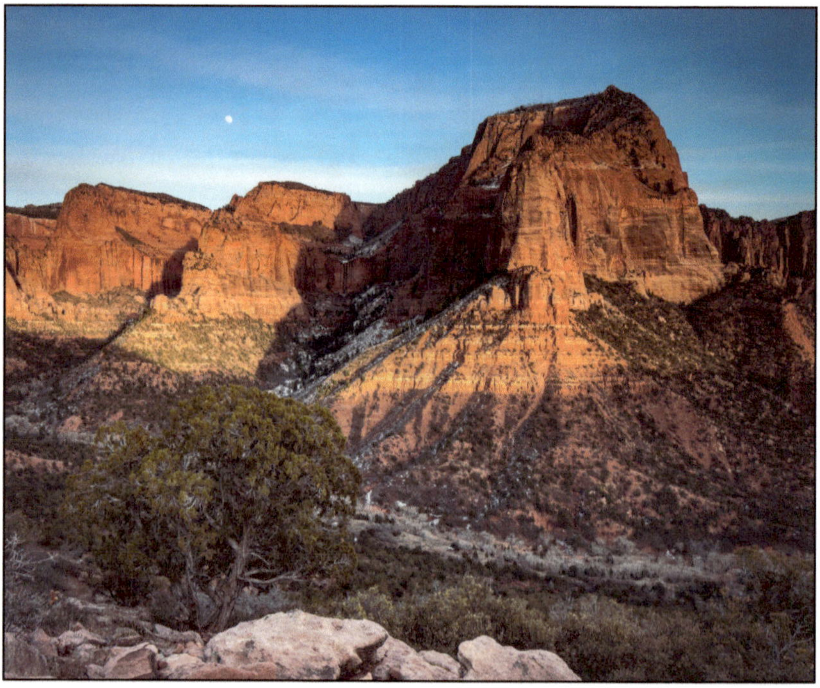

Shuntavi Butte and Finger Canyons   24mm f/16 1/5s ISO100

Outside Zion NP

Virgin and Grafton

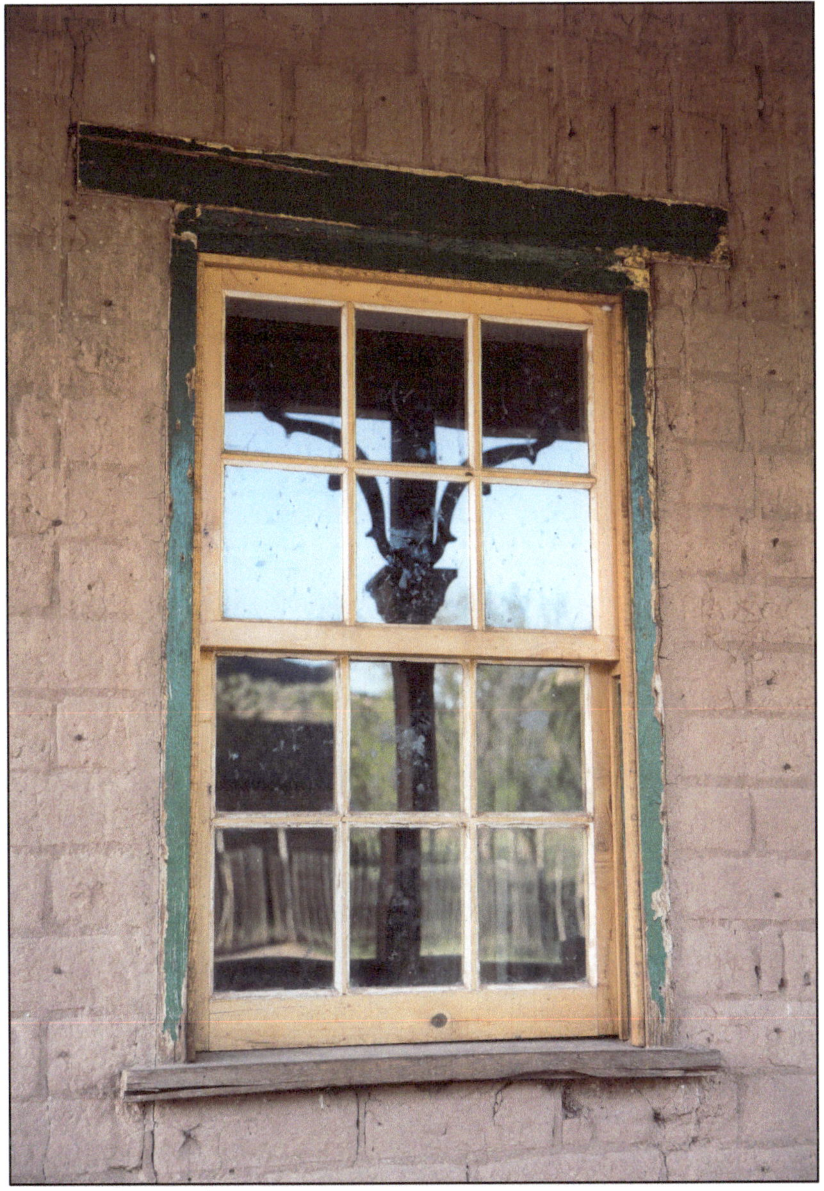

Grafton Ghost Town – Russell Home Window   50mm   f/4   1/80s   ISO200

Time	Best Good									Reward			
Budget	~5 min		Type		Roadside		Effort						
RT Distance	<200 ft		Δ Elev.		<10 ft		Zoom		Telephoto				

I provided a bit of a preview of this opportunity in The Five Park Areas section, specifically on page 26. The sunrise shot presented there is majestic, but I've already shared it! So here (below) is a midday capture.

After climbing the steep hill out of La Verkin, State Route 9 begins heading southeast. It will make its first gentle bend left, then a straightaway, then another gentle bend left... Now you will be heading more easterly. A brown sign reads "Historical Marker 800 ft." You crest a slight hill, then on your right is the well-pronounced pullout with a covered exhibit about Hurricane Mesa. This is your stop. (If you reach mile marker 16, you have just missed it.)

From this vista, to your east is a clear view of the West Temple (the highest, flat top feature on the horizon). These peaks define the west side of Zion Canyon.

Sunrise or otherwise, I love this vista as it symbolizes your approach to Zion National Park.

For the sunrise version, or for any sunrises / sunsets, my photography advice is to adjust your exposure compensation to -2 stops on your camera. This will help better capture the bold colors in the sky.

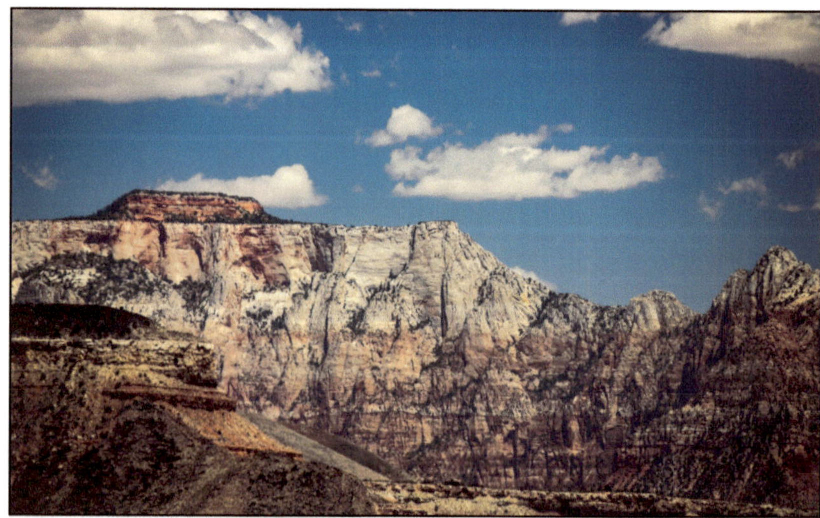

Magic Awaits on the Other Side...   350mm f/8 1/500s ISO100

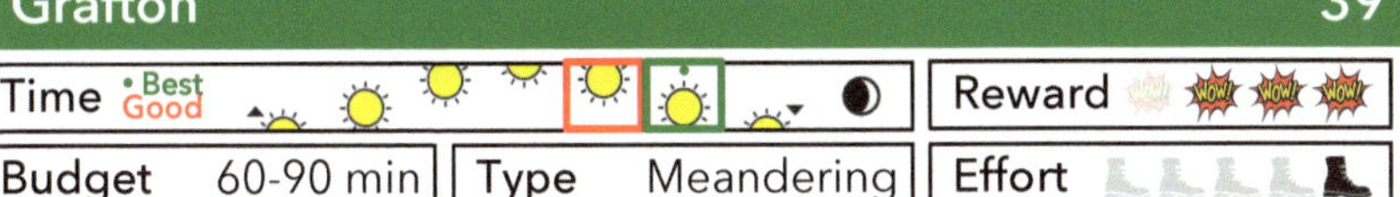

Time	Best Good		Reward
Budget	60-90 min	Type	Meandering	Effort
RT Distance	<0.5 mi	Δ Elev.	<10 ft	Zoom	Normal

Grafton, first settled in 1861, is now an abandoned town site (a "ghost town"). The remaining structures are few, but it is an interesting and short side trip from Zion National Park. If after visiting Zion for a few days and you're looking for an alternative side trip, this is a great one the area – definitely recommended.

It lies near the Virgin River, but on the opposite side of the river than State Route 9. So, to access Grafton, first you must cross the river via a one-lane bridge in Rockville, constructed by the National Park Service in 1924.

From Rockville, turn south on Bridge Road, and continue south over the bridge. Turn right on 250S / Grafton Road (heading west), and follow it to the Grafton town site. The route is well-marked. Be respectful of local residents and keep your speed down, for safety but also so as to not create an unnecessary dust cloud behind you. The drive from Rockville to Grafton takes about 15 minutes.

While some of the drive after the bridge is paved, its finale is

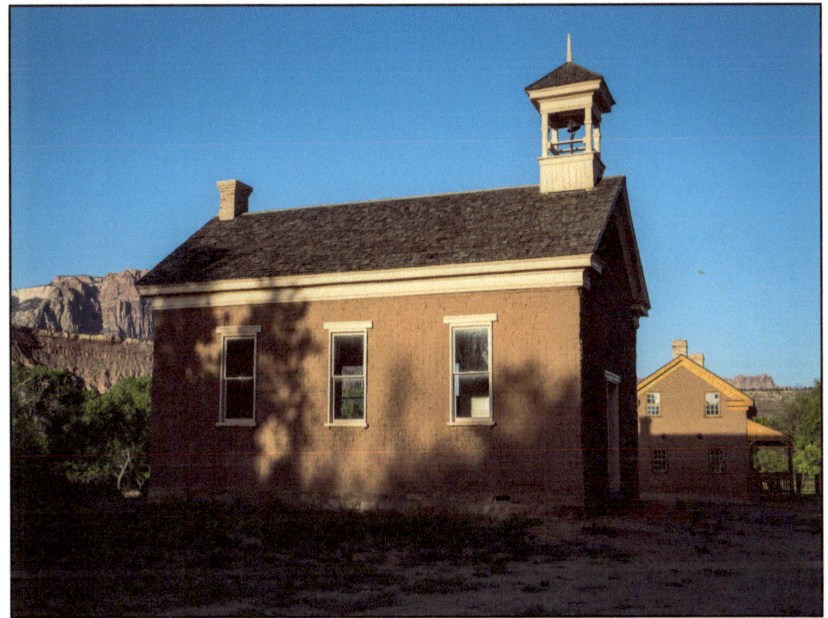

School House   35mm f/8 1/320s ISO100

unpaved, and can be bumpy in places... Be sure to secure loose items in your vehicle and beware of drinks without lids – or their contents may end up in your lap!

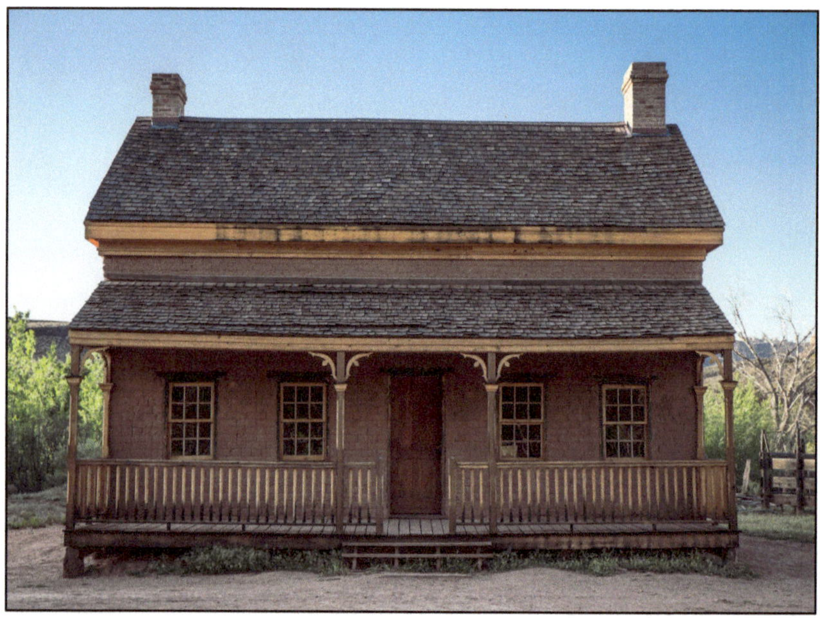

Russell Home   55mm f/5.6 1/200s ISO200

Fun fact: This site was used for the 1969 filming of "Butch Cassidy and the Sundance Kid." (As also was Zion Canyon, in the beginning of the film!)

The Grafton Heritage Partnership Project manages the town site today. They have an abundance of remarkable historic information on their website, **www.graftonheritage.org**.

The site is a bit spread out, with the two brick structures – the School House (circa 1886) and the Russell Home (circa 1862) – taking center stage.

Adjacent to the Russell Home is a lovely pasture and rustic (as in rusty!) tractor. Directly across from the Russell Home is *another* Russell's family home – this one of log construction, and built in the 1870's.

On your approach, near the main site, you will have passed the John Wood Home and its adjacent barn.

The Grafton Cemetery is south (also along the drive in), at the bend in the road. If interested, I recommend visiting it on your way out, back to Rockville.

134

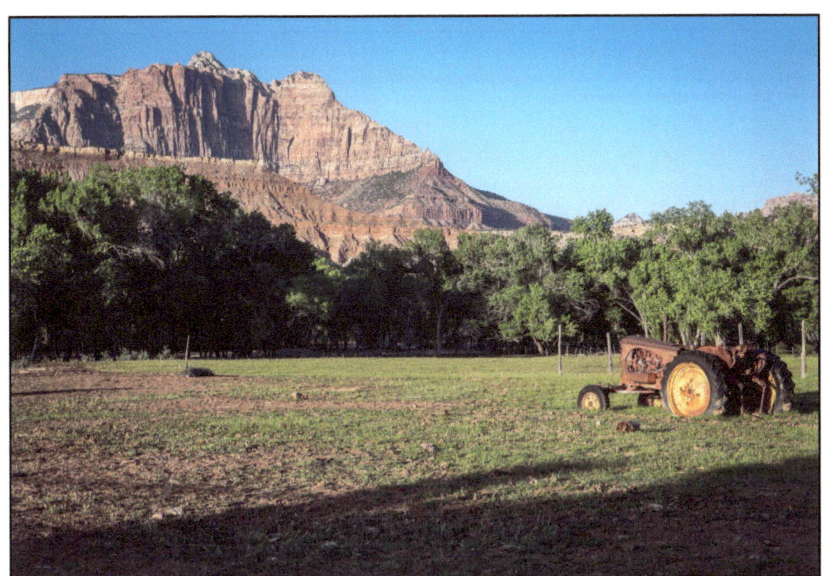

Quiet Pasture   55mm   f/11   1/160s   ISO200

Late afternoon is the best time to visit, as the soft sunlight will light the west-facing sides of these historic structures and the distant peaks in your background.

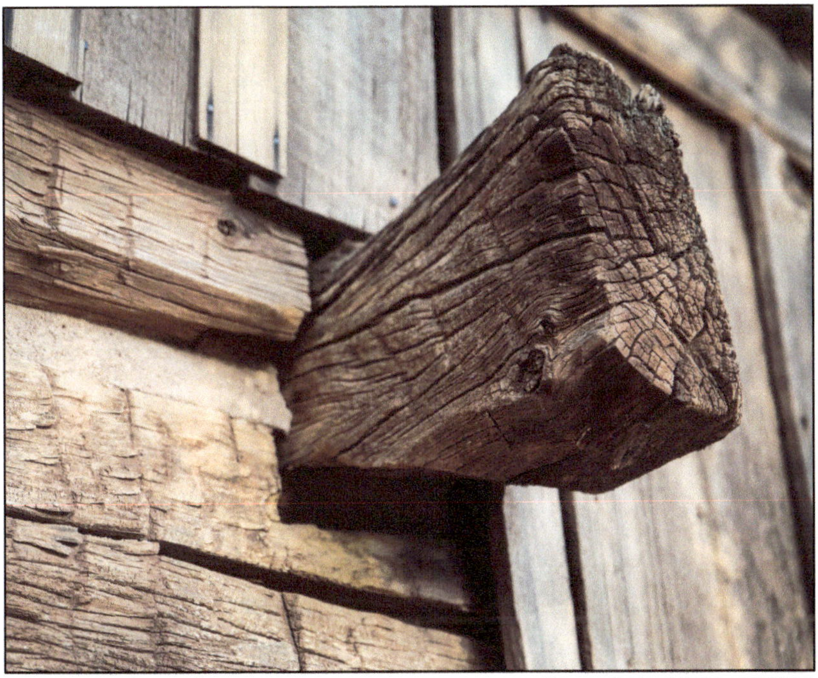

Pioneer's Craft Details   55mm   f/11   1/125s   ISO200

No.	Page	Site	Time	
			Best	Good
1	38	Watchman Trail	-AM	PM+
2	40	Towers of the Virgin	SR & AM+	-AM
3	41	The Watchman	PM+	SS
4	44	The Three Patriarchs	-AM	AM+
5	46	Historic Buildings	-AM & PM+	SS
6	47	Sand Bench Loop on Horse	-AM thru AM+	-PM thru PM+
7	51	Emerald Pools Trail	PM+	-PM
8	56	Kayenta Trail	PM+	-PM
9	59	Angels Landing	-PM thru PM+	-AM thru AM+
10	66	Weeping Rock	-AM	AM+
11	68	Hidden Canyon Trail	AM+ thru -PM	-AM & PM+
12	72	Great White Throne Viewpoint	-PM	MID & PM+
13	73	Big Bend	MID thru PM+	-AM thru AM+
14	74	Menu Falls	AM+ & -PM	MID
15	75	The Altar and The Pulpit	-PM	MID & PM+
16	76	Riverside Walk	AM+ & -PM	-AM & PM+
17	78	The Narrows	-AM thru AM+	-PM thru PM+
18	84	Lower Pine Creek Waterfall	-PM	MID & PM+
19	86	Nighttime Tail Light Trails	Nighttime	-
20	89	Great Arch	PM+	-AM
21	92	Zion-Mount Carmel Tunnel	AM+ thru -PM	-AM & PM+
22	93	Canyon Overlook Trail	SR & AM+	-AM
23	96	Pine Creek	AM+ thru -PM	-AM & PM+
24	98	Clear Creek	AM+ thru -PM	-AM & PM+
25	100	Many Pools	AM+ & -PM	-AM & PM+
26	102	Petroglyphs	-PM thru PM+	MID
27	104	White Wave	MID	AM+ & -PM
28	106	Prominent Pinyon Pine	-AM thru AM+	MID
29	108	Checkerboard Mesa	AM+	-AM
30	110	Grapevine Trail	AM+ & -PM	MID
31	112	The Subway (Bottom-Up Route)	SR thru -PM	-
32	120	Cave Knoll	-PM thru PM+	MID
33	121	Hoodoo Hill	-PM thru SS	-AM
34	124	Quaking Aspens	AM+ & -PM	-AM & PM+
35	126	Lava Point Overlook	PM+	-PM
36	128	Taylor Creek Trail	-AM thru AM+	-PM thru PM+
37	130	Timber Creek Overlook	PM+	-PM & SS
38	132	Park Approach from Virgin	SR	-PM thru PM+
39	133	Grafton	PM+	-PM

Reward (Wow's)	Budget	Type	Effort (Boots)	RT Distance	Δ Elevation	Zoom
2	1.5-2 hr	Lollipop Loop	3	~3.3 mi	~400 ft	Norm, Tele
3	15-30 min	Out & Back	0	~800 ft	<10 ft	Wide Angle
4	60-90 min	Out & Back	1	<1.6 mi	<60 ft	Normal
3	45-75 min	Out & Back	2	<0.4 mi	~30 ft	Wide Angle
1	15-30 min	Meandering	1	<0.2 mi	<10 ft	Normal
3	3-3.5 hr	Lollipop Loop	Yeehaw!	~7.6 mi	~500 ft	See Text
4	1-2 hr	Out & Back	3	~2.2 mi	~300 ft	Wide, Tele
3	1-1.5 hr	Out & Back	2	~2.0 mi	~150 ft	Norm, Tele
4	3-5 hr	Out & Back	5	~5.4 mi	~1,500 ft	Normal
2	30-45 min	Out & Back	2	~0.4 mi	~100 ft	Wide, Tele
3	2-4 hr	Out & Back	4	~2.8 mi	~900 ft	Wide, Tele
2	45-60 min	Through	1	~0.6 mi	~50 ft	Wide Angle
1	10-20 min	Meandering	1	<800 ft	<60 ft	Norm, Tele
2	60-90 min	Through	1	~1.1 mi	~30 ft	Normal
3	30-45 min	Out & Back	1	~0.5 mi	~20 ft	Normal
2	1-1.5 hr	Out & Back	2	~1.8 mi	~70 ft	Norm, Tele
4	6-8 hr	Out & Back	5	8-10 mi	~350 ft	Wide Angle
3	1-1.5 hr	Out & Back	3	~1.1 mi	~70 ft	Normal
3	30-45 min	Roadside	0	<200 ft	<10 ft	Wide Angle
1	5-10 min	Roadside	0	<200 ft	<10 ft	Normal
2	~5 min	Through	0	~1.1 mi	~300 ft	Normal
4	60-90 min	Out & Back	3	~0.9 mi	~180 ft	Whole Kit!
4	45-90 min	Meandering	3	0.3-1 mi	<60 ft	Wide Angle
3	1-1.5 hr	Meandering	3	0.5-2 mi	<120 ft	Wide Angle
3	45-75 min	Out & Back	3	~0.8 mi	<200 ft	Wide Angle
3	30-45 min	Out & Back	1	~0.3 mi	~30 ft	Norm, Tele
3	30-45 min	Meandering	3	~0.4 mi	~180 ft	Normal
3	15-30 min	Out & Back	1	~600 ft	~20 ft	Normal
2	10-20 min	Roadside	1	~200 ft	~10 ft	Normal
2	60-90 min	Out & Back	3	~0.8 mi	~400 ft	Normal
4	7-9 hr	Out & Back	5	~9 mi	~500 ft	Wide, Norm
2	5-10 min	Roadside	0	<200 ft	<10 ft	Norm, Tele
3	1-1.5 hr	Meandering	2	0.8-2 mi	<100 ft	Normal
2	15-30 min	Roadside	0	<200 ft	<10 ft	Norm, Tele
1	15-20 min	Out & Back	1	~700 ft	<20 ft	Telephoto
4	2.5-3.5 hr	Out & Back	4	~5.0 mi	~450 ft	Wide Angle
2	45-60 min	Out & Back	2	~1.0 mi	~100 ft	Wide Angle
2	~5 min	Roadside	0	<200 ft	<10 ft	Telephoto
3	60-90 min	Meandering	1	<0.5 mi	<10 ft	Normal

About the Author

Anthony Jones, who friends and family call "AJ," lives in the Seattle, Washington area with his wife and their two daughters.

In April 2011 he visited Joshua Tree National Park, laying the foundation for what would become regular photography pilgrimages to many other U.S. National Parks.

AJ enjoys the planning and logistics aspect of a trip as much as the trip itself, and in so he realized a shortage of available books focused on the photographer's specific needs while visiting national parks. Thus, his idea to write a series of these types of books was born...

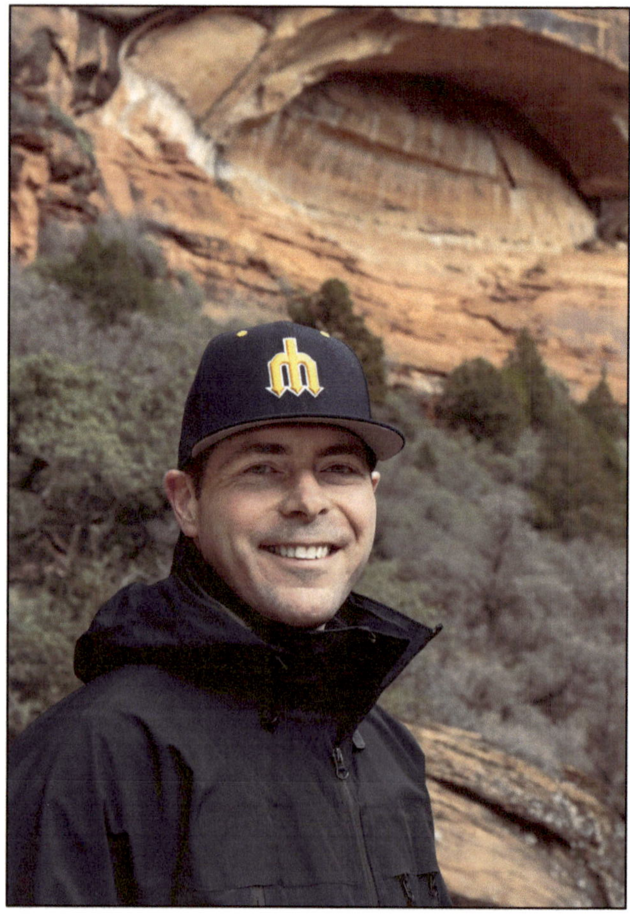

www.ingramcontent.com/pod-product-compliance
Lightning Source LLC
Chambersburg PA
CBHW041230050726
47599CB00007B/894